ELEMENTS OF *Writing*

REVISED EDITION

LANGUAGE SKILLS

PRACTICE AND ASSESSMENT

WORKSHEETS AND TESTS WITH ANSWER KEYS

► **First Course**

HOLT, RINEHART AND WINSTON

Harcourt Brace & Company

Austin • *New York* • *Orlando* • *Atlanta* • *San Francisco* • *Boston* • *Dallas* • *Toronto* • *London*

Staff Credits

Associate Director: Mescal Evler

Managing Editor: Steve Welch

Project Editors: Susan Sims Britt, Susan Lynch

Editorial Staff: *Editors,* Jonathan David Carson, Adrienne Greer; *Copy Editors,* Joseph S. Schofield IV, Atietie O. Tonwe; *Coordinators,* Susan G. Alexander, Amanda F. Beard, Rebecca Bennett, Wendy Langabeer, Marie Hoffman Price; *Support,* Ruth A. Hooker, Kelly Keeley, Margaret Sanchez, Pat Stover

Design: Christine Schueler

Editorial Permissions: Janet Harrington

Production Coordinator: Rosa Mayo Degollado

Electronic Publishing Supervisor: Barbara Hudgens

Electronic Publishing Staff: Heather Jernt, *Project Coordinator*
JoAnn Brown, David Hernandez, Rina May Ouellette, Charlie Taliaferro, Ethan Thompson

Contributing Writers

Judith Austin-Mills
Bill Martin
Matthew H. Pangborn
Raymond Teague

Printed in the United States of America

ISBN 0-03-051143-7

3 4 5 085 00 99 98

Contents

Contents (Continued)

Contents (Continued)

To the Teacher

The teacher support provided by the *Annotated Teacher's Edition* is further reinforced by the **Teaching Resources**.

The **Teaching Resources** have been designed to help you in your classroom—where the demands on your time and energy are great—to deal with each student as an individual.

This booklet, *Language Skills Practice and Assessment,* contains practice and reinforcement copying masters as well as Reviews (Forms A and B) covering material presented in Chapters 14–29 of the *Pupil's Edition.* Pretests and mastery tests with answer keys for grammar, usage, and mechanics are also included. The copying masters are arranged by chapter, and answer keys are provided at the end of each chapter.

A standardized test answer sheet to be used with the grammar, usage, and mechanics tests in Chapter 29 is located at the end of the booklet. Answers for these tests are located in the *Annotated Teacher's Edition.*

Language Skills Practice and Assessment is the fourth in a series of eight booklets comprising the **Teaching Resources.**

- *Practicing the Writing Process*
- *Strategies for Writing*
- *Word Choice and Sentence Style*
- ***Language Skills Practice and Assessment***
- *Academic and Workplace Skills*
- *Holistic Scoring: Prompts and Models*
- *Portfolio Assessment*
- *Practice for Assessment in Reading, Vocabulary, and Spelling*

Assessment: Pretests

Grammar Pretests (Form A)

Pretest A   Decide whether each of the following groups of words is a sentence or a sentence fragment. Then, on the line provided, write **S** for sentence or **F** for fragment. [20 points each]

_____ 1. Trying a double somersault.

_____ 2. She barely caught her partner's hands!

_____ 3. As she began the triple.

_____ 4. She fell to the net.

_____ 5. The crowd gasped.

Pretest B   In each of the following sentences, draw a line between the complete subject and the complete predicate. Underline each simple subject once and each simple predicate twice. [10 points each]

1. Teenagers need a balanced diet for good health.

2. Students in a hurry sometimes skip breakfast.

3. Cereal, milk, and fruit are good breakfast foods.

4. Grilled cheese sandwiches and juice also provide good nutrition.

5. A balanced diet helps students in school.

6. People need vegetables and proteins as well.

7. Meat, fish, and poultry supply protein.

8. Junk foods can kill your appetite.

9. Sweets cause tooth problems and provide many calories.

10. Good eating habits keep you healthy and help you live longer.

Pretest C   Read each sentence below and decide what kind it is. Write the correct punctuation mark at the end of each sentence. Then, on the line provided, identify what kind of sentence each is. Write **D** for declarative, **INT** for interrogative, **IMP** for imperative, or **EX** for exclamatory. [20 points each]

_____ 1. In 1752 the calendar was changed

_____ 2. Tell me the result

_____ 3. Eleven days in September were lost

_____ 4. That is the strangest thing I've ever heard

_____ 5. Were those days lost forever

Grammar Pretests (Form A)

Pretest D   For each of the following sentences, find the part of speech that is indicated in parentheses. Underline the word. Disregard the articles *a, an,* and *the.* [10 points each]

1. (noun)   A skunk is not large.

2. (adverb)   Skunks can easily protect themselves.

3. (interjection) Oh, you know what they do.

4. (pronoun)   They can squirt a smelly fluid.

5. (adjective)   First, a skunk gives a clear warning.

6. (preposition)   It stamps its feet and lifts its tail in the air.

7. (conjunction)   It rarely runs away or hides.

8. (verb)   A frightened skunk squirts at the face of an enemy.

9. (adverb)   The fluid is very smelly and can burn the eyes.

10. (verb)   Most times, skunks are friendly little animals.

Pretest E   Each of the following sentences contains an italicized complement. On the line provided, identify each complement. Write **DO** for direct object, **IO** for indirect object, **PA** for predicate adjective, or **PN** for predicate nominative. [10 points each]

> **Example:** __IO__ Dad made *me* a sandwich.

_____ 1. Pamela was the *star* of the play.

_____ 2. Dana gave me the wrong *directions.*

_____ 3. My papers are usually *neat.*

_____ 4. Manuel gave *Anita* some good advice.

_____ 5. Ms. Benton is our next-door *neighbor.*

_____ 6. Mr. Sumaki gives *us* piano lessons.

_____ 7. The box was *big* and awkward.

_____ 8. Rhoda Davis reads several *books* each week.

_____ 9. I just finished my *homework* a minute ago.

_____10. The new president of the bank is *Mrs. Morales.*

Grammar Pretests (Form A)

Pretest F Each sentence below contains a prepositional phrase. Underline each prepositional phrase. Then, on the line provided, write **ADJ** for an adjective phrase or **ADV** for an adverb phrase. [10 points each]

           Example: __ADV__ Juan ran to the finish line.

_____ 1. The jacket with the gray stripes is mine.

_____ 2. Kara helped with the laundry.

_____ 3. The man across the aisle is sleeping.

_____ 4. Mai spoke with confidence.

_____ 5. The stores close at 5:00 P.M. today.

_____ 6. A man in a blue uniform answered the phone.

_____ 7. Your order will be shipped in two days.

_____ 8. Jorge brought an apple and cheese for his snack.

_____ 9. Everyone in the bus fell asleep.

_____10. My doctor works at Emerson Hospital.

Pretest G Each of the following sentences contains a verbal phrase. First, underline the phrase. Then indicate what type of phrase it is. On the line provided, write **PP** for participial phrase or **IP** for infinitive phrase. [20 points each]

           Example: __PP__ Confused by the assignment, Laura raised her hand.

_____ 1. I hope to finish my homework soon.

_____ 2. Felice is the girl to ask.

_____ 3. The vase broken by the toddler was very old.

_____ 4. Kele began to sing with us.

_____ 5. Floating on his raft, Greg hummed a tune.

Pretest H Identify each of the following groups of words as a clause or not a clause. On the line provided, write **C** for clause or **N** for not a clause. [20 points each]

_____ 1. into the stormy waters

_____ 2. since it is raining

_____ 3. hiding under the bed

_____ 4. because they were hungry

_____ 5. after a terrible movie

Grammar Pretests (Form A)

Pretest I Each sentence below contains an italicized clause. Decide whether it is an adjective clause or an adverb clause. On the line provided, write **ADJ** for adjective clause or **ADV** for adverb clause. Then underline the word each clause modifies. [20 points each]

Example: _ADV_ *While Jason played the guitar,* Stacy <u>sang</u>.

_____ 1. We camped near Lake Arrowhead, *where we went fishing last year.*

_____ 2. *Because the weather was cold,* I stayed in the house.

_____ 3. The coat *that my mother bought* is blue.

_____ 4. *When she left her office,* Cletha heard the phone.

_____ 5. *After he made two strikes,* Vince hit a home run!

Pretest J Identify whether the italicized clause in each of the following sentences is an independent or a subordinate clause. On the line provided, write **IND** for independent clause or **SUB** for subordinate clause. [10 points each]

_____ 1. If the trip is cancelled, *we can play tennis.*

_____ 2. *If you think so,* you should do it.

_____ 3. The book *that I read* is very interesting.

_____ 4. Since we moved here, *we have met many people.*

_____ 5. As I walked to school, *I saw a strange sight.*

_____ 6. *When you finish dinner,* please wash the dishes.

_____ 7. The shells *that I found* are still in my pocket.

_____ 8. *I am asleep* when the newspaper is delivered.

_____ 9. The movie *that the reviewers liked* is sold out.

_____ 10. When you called, *I was still eating dinner.*

Pretest K Classify each of the following sentences as simple, compound, or complex. On the line provided, write **S** for simple sentence, **CD** for compound sentence, or **CX** for complex sentence. [20 points each]

_____ 1. Aunt Evelyn and Uncle Michael are both surgeons.

_____ 2. My sister, who lives in Colorado, owns a horse.

_____ 3. Chow wants to walk, but I want to take the bus.

_____ 4. I asked to try Japanese food, for I had never tasted it.

_____ 5. Neil prefers science fiction or fantasy stories.

Grammar Pretests (Form B)

Pretest A   Of the following twenty groups of words, some are complete sentences; others are not. In the blanks provided, identify each group. Use **S** for a sentence and **NS** for a word group that is not a sentence. [5 points each]

Example: __NS__ Since I began playing basketball.

_____ 1. Because the kittens keep escaping.

_____ 2. Most flowers will not bloom until the snow melts.

_____ 3. Under the warm woolen blanket.

_____ 4. A million and one reasons.

_____ 5. An artist painted my picture last summer.

_____ 6. Attending the Festival of American Folklore.

_____ 7. She dashes to the finish line!

_____ 8. Though the models are made out of bamboo.

_____ 9. He wandered about the forest.

_____10. A deadly snake slithered into the room.

_____11. Not everyone was glad when the telephone was invented.

_____12. Next, I cleaned the garage.

_____13. Along Guanabara Bay.

_____14. Keep out!

_____15. Outside the gate waited the knights.

_____16. A beautiful princess, in a high tower.

_____17. Unless the mountain can be crossed.

_____18. Should we carry an extra supply?

_____19. At last, beside the road.

_____20. I found the lost keys to the car.

Grammar Pretests (Form B)

Pretest B In the blanks provided, write the simple subject and the verb for each of the following ten sentences. Watch out for compound subjects and compound verbs and also for verb phrases. [5 points for each blank]

Example: ____types____ ____are____ Many types of answers are possible.

SUBJECT   VERB

_____ _____ 1. A new puppy should be treated gently.

_____ _____ 2. Several species of birds and reptiles can be found only on the Galápagos Islands.

_____ _____ 3. Ancient cities, books, and pottery give us clues about the past.

_____ _____ 4. Each day is a new chance for a better life and a happier future.

_____ _____ 5. Pride and envy can make a person sad and miserable.

_____ _____ 6. Did you see the shooting star?

_____ _____ 7. Tennis, track, and handball are good exercise.

_____ _____ 8. Terry's bottom drawer is full of baseball cards.

_____ _____ 9. Yesterday we learned about the importance of voting.

_____ _____ 10. Much of the state of Florida was once under water.

Pretest C The following passage contains twenty numbered, italicized words. In the numbered blanks that follow the paragraph, write the part of speech of each of these italicized words. Use these abbreviations: **N., PRON., ADJ., V., ADV., PREP., CONJ., INTERJ.** [5 points each]

Wherever people own (1) *land,* (2) *land* surveys are available. (3) *In* the past, surveyors used (4) *long* lengths of metal chain. Each chain (5) *measured* sixty-six feet. Surveyors used the chains as (6) *you* would use a tape measure. They (7) *simply* stretched out the chain (8) *from* point to point (9) *and* then calculated the footage (10) *by* multiplying the number of chains by the number of feet in a chain. For (11) *surveys* of large areas the surveyors took a compass reading and counted their steps as (12) *they* (13) *walked* along the compass reading. (14) *Then* they (15) *multiplied* the number of steps by the (16) *average* number of (17) *inches* that each step covered. (18) *Oh,* what hot and tiring work it was! (19) *Now* airplanes (20) *or* satellites can do the same job.

1. _____   6. _____   11. _____   16. _____

2. _____   7. _____   12. _____   17. _____

3. _____   8. _____   13. _____   18. _____

4. _____   9. _____   14. _____   19. _____

5. _____   10. _____   15. _____   20. _____

Grammar Pretests (Form B)

Pretest D   Each of the following sentences contains a prepositional phrase. First, underline each phrase. Then, in the first blank provided, write the word(s) that each phrase modifies. In the second blank, write the kind of prepositional phrase that it is. Write **ADJ** for an adjective phrase or **ADV** for an adverb phrase. [5 points for each blank]

Example: _searched_ _ADV_ The explorers searched <u>for the gold</u>.

WORD(S)   KIND OF
MODIFIED   PHRASE

_____ _____ 1. Take the one with the red cover.

_____ _____ 2. Before dinner we are going home.

_____ _____ 3. She quickly paddled the kayak to shore.

_____ _____ 4. The toddlers never went beyond their yard.

_____ _____ 5. Our neighbors across the street are moving.

_____ _____ 6. Have you ever ridden on a train?

_____ _____ 7. Lend me the book about sailboats, please.

_____ _____ 8. Everyone but Alicia was amazed.

_____ _____ 9. All the answers are in the book.

_____ _____ 10. A package from Grandmother is here.

Assessment: Pretests

Grammar Pretests (Form B)

Pretest E   Each of the following sentences contains one or two complements. Write each complement in the first blank provided. In the second blank, indicate what kind of complement it is. Write **DO** for a direct object, **IO** for an indirect object, **PA** for a predicate adjective, and **PN** for a predicate nominative. [5 points for each blank]

Example: ___me, watch___ ___IO, DO___ Grandfather sent me a watch.

COMPLE-   KIND OF COM-
MENT(S)   PLEMENT

_____ _____ 1. Angel is a professional jai alai player.

_____ _____ 2. My mother is an airplane pilot.

_____ _____ 3. The glow from the diamond was brilliant.

_____ _____ 4. Mr. Edison gave people electric light bulbs.

_____ _____ 5. What is the capital of Spain?

_____ _____ 6. They showed us slides of China.

_____ _____ 7. My chair was hard and uncomfortable.

_____ _____ 8. The machine can produce two crates a day.

_____ _____ 9. Have you seen my yellow sweater?

_____ _____ 10. The house appeared empty and forbidding.

Assessment Tests

Grammar Pretests (Form A)

Pretest A [20 points each]

1. F
2. S
3. F
4. S
5. S

Pretest B [10 points each]

1. <u>Teenagers</u> | <u>need</u> a balanced diet for good health.
2. <u>Students</u> in a hurry | sometimes <u>skip</u> breakfast.
3. <u>Cereal</u>, <u>milk</u>, and <u>fruit</u> | <u>are</u> good breakfast foods.
4. Grilled cheese <u>sandwiches</u> and <u>juice</u> | also <u>provide</u> good nutrition.
5. A balanced <u>diet</u> | <u>helps</u> students in school.
6. <u>People</u> | <u>need</u> vegetables and proteins as well.
7. <u>Meat</u>, <u>fish</u>, and <u>poultry</u> | <u>supply</u> protein.
8. Junk <u>foods</u> | <u>can kill</u> your appetite.
9. <u>Sweets</u> | <u>cause</u> tooth problems and <u>provide</u> many calories.
10. Good eating <u>habits</u> | <u>keep</u> you healthy and <u>help</u> you live longer.

Pretest C [20 points each]

1. In 1752 the calendar was changed. —D
2. Tell me the result. —IMP
3. Eleven days in September were lost.—D
4. That is the strangest thing I've ever heard!—EX
5. Were those days lost forever?—INT

Pretest D [10 points each]

1. A <u>skunk</u> is not large.
2. Skunks can <u>easily</u> protect themselves.
3. <u>Oh</u>, you know what they do.
4. <u>They</u> can squirt a smelly fluid.
5. First, a skunk gives a <u>clear</u> warning.
6. It stamps its feet and lifts it tail <u>in</u> the air.
7. It rarely runs away <u>or</u> hides.

8. A frightened skunk <u>squirts</u> at the face of an enemy.
9. The fluid is <u>very</u> smelly and can burn the eyes.
10. Most times, skunks <u>are</u> friendly little animals.

Pretest E [10 points each]

1. PN
2. DO
3. PA
4. IO
5. PN
6. IO
7. PA
8. DO
9. DO
10. PN

Pretest F [10 points each]

1. The jacket <u>with the gray stripes</u> is mine.—ADJ
2. Kara helped <u>with the laundry</u>.—ADV
3. The man <u>across the aisle</u> is sleeping.—ADJ
4. Mai spoke <u>with confidence</u>.—ADV
5. The stores close <u>at 5:00 P.M. today</u>.—ADV
6. A man <u>in a blue uniform</u> answered the phone.—ADJ
7. Your order will be shipped <u>in two days</u>.—ADV
8. Jorge brought an apple and cheese <u>for his snack</u>.—ADV
9. Everyone <u>in the bus</u> fell asleep.—ADJ
10. My doctor works <u>at Emerson Hospital</u>.—ADV

Pretest G [20 points each]

1. I hope <u>to finish my homework soon</u>.—IP
2. Felice is the girl <u>to ask</u>.—IP
3. The vase <u>broken by the toddler</u> was very old.—PP
4. Kele began <u>to sing with us</u>.—IP
5. <u>Floating on his raft</u>, Greg hummed a tune.—PP

Assessment Tests

Pretest H [20 points each]

1. N
2. C
3. N
4. C
5. N

Pretest I [20 points each]

1. Lake Arrowhead—ADJ
2. stayed—ADV
3. coat—ADJ
4. heard—ADV
5. hit—ADV

Pretest J [10 points each]

1. IND
2. SUB
3. SUB
4. IND
5. IND
6. SUB
7. SUB
8. IND
9. SUB
10. IND

Pretest K [20 points each]

1. S
2. CX
3. CD
4. CD
5. S

Grammar Pretests (Form B)

Pretest A [5 points each]

1. NS
2. S
3. NS
4. NS
5. S
6. NS
7. S
8. NS

9. S
10. S
11. S
12. S
13. NS
14. S
15. S
16. NS
17. NS
18. S
19. NS
20. S

Pretest B [5 points for each blank]

	SIMPLE SUBJECT	VERB
1.	puppy	should be treated
2.	species	can be found
3.	cities, books, pottery	give
4.	day	is
5.	Pride, envy	can make
6.	you	Did see
7.	Tennis, track, handball	are
8.	drawer	is
9.	we	learned
10.	Much	was

Pretest C [5 points each]

1. N.
2. ADJ.
3. PREP.
4. ADJ.
5. V.
6. PRON.
7. ADV.
8. PREP.
9. CONJ.

Assessment Tests

10. PREP.
11. N.
12. PRON.
13. V.
14. ADV
15. V.
16. ADJ.
17. N.
18. INTERJ.
19. ADV.
20. CONJ.

Pretest D [5 points for each blank]

WORD(S) MODIFIED	KIND OF PHRASE		
one	ADJ	1.	with the red cover
are going	ADV	2.	Before dinner
paddled	ADV	3.	to shore
went	ADV	4.	beyond their yard
neighbors	ADJ	5.	across the street
Have ridden	ADV	6.	on a train
book	ADJ	7.	about sailboats
Everyone	ADJ	8.	but Alicia
are	ADV	9.	in the book
package	ADJ	10.	from Grandmother

Pretest E [5 points for each blank]

COMPLEMENT(S)	KIND OF COMPLEMENT
1. player	PN
2. pilot	PN
3. brilliant	PA
4. people, bulbs	IO, DO
5. What	PN
6. us, slides	IO, DO
7. hard, uncomfortable	PA, PA
8. crates	DO
9. sweater	DO
10. empty, forbidding	PA, PA

The Sentence

A **sentence** is a group of words that expresses a complete thought. Every sentence begins with a capital letter and ends with a period, a question mark, or an exclamation point.

Lori will give a speech about whales.

Speak clearly into the microphone.

Have you prepared your speech?

What a great speech that was!

A group of words that looks like a sentence but does not express a complete thought is a **sentence fragment.**

Sentence Fragment: Markings on their tails. (This is not a complete thought. What about the markings?)

Sentence: The whales were identified by the markings on their tails.

Exercise A   Decide whether each group of words is a sentence or a sentence fragment. Then on the line provided, write **S** if the group of words is a sentence or **SF** if the group of words is a sentence fragment.

_____ 1. Whales are the largest mammals.

_____ 2. Water helps support the gigantic body of the whale.

_____ 3. Unable to survive on land.

_____ 4. A beached whale cannot expand its lungs.

_____ 5. Prevented by its tremendous weight.

_____ 6. The blue whale which can weigh over 100 tons.

Exercise B: Correction Modeling   Each item below shows one way a sentence fragment can be corrected. Study each correction. Then on the line provided, show another way the fragment can be corrected.

Example: Fragment: A walk in the woods.
Correction: The children are taking a walk in the woods.
Another correction: Let's go for a walk in the woods.

1. Fragment: After she spoke.   Correction: After she spoke, the audience applauded.

_____

2. Fragment: Seen from shore.   Correction: A school of whales was seen from shore.

_____

3. Fragment: The girl in the boat.   Correction: The girl in the boat waved to me.

_____

4. Fragment: Walking on the beach.   Correction: Walking on the beach is good exercise.

_____

Chapter 13: The Sentence

Subject and Predicate

Every sentence is made up of two parts, a *subject* and a *predicate*.

A **subject** tells whom or what the sentence is about. The subject may come at the beginning, in the middle, or at the end of a sentence.

> *Davy Crockett* is a popular legendary hero.
>
> In folk tales, *the bigger-than-life hero* rode his tame bear, Death Hug.
>
> Telling many of these tall tales was *Davy Crockett himself.*

A **predicate** is the part of the sentence that says something about the subject. The predicate may be found anywhere in the sentence.

> Davy Crockett *died at the Battle of the Alamo.*
>
> *Killed in that attack were* all the defenders of the Alamo.

Exercise A   Decide whether the underlined word or group of words in each of the sentences below makes up the subject or the predicate. Then on the line provided, write **S** if the underlined word or group of words is the subject or **P** if it is the predicate.

_____ 1. According to his neighbors, <u>Davy Crockett</u> was a remarkable child.

_____ 2. At eight years old, Crockett <u>weighed 200 pounds with his shoes off.</u>

_____ 3. In one story, a <u>wild stallion</u> carried Davy on his back for three days.

_____ 4. Did <u>you</u> ever hear the story about Davy's conversation with a raccoon?

_____ 5. Most of the remarkable stories about Crockett <u>are obviously not true.</u>

_____ 6. Born in 1786 in Tennessee, Davy Crockett <u>did really exist.</u>

_____ 7. After a campaign loss in 1823 came <u>Crockett's election to Congress in 1827.</u>

_____ 8. <u>The people of Tennessee</u> elected Crockett to Congress again in 1829.

_____ 9. <u>Was</u> the Mexican leader Santa Anna defeated by Crockett?

_____ 10. <u>The legendary Davy Crockett</u> continues to capture our imaginations.

Exercise B   Draw one line under the complete subject and two lines under the complete predicate in each of the following sentences.

1. Norwegian explorer Roald Amundsen led the first expedition to the South Pole in 1911.

2. Who first reached the North Pole?

3. Claiming to be first were the U.S. explorers Frederick Cook and Robert Peary.

4. Peary's claim was recognized by Congress.

5. The U.S. explorer and aviator Admiral Richard Byrd flew a plane over the South Pole on November 29, 1929.

Chapter 13: The Sentence

Complete Subject and Simple Subject

The **complete subject** consists of all the words needed to tell *who* or *what* a sentence is about. The **simple subject** is the main word or word group in the complete subject.

           Sentence: The study of wildlife is fascinating and fun.

    Complete subject: The study of wildlife

      Simple subject: study

           Sentence: Aunt Mai teaches an ecology course.

    Complete subject: Aunt Mai

      Simple subject: Aunt Mai

Exercise A   Decide whether the underlined word or group of words in each of the following sentences is the complete subject or the simple subject. Then on the line provided, write **CS** for complete subject or **SS** for simple subject.

_____ 1. This particular course concentrates on endangered species.

_____ 2. A large variety of plants and animals have become endangered.

_____ 3. The U.S. Fish and Wildlife Service keeps a list of endangered animals.

_____ 4. Some animals are threatened by a change in their surroundings.

_____ 5. Considered the greatest threat to animals are the activities of human

         beings.

_____ 6. The rain forests of the world are being destroyed at an alarming rate.

_____ 7. With the destruction of the rain forests comes the elimination of

         thousands of species of living things.

_____ 8. The existence of all living things depends on a delicate balance of nature.

_____ 9. Earth Day 1990 had the slogan "Save the Planet."

_____10. People from more than 140 countries took part in Earth Day festivities.

Exercise B   Find the complete subject in each of the following sentences. Draw a line between the complete subject and the rest of the sentence. Then underline the simple subject.

        Example: One fascinating nocturnal animal / is the aardvark.

1. That strange name used to make me laugh.

2. Another animal with a strange name is the aardwolf.

3. The biggest moth in all the world was named for Atlas, a Titan in Greek mythology.

4. The larva of the ant lion is the doodlebug.

5. The armadillo of the forests of eastern South America has a body three feet long.

Chapter 13: The Sentence

Complete Predicate and Verb

The **complete predicate** of a sentence is the part that says something about the subject. The **simple predicate,** or **verb,** is the main word or group of words in the complete predicate.

Sentence: Families entertained themselves one hundred years ago.

Complete predicate: entertained themselves one hundred years ago

Simple predicate (verb): entertained

Sentence: They would have been astonished by television.

Complete predicate: would have been astonished by television

Simple predicate (verb): would have been astonished

Exercise A   Decide whether the underlined word or group of words in each of the following sentences is the complete predicate or the verb (simple predicate). Then on the line provided, write **CP** for complete predicate or **V** for verb.

_____ 1. Movie machines were invented in 1894.

_____ 2. The first movie was shown in Paris in 1895.

_____ 3. Thomas Edison helped develop the movie projector.

_____ 4. At first, movies must have amazed people.

_____ 5. For many years, moviegoers watched newsreels at movie theaters.

_____ 6. Then came the invention of television.

_____ 7. Television news could inform people completely and rapidly.

_____ 8. Newsreels ended in the 1950s.

_____ 9. Today, people can watch news programs at any time.

_____10. A world without television is unimaginable.

Exercise B   Draw a line under the complete predicate in each of the following sentences. Then on the line provided, write the verb.

Example: The temperature had reached 70°F before breakfast.
had reached

1. Our trip took us through misty mountains and shady,

   green forests.   _____

2. Dairy cows were grazing on the lower slopes of the hills.   _____

3. We arrived at our destination before late afternoon.   _____

4. The whole family was looking forward to a fun vacation.   _____

Compound Subjects and Verbs

A **compound subject** consists of two or more connected subjects that have the same verb. A **compound verb** consists of two or more connected verbs that have the same subject. Compound sentence parts can be connected with *and, or,* or *but.*

> **Compound subject:** *Branches* and *animal skins* were used to make tepees.
>
> **Compound verb:** Plains people *could assemble* or *dismantle* tepees quickly.

Exercise A   Underline the compound part in each of the following sentences. Then on the lines provided, write **CS** if the compound part is a compound subject or **CV** if it is a compound verb.

_____ 1. The Arapaho and the Pawnees belonged to the Plains nations of Native

Americans.

_____ 2. Members of the Plains nations made and decorated gorgeous feather

headdresses.

_____ 3. Native Americans farmed, hunted, and fished for survival.

_____ 4. Delicate silver jewelry, colorful rugs, and wool blankets were made by the

Navajo.

_____ 5. Mexico and South America also had great native empires.

Exercise B: Sentence Combining   Combine each pair of sentences to create one sentence with a compound subject or a compound verb. Write the new sentence on the line provided. When you create a sentence with a compound subject, make sure that the other words in the sentence agree in number with the subject.

> **Example:** Than's father is an excellent cook. Lily's mother is an
> excellent cook, too.
>
> Than's father and Lily's mother are excellent cooks.
> _____
> (Notice that the verb *are* and the noun *cooks* agree in
> number with the plural subject.)

1. The sausage sizzled in the pan. It sputtered too.

_____

2. The birdbath attracts many birds. So does the small wooden birdhouse.

_____

3. The workman didn't ask for our help. He didn't need our help.

_____

4. The plane lifted off. It soared out of sight.

_____

5. Tweedledum is a character created by Lewis Carroll. So is Tweedledee.

_____

Chapter 13: The Sentence

Kinds of Sentences

A **declarative sentence** makes a statement. It is followed by a period.

President Abraham Lincoln was elected in 1860.

An **imperative sentence** gives a command or makes a request. It is followed by a period. A strong command is followed by an exclamation point.

Consider the similarities between President Lincoln and President Kennedy.

Consider the startling facts!

The subject of an imperative sentence is always *you*, although *you* may not appear in the sentence.

An **interrogative sentence** asks a question. It is followed by a question mark.

Did you know that John Kennedy was elected president in 1960?

An **exclamatory sentence** shows excitement or expresses strong feeling. It is followed by an exclamation point.

How tragic that both Lincoln and Kennedy were assassinated!

Exercise A   Decide what kind of sentence each of the following sentences is. Then on the line provided, write **DEC** if the sentence is declarative, **IMP** if it is imperative, **INT** if it is interrogative, or **EXC** if it is exclamatory. Then write the punctuation that should follow the sentence.

1. The vice-presidents under both Lincoln and Kennedy

   were named Johnson   _____

2. What a strange coincidence that is   _____

3. Read about the investigations into the deaths of both men   _____

4. How many people believe that there was a conspiracy   _____

5. There are still unanswered questions about these deaths   _____

Exercise B: Proofreading   The following paragraph contains three errors in end punctuation, one error in capitalization, and one spelling error. Can you find these errors? Proofread the paragraph to correct the errors.

   Imagine building a boat with no nails or screws what a difficult job that

would be However, there is evidence that ancient African and South American

cultures built reed ships that were held together with rope. The two cultures

were similar in other ways as well. Did you know, for instance, that both cultures

built pyramids and wrote in hieroglyphics

Chapter 13: The Sentence

Review (Form A)

Exercise A   Decide whether each group of words is a sentence or a sentence fragment. Then on the line provided, write **S** if the group of words is a sentence or **F** if the group of words is a sentence fragment.

_____ 1. Thought she had missed the bus.

_____ 2. Pasta salad is being served for lunch today.

_____ 3. In the bedroom closet behind the ironing board.

_____ 4. His latest excuse but not his most original.

_____ 5. Please take this note home to your family.

_____ 6. I would appreciate help with this project.

_____ 7. The space shuttle on the launching pad.

_____ 8. Stretching for miles in every direction.

_____ 9. Whenever he goes out into the sun.

_____ 10. That was a dazzling display of fireworks!

Exercise B   In each of the following sentences, draw a line between the complete subject and the complete predicate. Then underline the simple subject once and the verb twice.

1. An unusual event occurred at our beach last summer.

2. Two girls were jogging along the beach.

3. They heard a strange sound.

4. Thrashing around in the water was a dark object.

5. A helpless dolphin was being tossed around by the waves.

6. The worried joggers called the Center for Coastal Studies.

7. Two dolphin experts soon arrived at the beach.

8. They moved into the cold surf to rescue the dolphin.

9. Scientists at the local aquarium nursed the dolphin.

10. A healthy dolphin was released into the ocean several months later.

Review (Form A)

Exercise C   Each of the following sentences contains a compound verb. Underline the compound verb. Then on the line provided, rewrite the sentence so that it has a compound subject as well. Use *and* or *or* to join the parts of the compound subject. Remember that the other words in the sentence must agree in number with the compound subject.

1. Today my cousin Luke will hike and ride a mountain bike through the

   conservation land behind his house.

   _____

2. For tests, Shanti studies and memorizes all her notes from class.

   _____

3. The pilot greeted us and introduced himself as we boarded the plane.

   _____

4. The fog reduced visibility at the airport and delayed the flight.

   _____

5. A bushy-tailed squirrel races across the lawn and scurries up the tree.

   _____

Exercise D   On the line provided, write whether each of the following sentences is declarative, imperative, interrogative, or exclamatory. Then write the last word of each sentence, and provide the appropriate end punctuation.

1. The sixth month of the year was named for the Roman goddess Juno

   _____

2. Please bring me that calendar

   _____

3. When exactly is the birthday party for Julio

   _____

4. How exciting it was to win a gold medal

   _____

5. Watch out for that speeding car

   _____

Chapter 13: The Sentence

Review (Form B)

Exercise A   Decide whether each group of words is a sentence or a sentence fragment. Then on the line provided, write **S** if the group of words is a sentence or **F** if the group of words is a sentence fragment.

_____ 1. Because of the loud buzzing.

_____ 2. After a short while, the beaver began building his dam again.

_____ 3. You must have heard about the mysterious Bermuda Triangle.

_____ 4. When she wrote her story.

_____ 5. Although everyone with a good reason.

_____ 6. Scientists keep searching for the answer to the problem.

_____ 7. On the other side of the basketball court.

_____ 8. Very few people actually saw what happened.

_____ 9. Without the benefit of modern medicine.

_____10. The car swerved sharply to avoid hitting the pedestrian.

Exercise B   In each of the following sentences, draw a line between the complete subject and the complete predicate. Then underline each simple subject once and each verb twice.

1. The thousand-mile migration of the salmon fascinates me.

2. Fish "ladders" have been built near dams to help the salmon in their voyage.

3. Leaps of more than ten feet have been recorded.

4. The longest spawning trip exceeds 2,400 miles.

5. Salmon spawn in fresh water.

6. A Pacific salmon spawns in the stream of its birth and then dies.

7. An Atlantic salmon may return to a spawning spot three or four times in its

    lifetime.

8. The female fish digs several saucer-shaped nests in the bed of a stream.

9. One ten-pound female may deposit up to eight thousand eggs at spawning time.

10. A smolt is a young salmon.

Review (Form B)

Exercise C   Each of the following sentences contains a compound verb. Underline the compound verb. Then on the line provided, rewrite the sentence so that it has a compound subject as well. Use *and* or *or* to join the parts of the compound subject. Remember that the other words in the sentence must agree in number with the compound subject.

1. The table was cleaned thoroughly and given a fresh coat of paint.

_____

2. Rachel is singing a song and playing the guitar for the talent show.

_____

3. My brother Angelo frowned and sighed but finally did the yardwork.

_____

4. His aunt Ester takes ice-skating lessons and hopes to become a professional skater.

_____

5. Cars lined the road and created a massive traffic jam.

_____

Exercise D   On the line provided, write whether each of the following sentences is declarative, imperative, interrogative, or exclamatory. Then write the last word of each sentence, and provide the appropriate end punctuation.

1. Emily and Rosa climbed slowly up the side of the hill

_____

2. How magnificent the scenery was

_____

3. Can you see the village from there

_____

4. Hand me the binoculars, please

_____

5. The girls watched as a hawk soared gracefully over the valley

_____

Answer Key

Practice and Reinforcement (1)
The Sentence

Exercise A

1. S
2. S
3. SF
4. S
5. SF
6. SF

Exercise B: Correction Modeling

(Answers will vary. Possible responses are given.)

1. Lori went back to her seat after she spoke.
2. Seen from shore, the boat looked like a toy.
3. The girl in the boat is my sister.
4. The boys are walking on the beach.

Practice and Reinforcement (2)
Subject and Predicate

Exercise A

1. S
2. P
3. S
4. S
5. P
6. P
7. S
8. S
9. P
10. S

Exercise B

1. <u>Norwegian explorer Roald Amundsen</u> <u>led the first expedition to the South Pole in 1911.</u>
2. <u>Who</u> <u>first reached the North Pole?</u>
3. <u>Claiming to be the first were</u> <u>the U.S. explorers Frederick Cook and Robert Peary.</u>
4. <u>Peary's claim</u> <u>was recognized by Congress.</u>

5. <u>The U.S. explorer and aviator Admiral Richard Byrd</u> <u>flew a plane over the South Pole on November 29, 1929.</u>

Practice and Reinforcement (3)
Complete Subject and Simple Subject

Exercise A

1. CS
2. SS
3. SS
4. CS
5. CS
6. SS
7. CS
8. SS
9. CS
10. CS

Exercise B

1. That strange <u>name</u> / used to make me laugh.
2. Another <u>animal</u> with a strange name / is the aardwolf.
3. The biggest <u>moth</u> in all the world / was named for Atlas, a Titan in Greek mythology.
4. The <u>larva</u> of the ant lion / is the doodlebug.
5. The <u>armadillo</u> of the forests of eastern South America / has a body of three feet long.

Practice and Reinforcement (4)
Complete Predicate and Verb

Exercise A

1. V
2. CP
3. CP
4. V
5. V
6. CP
7. V

Answer Key

8. CP
9. V
10. CP

Exercise B

1. Our trip <u>took</u> us through misty mountains and shady, green forests./took
2. Dairy cows <u>were grazing</u> on the lower slopes of the hills./ were grazing
3. We <u>arrived</u> at our destination before late afternoon./ arrived
4. The whole family <u>was looking</u> forward to a fun vacation./ was looking

Practice and Reinforcement (5)
Compound Subjects and Verbs

Exercise A

1. The <u>Arapaho</u> and the <u>Pawnees</u> belonged to the Plains nations of Native Americans./ CS
2. Members of the Plains nations <u>made</u> and <u>decorated</u> gorgeous feather headdresses./ CV
3. Native Americans <u>farmed</u>, <u>hunted</u>, and <u>fished</u> for survival./ CV
4. Delicate silver <u>jewelry</u>, colorful <u>rugs</u>, and wool <u>blankets</u> were made by the Navajo./ CS
5. <u>Mexico</u> and <u>South America</u> also had great native empires./ CS

Exercise B: Sentence Combining

1. The sausage sizzled and sputtered in the pan.
2. The birdbath and the small wooden birdhouse attract many birds.
3. The workman didn't ask for or need our help.
4. The plane lifted off and soared out of sight.
5. Tweedledum and Tweedledee are characters created by Lewis Carroll.

Practice and Reinforcement (6)
Kinds of Sentences

Exercise A

1. DEC/.
2. EXC/!
3. IMP/.
4. INT/?
5. DEC/.

Exercise B: Proofreading

Imagine building a boat with no nails or screws⊙ᵹwhat a difficult job that would be./ However, there is evidence that ancient African and South American cultures built reed ships that were held together with rope. The two cultures were similar in other ways as well. Did you know, for instance, that both cultures built pyramids and wrote in hieroglyphics?

Chapter Review
Form A

Exercise A

1. F
2. S
3. F
4. F
5. S
6. S
7. F
8. F
9. F
10. S

Answer Key

Exercise B

1. An unusual <u>event</u> /<u>occurred</u> at our beach last summer.
2. Two <u>girls</u>/<u>were jogging</u> along the beach.
3. <u>They</u> /<u>heard</u> a strange sound.
4. <u>Thrashing</u> around in the water <u>was</u> /a dark <u>object</u>.
5. A helpless <u>dolphin</u> /<u>was being tossed</u> around by the waves.
6. The worried <u>joggers</u> /<u>called</u> the Center for Coastal Studies.
7. Two dolphin <u>experts</u> /soon <u>arrived</u> at the beach.
8. <u>They</u> /<u>moved</u> into the cold surf to rescue the dolphin.
9. <u>Scientists</u> at the local aquarium /<u>nursed</u> the dolphin.
10. A healthy <u>dolphin</u> /<u>was released</u> into the ocean several months later.

Exercise C

(Answers will vary for the second part of the exercise. Possible responses are given.)

1. Today my cousin Luke <u>will hike</u> and <u>ride</u> a mountain bike through the conservation land behind his house./Today my cousin Luke and I will hike and ride mountain bikes through the conservation land behind his house.
2. For tests, Shanti <u>studies</u> and <u>memorizes</u> all her notes from class. /For tests, Shanti and her best friend Peter study and memorize all their notes from class.
3. The pilot <u>greeted</u> us and <u>introduced</u> himself as we boarded the plane. /The pilot and the flight attendants greeted us and introduced themselves as we boarded the plane.
4. The fog <u>reduced</u> visibility at the airport and <u>delayed</u> the flight./ The fog and mist reduced visibility at the airport and delayed the flight.
5. A bushy-tailed squirrel <u>races</u> across the lawn and <u>scurries</u> up the tree./ A bushy-tailed squirrel and a small, furry chipmunk race across the lawn and scurry up the tree.

Exercise D

1. declarative/Juno.
2. imperative/calendar.
3. interrogative/Julio?
4. exclamatory/medal!
5. imperative/car!

Chapter Review Form B

Exercise A

1. F
2. S
3. S
4. F
5. F
6. S
7. F
8. S
9. F
10. S

Exercise B

1. The thousand-mile <u>migration</u> of the salmon / <u>fascinates</u> me.
2. Fish "<u>ladders</u>" / <u>have been built</u> near dams to help the salmon in their voyage.
3. <u>Leaps</u> of more than ten feet / <u>have been recorded</u>.
4. The longest spawning <u>trip</u> /<u>exceeds</u> 2,400 miles.
5. <u>Salmon</u> / <u>spawn</u> in fresh water.
6. A Pacific <u>salmon</u> / <u>spawns</u> in the stream of its birth and then <u>dies</u>.
7. An Atlantic <u>salmon</u> / <u>may return</u> to a spawning spot three or four times in its lifetime.
8. The female <u>fish</u> / <u>digs</u> several saucer-shaped nests in the bed of a stream.
9. One ten-pound <u>female</u> /<u>may deposit</u> up to eight thousand eggs at spawning time.
10. A <u>smolt</u> / <u>is</u> a young salmon.

Answer Key

Exercise C

(Answers will vary for the second part of the exercise. Possible responses are given.)

1. The table <u>was cleaned</u> thoroughly and <u>given</u> a fresh coat of paint./The table and chairs were cleaned thoroughly and given a fresh coat of paint.

2. Rachel <u>is singing</u> a song and <u>playing</u> the guitar for the talent show./Rachel and María are singing a song and playing guitars for the talent show.

3. My brother Angelo <u>frowned</u> and <u>sighed</u> but finally <u>did</u> the yardwork./My brothers Angelo and Tony frowned and sighed but finally did the yardwork.

4. His aunt Ester <u>takes</u> ice-skating lessons and <u>hopes</u> to become a professional skater./His aunt Ester and uncle Hector take ice-skating lessons and hope to become professional skaters.

5. Cars <u>lined</u> the road and <u>created</u> a massive traffic jam./Cars, trucks, and buses lined the road and created a massive traffic jam.

Exercise D

1. declarative/hill.
2. exclamatory/was!
3. interrogative/there?
4. imperative/please.
5. declarative/valley.

Chapter 14: The Parts of Speech

The Noun

A **noun** is a word that names a person, a place, a thing, or an idea. Some nouns contain more than one word. Such nouns are called **compound nouns.**

Persons: Diana Chang, poet, police officer, Cherokees
Places: living room, ceiling, New South Wales, island
Things: sandwich, television, Father's Day, Statue of Liberty
Ideas: fear, self-control, truth, sympathy

Exercise A   Underline all the nouns in the following sentences.

Example: A <u>letter</u> from <u>Uncle Rufino</u> arrived last <u>week</u>.

1. Our sun is actually a star.

2. My sister, a student, is studying chemistry this summer.

3. Mr. Morales was fascinated by the koalas at the San Diego Zoo.

4. Mingan is the new goalie on the team.

5. Earline is having a party after the play.

6. Did your parents go to Hawaii for a convention?

7. The storm interrupted the final game of the World Series.

8. The actors had faith in their director.

9. Lucy, a young chimpanzee, learned several words in sign language.

10. Ryan always puts humor into his essays.

Exercise B   The paragraph below contains twenty nouns. Underline each noun in the paragraph.

When a volcano erupted on the island of Krakatoa in Indonesia, the whole world felt the effects. The noise from the eruption could be heard at great distances, and the force from the blast could be felt as far as California. A cloud of ash circled the globe and dimmed the light from the sun. Volcanic eruptions are powerful forces that can affect the entire planet.

Chapter 14: The Parts of Speech

Types of Nouns

A **proper noun** names a particular person, place, thing, or idea. It begins with a capital letter. A **common noun** names any one of a group of persons, places, or things. It generally is not capitalized.

> **Proper:** Willa Brown
> **Common:** pilot

A **concrete noun** names a person, place , or thing that can be perceived by the senses. An **abstract noun** names an idea, a feeling, a quality, or a characteristic.

> **Concrete:** song
> **Abstract:** beauty

Exercise A   Decide whether each noun is common or proper, concrete or abstract. On the lines provided, write **COM** for common, **PRO** for proper, **CON** for concrete, or **ABS** for abstract.

> **Examples:** Marlene Childress—PRO, CON
> imagination—COM, ABS

1. humor   _____

2. Brazil   _____

3. computer   _____

4. sympathy   _____

5. Great Barrier Reef _____

6. bridge   _____

7. dishonesty   _____

8. Jupiter   _____

9. kangaroo   _____

10. Queen Elizabeth II _____

Exercise B: Proofreading   The following paragraph contains five errors in capitalization and five spelling errors. Can you find these errors? Proofread the paragraph and correct all the errors.

Jules verne allways loved adventure. As a boy, he worked on a Ship, the

coralie. Later, the young man wrote plays, which provided little income. Verne

needed monnie, so he started writing books about real and imaginary jurneys.

the Public loved these stories and eegerly awaited each new novvel.

Chapter 14: The Parts of Speech

The Pronoun

A **pronoun** is a word used in place of one or more nouns or pronouns. The word that a pronoun stands for is called the **antecedent**. Sometimes the antecedent is not stated.

> *Ms. Cato* is my math teacher. *She* made everything clear. (*Ms. Cato* is the antecedent of the pronoun *she*.)

> *He* swung from one trapeze to the other. (The pronoun *He* has no antecedent in this sentence. Trapeze is the antecedent of the pronoun *other*.)

A **personal pronoun** refers to the person speaking, to the person spoken to, or to the person spoken about.

> Ask *them* where the stadium is.   *I* will call *you* after school.

A **reflexive pronoun** refers to the subject and directs the action of the verb back to the subject. An **intensive pronoun** emphasizes a noun or another pronoun.

> **Reflexive:** Consuelo prepared *herself* for the quiz.
> **Intensive:** My younger brother prepared dinner *himself*.

Exercise A   Underline the pronoun or pronouns in each sentence. Then decide what kind of pronoun each is. On the line provided, in the order in which the pronouns appear, write **P** for personal, **R** for reflexive, or **I** for intensive.

_____ 1. The baby cried herself to sleep.

_____ 2. We should not let ourselves overlook the plight of the homeless.

_____ 3. Are you aware of the dangers of smoking?

_____ 4. "I will not tolerate lateness," the band leader told us.

_____ 5. The principal himself called me with the good news.

_____ 6. "Jogging is not for me," said Dr. Wong.

_____ 7. When the smoke detector sounded, the cat hid itself behind the couch.

_____ 8. After the twins frosted the cake, they looked for the candles.

_____ 9. Before you wash the floor, please move the chairs.

_____10. Don't wear the new boots until you waterproof them.

Exercise B   The following paragraph contains six pronouns. Circle the pronouns. If a pronoun has an antecedent, underline the antecedent.

> If a maple tree could not shed its leaves in winter, the tree would die. Trees
>
> lose gallons of water each day through their leaves. In winter, when the ground
>
> freezes, the trees cannot take in much water from the soil. To save themselves
>
> from drying out, many trees drop their leaves. With no leaves, a tree can keep
>
> more of its moisture and prevent itself from drying out.

Chapter 14: The Parts of Speech

Types of Pronouns

A **demonstrative pronoun** points out a person, a place, a thing, or an idea.

>*This* is the machine we use.   *These* are the instructions.

An **interrogative pronoun** introduces a question.

>*Which* of the seats is mine?   *Who* knows the words to the song?

An **indefinite pronoun** refers to a person, a place, a thing, or an idea that is not specifically named.

>*Anyone* can do this simple trick.   *Few* have failed to succeed.

A **relative pronoun** introduces a subordinate clause.

>Yeager's plane, *which* was named *Glamorous Glennis,* flew 700 miles per hour.

>The book *that* you need is in the reference section of the library.

Exercise A   On the line provided, write the pronoun in each sentence.

1. What are guppies? _____

2. Guppies are small fish that people often keep as pets. _____

3. These are called rainbow fish. _____

4. All are named for R. J. Lechmere Guppy. _____

5. Guppy, who introduced the fish to England in 1866, lived in Trinidad. _____

Exercise B   Underline the pronoun or pronouns in each sentence. Then decide what kind of pronoun each is. On the line provided, write **DEM** for demonstrative, **INT** for interrogative, **IND** for indefinite, or **REL** for relative.

_____ 1. This is an Elberta peach, which is very popular in the United States.

_____ 2. Nobody really knows where the fruit came from.

_____ 3. Toby told a story that may or may not be true.

_____ 4. Who started the story?

_____ 5. A man in Georgia, whose wife was named Elberta, grew peach trees.

_____ 6. These had been sent by a friend in another state.

_____ 7. Elberta, who liked to sew, tucked some peach pits in a sewing basket.

_____ 8. What happened to the peach pits?

_____ 9. Elberta's grandson planted several.

_____10. Those were crossed with another kind of peach.

Chapter 14: The Parts of Speech

The Adjective

An **adjective** is a word that modifies, or describes, a noun or a pronoun. Adjectives are used to tell *what kind, which one, how much,* or *how many.*

> **What kind:** Anzu bought a *red* dress.
> **Which one:** Viktor is the *oldest* brother.
> **How much:** There is *no* water on the moon.
> **How many:** I discovered *several* photographs.

The adjectives *a, an,* and *the* are called **articles**. *A* and *an* are **indefinite articles**. They refer to someone or something in general terms. *The* is a **definite article** because it refers to a particular, or definite, person or thing.

> **Indefinite article:** Julio stayed up late to see a movie.
> **Definite article:** The U.S. flag is red, white, and blue.

Exercise A Underline the adjectives in each sentence. Then decide whether each article is definite or indefinite. On the line provided, write **D** for definite or **I** for indefinite.

_____ 1. Yes, Sylvia has an older brother.

_____ 2. The sudden wind chilled us.

_____ 3. Someday you may own a small electric car.

_____ 4. Edna ordered a medium hamburger with extra onions.

_____ 5. The mysterious tapping terrified everyone.

Exercise B In each of the following sentences, underline all the adjectives except *a, an,* and *the.* Then draw an arrow from each adjective to the word that it modifies.

1. Mary Shelley wrote a horror story.

2. The plot of the story was imaginative.

3. One stormy night, she had listened to several stories about ghosts.

4. Friends had made up scary stories about monsters.

5. Mary knew she would have a terrible night.

6. Mary thought about the stories all night and had a strange nightmare.

7. She dreamed of a young doctor who created a monster.

8. Mary wrote a story of the ghastly nightmare and called it *Frankenstein.*

9. The eerie novel was a great success.

10. Several movies have been made from it.

Chapter 14: The Parts of Speech

Types of Adjectives

How a word is used in a sentence determines what part of speech it is. Some words may be either nouns or adjectives. Others can be either pronouns or adjectives.

Noun: I like *school* most of the time.

Adjective: The *school* bus had a flat tire.

Pronoun: Please hold *these* for me.

Adjective : *These* bags are heavy.

A **proper adjective** is formed from a proper noun. It always begins with a capital letter.

Proper Noun: This butterfly is found in *Africa*.

Proper Adjective: The *African* swallowtail is a large butterfly.

Exercise A   Decide whether the italicized word in each sentence is being used as a noun, a pronoun, or an adjective. Then, on the line provided, write **N** for noun, **P** for pronoun, or **A** for adjective.

_____ 1. This town needs a good *dress* shop.

_____ 2. The *glass* top on that table is difficult to clean.

_____ 3. Tomorrow is my *birthday*.

_____ 4. Put some of this good *Texas* barbecue sauce on your sandwich.

_____ 5. Sam Houston was the president of *Texas* before it became a state.

_____ 6. This *glass* is still dirty.

_____ 7. Allison bought a white *dress* for the dance.

_____ 8. *Many* attended the holiday festival.

_____ 9. Ramona mailed a *birthday* card to her grandmother.

_____10. When I was sick, I received *many* cards.

Exercise B   Underline all ten adjectives in the following paragraph. Do not include the articles *a, an,* and *the*.

Louis Braille invented a special alphabet that allows people with visual impairments

to read. The alphabet uses raised dots that the visually impaired can feel. The dots

are arranged in patterns, with different patterns standing for individual letters or

sounds. A person reads Braille by rubbing one or two fingertips over the elevated

dots. A person can write Braille by hand, using a pointed stylus and a metal slate.

Or, a person can use a Braille typewriter or computer.

Chapter 14: The Parts of Speech

Review (Form A)

Exercise A   Underline the nouns in the following sentences.

1. William Sydney Porter had talent.

2. The man was a writer.

3. His pen name was O. Henry.

4. Porter spent three years in jail.

5. His first story was published by *McClure's Magazine* while he was a prisoner.

Exercise B   Decide whether each italicized noun is common or proper, concrete or abstract. Then, on the line provided, write **COM** for common or **PRO** for proper, **CON** for concrete or **ABS** for abstract.

_____ 1. Maps change over *time*.

_____ 2. Some changes are caused by *human beings*.

_____ 3. Old maps do not show the *Suez Canal*.

_____ 4. Nature also changes the outlines of *countries* and oceans.

_____ 5. The Caspian Sea is a good *example*.

_____ 6. This small inland *sea* is filling up with sediment.

_____ 7. *Centuries* ago, the Caspian Sea was larger.

_____ 8. The *Red Sea* seems to be growing.

_____ 9. Many different forces affect the surface of the *earth*.

_____10. Wind, *water,* and movement of the earth's crust are powerful forces.

Exercise C   Underline the pronouns in the following sentences. Then decide what kind of pronoun each is. On the line provided, write **P** for personal, **R** for reflexive, or **I** for intensive.

_____ 1. The instructor herself first demonstrated the dive.

_____ 2. The spokes of a bicycle's wheel help it absorb shock.

_____ 3. King Charles liked to say, "In my empire the sun never sets."

_____ 4. A frightened hedgehog curls itself into a ball.

_____ 5. The artist wanted you to come to the gallery opening.

Chapter 14: The Parts of Speech

Review (Form A)

Exercise D On the line provided, write the pronoun or pronouns in each sentence. Then decide what kind of pronoun each is. Write **DEM** for demonstrative, **INT** for interrogative, **IND** for indefinite, or **REL** for relative.

1. Jorge is the boy who wore the red wig in the first act. _____

2. Hairstyle is one of the details that help scholars date pictures. _____

3. Everyone who enters the lab must wear a coverall. _____

4. Whom will the class choose as a representative? _____

5. What should Susan bring to the party? _____

6. Of all the fruits, these have the most vitamin C. _____

7. Jamal called the house, but no one answered. _____

8. Please put away the boxes, and then help Marvin move this. _____

9. Lily was the only person who voted against the measure. _____

10. Think about different scenes, and then decide what Alicia should paint. _____

Exercise E Underline the adjectives in each sentence. Then decide whether each article is definite or indefinite. On the line provided, write **D** for definite or **I** for indefinite. If there are two articles in a sentence, write your answers in the same order in which the articles appear.

_____ 1. Have you ever seen the huge rosebush in Tombstone?

_____ 2. Every spring, the bush is covered with white flowers.

_____ 3. The bush was planted by a Scottish woman.

_____ 4. She came to Tombstone in the late 1800's.

_____ 5. She was a young bride at the time.

_____ 6. Now the plant is very old.

_____ 7. Many people travel to Tombstone to see the bush.

_____ 8. It grows beside the old Rose Tree Inn.

_____ 9. The rosebush is very large.

_____10. Several sources call it the largest rosebush in the world.

Chapter 14: The Parts of Speech

Review (Form A)

Exercise F   Decide whether the italicized word in each sentence is being used as a noun, a pronoun, or an adjective. Then, on the line provided, write **N** for noun, **P** for pronoun, or **A** for adjective.

_____ 1. *Many* have heard about the Pony Express.

_____ 2. However, it lasted only a *few* years.

_____ 3. Among its *young* riders was William Cody, later known as Buffalo Bill.

_____ 4. The arrival of transcontinental *telegraph* lines put an end to the pony

express.

_____ 5. Even the fastest riders could not compete with the *telegraph*.

Chapter 14: The Parts of Speech

Review (Form B)

Exercise A   Underline the nouns in the following sentences.

1. Owney was a stray dog found behind a post office in New York.

2. The mail clerks gave food to the friendly animal.

3. Owney traveled all over the United States, hitching rides in the mail cars of trains.

4. Soon, the tags on his collar were covered with stamps from cities all over the country.

5. Owney traveled to Japan by boat and then continued around the world.

Exercise B   Decide whether each italicized noun is common or proper, concrete or abstract. Then, on the line provided, write **COM** for common or **PRO** for proper, **CON** for concrete or **ABS** for abstract.

_____ 1. At the time of the *Civil War*, three banks were robbed.

_____ 2. The *banks* were robbed by a band of Confederate soldiers.

_____ 3. The robbers stole more than $100,000—a *fortune* at that time.

_____ 4. More than half of the *robbers* were captured in Canada.

_____ 5. The men had only a small amount of *money* on them.

_____ 6. A large *amount* of gold was still missing.

_____ 7. This *treasure* has never been found.

_____ 8. Searchers believe that it is hidden somewhere near St. Albans, *Vermont*.

_____ 9. People think it may be near *Lake Champlain*.

_____ 10. Many treasure hunters have tried to find the money, with no *success*.

Exercise C   Underline the pronouns in the following sentences. Then decide what kind of pronoun each is. On the line provided, write **P** for personal, **R** for reflexive, or **I** for intensive.

_____ 1. When the popcorn gets hot, the steam inside the kernels makes them pop.

_____ 2. The swim team outdid itself in the freestyle event.

_____ 3. Consuelo smiled and said, "I know the words to the song."

_____ 4. The senator herself signed the letter.

_____ 5. Is the sponge you bought natural or artificial?

Chapter 14: The Parts of Speech

Review (Form B)

Exercise D   On the line provided, write the pronoun or pronouns in each sentence. Then decide what kind of pronoun each is. Write **DEM** for demonstrative, **INT** for interrogative, **IND** for indefinite, or **REL** for relative.

1. Rebecca, whose picture is on the poster, is now fourteen. _____

2. What did Silas order from the bookstore? _____

3. Before Dad cooks these, peel off the shells. _____

4. Early bikes had to have bells, which were rung constantly. _____

5. Don't tell anyone about the surprise visitor. _____

6. Which gets the best gas mileage in city traffic? _____

7. Now try this on for size. _____

8. Salim wanted to buy both but could not afford to. _____

9. Sarah Winchester, who inherited a fortune, built an enormous house. _____

10. Who has the lead role? _____

Exercise E   Underline the adjective or adjectives in each sentence. Then decide whether each article is definite or indefinite. On the line provided, write **D** for definite or **I** for indefinite. If there are two or more articles in a sentence, write your answers in the same order in which the articles appear. Some sentences have no articles.

_____ 1. In 1906, photography was still new.

_____ 2. Many people were fascinated by photographs.

_____ 3. The interest started a new fad.

_____ 4. People started wearing tiny photographs on fingernails.

_____ 5. Young brides wore pictures on their ring fingers.

_____ 6. First, the photographic print was put onto a special, wet paper.

_____ 7. The paper could transfer a picture onto a smooth fingernail.

_____ 8. When the picture became dry, it stuck.

_____ 9. Later the owner put clear polish over the picture.

_____ 10. The hard polish protected the picture for a long time.

Chapter 14: The Parts of Speech

Review (Form B)

Exercise F   Decide whether the italicized word in each sentence is being used as a noun, a pronoun, or an adjective. Then, on the line provided, write **N** for noun, **P** for pronoun, or **A** for adjective.

_____ 1. Years ago, people in New England tried farming *silkworms*.

_____ 2. The scarf made of wool will be warmer than the *silk* scarf.

_____ 3. *These* plants have poisonous leaves.

_____ 4. I can't believe you said *that*!

_____ 5. This is just a *summer* shower, so it won't last long.

Answer Key

Practice and Reinforcement (1)
The Noun

Exercise A

1. sun, star
2. sister, student, chemistry, summer
3. Mr. Morales, koalas , San Diego Zoo
4. Mingan, goalie, team
5. Earline, party, play
6. parents, Hawaii, convention
7. storm, game, World Series
8. actors, faith, director
9. Lucy, chimpanzee, words, sign language
10. Ryan, humor, essays

Exercise B

When a volcano erupted on the island of Krakatoa in Indonesia, the whole world felt the effects. The noise from the eruption could be heard at great distances, and the force from the blast could be felt as far as California. A cloud of ash circled the globe and dimmed the light from the sun. Volcanic eruptions are powerful forces that can affect the entire planet.

Practice and Reinforcement (2)
Types of Nouns

Exercise A

1. COM, ABS
2. PRO, CON
3. COM, CON
4. COM, ABS
5. PRO, CON
6. COM, CON
7. COM, ABS
8. PRO, CON
9. COM, CON
10. PRO, CON

Exercise B: Proofreading

Jules verne always loved adventure. As a boy, he worked on a ship, the *coralie*. Later, the young man wrote plays, which provided little income. Verne needed ~~monnie~~ *money*, so he started writing books about real and imaginary ~~jurneys~~ *journeys*. the public loved these stories and ~~eegerly~~ *eagerly* awaited each new novel.

Practice and Reinforcement (3)
The Pronoun

Exercise A

1. R—The baby cried herself to sleep.
2. P, R—We should not let ourselves overlook the plight of the homeless.
3. P—Are you aware of the dangers of smoking?
4. P, P—"I will not tolerate lateness," the band leader told us.
5. I, P—The principal himself called me with the good news.
6. P —"Jogging is not for me," said Dr. Wong.
7. R—When the smoke detector sounded, the cat hid itself behind the couch.
8. P—After the twins frosted the cake, they looked for the candles.
9. P—Before you wash the floor, please move the chairs.
10. P, P—Don't wear the new boots until you waterproof them.

Exercise B

If a maple tree could not shed its leaves in winter, the tree would die. Trees lose gallons of water each day through their leaves. In winter, when the ground freezes, the trees cannot take in much water from the soil. To save themselves from drying out, many trees drop their leaves. With no leaves, a tree can keep more of its moisture and prevent itself from drying out.

Answer Key

Practice and Reinforcement (4)
Types of Pronouns

Exercise A

1. What
2. that
3. These
4. All
5. who

Exercise B

1. DEM, This; REL, which
2. IND, Nobody
3. REL, that
4. INT, Who
5. REL, whose
6. DEM, These
7. REL, who
8. INT, What
9. IND, several
10. DEM, Those

Practice and Reinforcement (5)
Adjectives

Exercise A

1. I,—an, older
2. D,—The, sudden
3. I,—a, small, electric
4. I,—a, medium, extra
5. D,—The, mysterious

Exercise B

1. Mary Shelley wrote a horror story.
2. The plot of the story was imaginative.
3. One stormy night, she had listened to several stories about ghosts.
4. Friends had made up scary stories about monsters.
5. Mary knew she would have a terrible night.
6. Mary thought about the stories all night and had a strange nightmare.
7. She dreamed of a young doctor who created a monster.

8. Mary wrote a story of the ghastly nightmare and called it *Frankenstein*.
9. The eerie novel was a great success.
10. Several movies have been made from it.

Practice and Reinforcement (6)
Types of Adjectives

Exercise A

1. A
2. A
3. N
4. A
5. N
6. N
7. N
8. P
9. A
10. A

Exercise B

Louis Braille invented a special alphabet that allows the visually impaired to read. The alphabet uses raised dots that the visually impaired can feel. The dots are arranged in patterns, with different patterns standing for individual letters or sounds. A person reads Braille by rubbing one or two fingertips over the elevated dots. A person can write Braille by hand, using a pointed stylus and a metal slate. Or, a person can use a Braille typewriter or computer.

Chapter Review
Form A

Exercise A

1. William Sydney Porter had talent.
2. The man was a writer.
3. His pen name was O. Henry.
4. Porter spent three years in jail.
5. His first story was published by *McClure's Magazine* while he was a prisoner.

Answer Key

Exercise B

1. COM, ABS
2. COM, CON
3. PRO, CON
4. COM, CON
5. COM, ABS
6. COM, CON
7. COM, ABS
8. PRO, CON
9. COM, CON
10. COM, CON

Exercise C

1. I—The instructor herself first demonstrated the dive.
2. P—The spokes of a bicycle's wheel help it absorb shock.
3. P—King Charles liked to say, "In my empire the sun never sets."
4. R—A frightened hedgehog curls itself into a ball.
5. P—The artist wanted you to come to the gallery opening.

Exercise D

1. who—REL
2. one—IND; that—REL
3. Everyone—IND; who—REL
4. Whom—INT
5. What—INT
6. all—IND; these—DEM
7. no one—IND
8. this—DEM
9. who—REL
10. those—DEM

Exercise E

1. D—Have you ever seen the huge rosebush in Tombstone?
2. D—Every spring, the bush is covered with white flowers.
3. D, I—The bush was planted by a Scottish woman.
4. D—She came to Tombstone in the late 1800s.
5. I, D—She was a young bride at the time.
6. D—Now the plant is very old.
7. D—Many people travel to Tombstone to see the bush.
8. D—It grows beside the old Rose Tree Inn.
9. D—The rosebush is very large.
10. D, D—Several sources call it the largest rosebush in the world.

Exercise F

1. P
2. A
3. A
4. A
5. N

Chapter Review
Form B

Exercise A

1. Owney was a stray dog found behind a post office in New York.
2. The mail clerks gave food to the friendly animal.
3. Owney traveled all over the United States, hitching rides in the mail cars of trains.
4. Soon, the tags on his collar were covered with stamps from cities all over the country.
5. Owney traveled to Japan by boat and then continued around the world.

Exercise B

1. PRO, CON
2. COM, CON
3. COM, ABS
4. COM, CON
5. COM, CON
6. COM, ABS
7. COM, CON
8. PRO, CON
9. PRO, CON
10. COM, ABS

Answer Key

Exercise C
1. P—them
2. R—itself
3. P—I
4. I—herself
5. P—you

Exercise D
1. whose—REL
2. What—INT
3. these—DEM
4. which—REL
5. anyone—IND
6. Which—INT
7. this—DEM
8. both—IND
9. who—REL
10. Who—INT

Exercise E
1. new
2. Many
3. The , a, new—D, I
4. tiny
5. Young, their, ring
6. the, photographic, a, special, wet—D, I
7. The , a, a, smooth —D, I, I
8. the, dry—D
9. the, clear, the—D, D
10. The, hard, the, a, long —D, D, I

Exercise F
1. N
2. A
3. A
4. P
5. A

Chapter 15: The Parts of Speech

Transitive and Intransitive Verbs

A **transitive verb** is an action verb that expresses an action directed toward a person or thing.

Ingrid *left* her sneakers in the gym. (The action of *left* is directed toward *sneakers*. *Sneakers* is the object of the verb *left*.)

An **intransitive verb** expresses action (or tells something about the subject) without passing the action to a receiver.

The runner *stretched*. (The action of *stretched* is not passed to a receiver.)

A verb may be transitive in one sentence and intransitive in another.

Transitive: The settlers *endured* many hardships.

Intransitive: Many died, but a few *endured*.

Exercise A   Decide whether the italicized verb in each sentence is transitive or intransitive. On the line provided, write **T** for transitive or **I** for intransitive.

_____ 1. At this airport, no planes *land* after dark.

_____ 2. My sister and I *planted* tomatoes.

_____ 3. Rick's parrot *screams* all day.

_____ 4. Everyone *ran* toward the exits.

_____ 5. Ming Chin *caught* the largest fish.

_____ 6. Ira *is finishing* his homework.

Exercise B: Expanding Sentences   Sometimes adding a word or phrase can make an intransitive verb transitive. Add a word or phrase to each sentence below to change each intransitive verb into a transitive one. Write your expanded sentences on the lines provided.

Example: Amos is driving to Seattle.

Amos is driving a truck to Seattle.

1. Erin will not forget. _____

_____

2. Ernesto will recite next. _____

_____

3. Today we can draw with charcoal. _____

_____

4. While one partner works, the other watches. _____

_____

Chapter 15: The Parts of Speech

Action Verbs and Linking Verbs

An **action verb** is a verb that expresses physical or mental action.

    John Muir *wrote* about Yosemite National Park.

    Eileen *imagined* the scene.

A **linking verb** expresses a state of being. A linking verb connects the subject of a sentence with a word in the predicate that explains or describes the subject.

    Your painting *is* beautiful!

Some verbs may be either action or linking verbs, depending on how they are used.

        Action verb: Paco *tasted* the soup.

        Linking verb: Those vegetables *tasted* fresh.

Exercise A   Underline the verbs in the sentences below. Then decide whether each is an action verb or a linking verb. On the line provided, write **A** for action verb or **L** for linking verb.

          Example: ___L___   Aaron Burr <u>was</u> the third vice-president of the United States.

_____ 1. Burr became one of the most colorful characters in U.S. history.

_____ 2. Although a brave man, he felt unhappy in the army.

_____ 3. He resigned in 1779 because of ill health.

_____ 4. Later, Burr practiced law.

_____ 5. He always seemed wealthy and successful.

_____ 6. He fought a duel with Alexander Hamilton.

_____ 7. Although illegal, duels were fairly common at the time.

_____ 8. Onlookers heard two shots.

_____ 9. Hamilton died from his wound.

_____ 10. Burr's career was over.

Exercise B   Underline the linking verb in each of the following sentences. Then draw an arrow between the words joined by the linking verb.

        Example: The old house <u>looked</u> deserted.

1. The farm animals looked quite content.

2. The computerized voice sounds human.

3. After the storm, the islanders grew fearful of all dark clouds.

4. Some of the bristlecone pines are very old.

5. The huge diamond mine is now a museum.

Chapter 15: The Parts of Speech

Verb Phrases and Helping Verbs

A **verb phrase** contains one main verb and one or more helping verbs.

The code *was hidden* inside an old book. (The main verb is *hidden*.)

Sometimes a verb phrase is interrupted by another part of speech.

Sparky *will* not *bite* you.

Our customers *can* always *use* cash, checks, or credit cards.

Exercise A   Underline the verb phrase in each sentence. Then draw another line under each main verb.

> **Example:** People <u>have <u>celebrated</u></u> birthdays for thousands of
> years.

1. Ancient Egyptians would sometimes buy birthday garlands.

2. The Persians would hold special feasts.

3. In nineteenth-century literature, birthdays were often described as sad affairs.

4. Some people do not like birthday celebrations.

5. Other people have celebrated in spectacular ways.

6. On one occasion, Julius Caesar had declared himself a god!

7. Perhaps we should copy certain Scandinavian celebrations.

8. On certain birthdays, the entire village will congratulate someone.

9. Festivities may include loud cannons and numerous speeches.

10. Maybe I will celebrate my birthday like that next year.

Exercise B   Underline the ten verb phrases in the following paragraph. Draw another line under the main verb in each phrase.

> Scientists can explain the causes of thunder. Thunder is caused by the heat of
> lightning. A stroke of lightning can heat nearby air molecules. The heated air
> molecules will then expand. They will also move. Their movement can create
> sound waves. Because light can travel faster than sound, you will first see the
> lightning. The flash will occur almost immediately. Only afterwards will you
> hear the thunder.

Chapter 15: The Parts of Speech

The Adverb

An **adverb** is a word that modifies a verb, an adjective, or another adverb. An adverb tells *where, when, how, how often, how long, to what extent,* or *how much.*

> *Yesterday* my next-door neighbor was *extremely* kind. (The adverb *Yesterday* modifies the verb *was* and tells when. The adverb *extremely* modifies the adjective *kind* and tells to what extent.)

Exercise A   On the line provided, write the adverb or adverbs in each sentence. Then underline the word that each adverb modifies.

> **Example:** ___rarely___   You <u>can</u> rarely <u>get</u> tickets for this horse show.

_____ 1. Vivi Malloy rides her horse daily.

_____ 2. She has always wanted to make the U. S. Equestrian Team.

_____ 3. Vivi rides a very attractive chestnut horse named Penny Red.

_____ 4. Vivi usually cleans the horse's stall after school.

_____ 5. Then she grooms her horse.

_____ 6. Vivi mounts Penny Red cheerfully.

_____ 7. Penny Red trots briskly around the ring.

_____ 8. Penny Red and Vivi especially enjoy jumping.

_____ 9. They have competed successfully in several shows.

_____10. Vivi's parents always attend her shows.

Exercise B: Revising   On the line provided, rewrite each of the following sentences, adding one or more adverbs.

1. Many medieval castles were protected by moats.

_____

2. The moats were filled with water.

_____

3. People crossed the moats on drawbridges.

_____

4. These bridges could be raised.

_____

5. The gate to the castle was covered with iron.

_____

Chapter 15: The Parts of Speech

Prepositions and Prepositional Phrases

A **preposition** is a word that shows the relationship between a noun or pronoun and another word in the sentence.

The dog jumped *through* the hoop. (The preposition *through* shows the relationship between *dog* and *hoop*.)

A **prepositional phrase** includes a preposition, a noun or pronoun called the **object of the proposition**, and any modifiers of that object.

Dr. Okana peered *through the huge telescope.* (The preposition is *through* and the object of the preposition is *telescope. The* and *huge* modify *telescope.*)

Exercise A   Underline the prepositional phrase in each sentence. Then write the preposition on the line provided.

_____ 1. A copper-colored snake slithered along the rotting log.

_____ 2. During a crisis David sometimes loses his self-control.

_____ 3. The newscaster slipped on the ice.

_____ 4. The ancient Pont du Gard was built 160 feet above the Gard River.

_____ 5. A fungus caused the nineteenth-century potato famine in Ireland.

_____ 6. The pigs found their food under the shallow water.

Exercise B: Expanding Sentences   Prepositional phrases add interest and information to sentences. Add prepositional phrases to the following sentences. Rewrite the sentences on the lines provided.

1. The frightened soldier hid.

_____

2. Canditha wore a beautiful scarf.

_____

3. Suddenly, the prisoners heard a faint scratching noise.

_____

4. The creature had hideous, green tentacles.

_____

Types of Conjunctions

A **conjunction** is a word that joins words or groups of words.

Coordinating conjunctions connect words or groups of words used in the same way.

You can eat *or* sleep first. (The conjunction *or* connects the verbs *can eat* and *sleep*.)

Correlative conjunctions are pairs of conjunctions. They also connect words or groups of words used in the same way.

Your tropical fish *not only* will survive *but also* will thrive.

Exercise A   Underline the conjunctions in the following sentences.

1. I pressed the button, but the elevator did not stop.

2. Either Eddie or Pang will deliver the furniture.

3. We wanted to go sledding, but the snow was starting to melt.

4. Jennifer repeated the caller's number and wrote it on the pad.

5. Neither strawberries nor raspberries are in season right now.

6. Pandora was curious but frightened.

7. Don't sail now, for the winds are too strong.

8. I'd like to visit California, but I can't go right now.

9. Leotie wondered whether she should go or stay home.

10. Do you want me to make the fruit punch or blow up the balloons?

Exercise B: Sentence Combining   Combine each pair of sentences by using one or more conjunctions to create a compound subject, a compound object, or a compound verb.

1. Rudy plays the trumpet. Rudy plays the trombone.

_____

2. The horse bucked. The horse reared.

_____

3. Scott served the first course. Paco served the first course.

_____

4. My sister does not speak Russian. My sister does not read Russian.

_____

5. The building trembled. The building did not collapse.

_____

Chapter 15: The Parts of Speech

The Interjection

An **interjection** is a word that expresses strong emotion. An interjection is set off from the rest of the sentence by an exclamation point or by a comma or commas.

Hey! Come back here!

Well, you could try a lighter bat.

Exercise A   Underline the interjections in the following sentences.

1. Ouch! I stubbed my toe.

2. Oh, maybe we should wait.

3. Help! My experiment blew up!

4. Well, it isn't raining as hard now.

5. You won that much? Wow!

6. Eureka! I have found it!

7. Gee, it sounds like fun, but I have to work.

8. Hooray! We won first place!

9. Oops! I spilled juice on the floor.

10. Shucks, that's not so fast.

Exercise B: Proofreading   The following paragraph is missing two punctuation marks and contains two spelling errors and one error in capitalization. Can you find all five errors? Proofread the paragraph to correct the errors.

You should try to come to the Harvest Festival our town holds each october.

Oh it can get cold, but evryone bundles up. People bring in enormus pumpkins

for one contest. Maybe you saw the picture in the newspaper last year. The

winning pumpkin was bigger than the judge's young daughter. I tried to move

it, but I couldn't. Wow That pumpkin was heavy!

Chapter 15: The Parts of Speech

Reviewing the Parts of Speech

You can't tell what part of speech a word is until you know how it is used in a sentence. Words can often be used as more than one part of speech.

The two contestants always *shake* hands. (The word *shake* is used as a verb.)

Give the jar a *shake* before you pour the juice. (The word *shake* is used as a noun.)

Exercise A Each sentence contains an italicized word. Decide what part of speech that word is. On the line provided, write **N** for noun, **PRO** for pronoun, or **ADJ** for adjective.

_____ 1. I found *this* unusual plant in our meadow.

_____ 2. A hayfield is a wonderful *place* to observe nature.

_____ 3. Once I asked my sister to help *me* collect flowers.

_____ 4. I especially like the *colorful* flowers.

_____ 5. *Those* look pretty when they are dried.

Exercise B Each sentence contains one or more italicized words. Decide what part of speech each italicized word is. On the line provided, write **V** for verb, **ADV** for adverb, **PREP** for preposition, **C** for conjunction, or **I** for interjection.

_____ 1. Maps are *very* popular with collectors.

_____ 2. Some *have sold* for very high prices.

_____ 3. High prices have encouraged the publication of special books *and* magazines.

_____ 4. Valuable maps must be *carefully* protected from light and dust.

_____ 5. Many of the most valuable maps are kept *inside* closed drawers.

_____ 6. *Oh,* that really is a treasure map.

_____ 7. The Library of Congress houses the world's most valuable collection *of* maps.

_____ 8. *Within* its vault lies the original layout of Washington, D.C.

_____ 9. *Either* Thomas Jefferson *or* Pierre L'Enfant wrote the comments on the map.

_____ 10. In this collection *are* many unusual maps.

Chapter 15: The Parts of Speech

Review (Form A)

Exercise A   Decide whether each italicized verb is transitive or intransitive. Then, on the line provided, write **T** for transitive or **I** for intransitive.

_____ 1. The end of the rope *fell* into the water.

_____ 2. All the antelopes *raised* their heads.

_____ 3. Sean *was given* an award for bravery.

_____ 4. During the scavenger hunt, we *raced* into every store on Main Street.

_____ 5. Mu Lan *finished* her picture just in time for the show.

Exercise B   Decide whether each italicized verb is an action verb or a linking verb. On the line provided, write **A** for action verb or **L** for linking verb.

_____ 1. The apartment *has been* warm all week.

_____ 2. Before diving, always *look* below you for possible hazards.

_____ 3. In his old age, my dog *has become* quite gray around the mouth and eyes.

_____ 4. We may be lost, because this *doesn't look* familiar to me.

_____ 5. Most of the subjects *dreamed* about flying or sailing.

_____ 6. My father *is* worried about his job.

_____ 7. Quartz crystals *vibrate* at a constant rate.

_____ 8. Alicia *wore* kneepads and a helmet.

_____ 9. The baby rabbit *remained* still until the dog passed by.

_____10. As he climbed up the tower, Willis *felt* totally confident.

Exercise C   In each of the following sentences, underline the helping verb once and the main verb twice.

1. A chameleon's body may grow six inches long.

2. The animal's tongue might be even longer.

3. This long tongue is kept rolled up inside the animal's mouth.

4. The chameleon can unroll its tongue very quickly.

5. Chameleons have caught insects eight inches away.

Chapter 15: The Parts of Speech

Review (Form A)

Exercise D   In each of the following sentences, underline the prepositional phrase. Then underline the object of the preposition a second time.

1. Mildred Didrikson Zaharias came from Texas.

2. She was known by her nickname, Babe.

3. During her teens, she played basketball.

4. She scored more than one hundred points in a single game.

5. At eighteen, she set several track records.

6. Before the year's end, she won two Olympic medals.

7. Babe won one medal for the javelin toss.

8. She played baseball with a professional team.

9. Until her early death, she played golf.

10. She won more than fifty golf tournaments in her life.

Exercise E   Identify the italicized word in each of the following sentences as an adverb, conjunction, or interjection. On the line provided, write **ADV** for adverb, **C** for conjunction, or **I** for interjection.

_____ 1. *Sometimes* beachcombers find interesting things on beaches.

_____ 2. Usually they find bottles *or* driftwood.

_____ 3. The *most* common items are the least interesting.

_____ 4. A local woman *once* found a narwhal tusk.

_____ 5. But aren't narwhals *really* imaginary creatures?

_____ 6. *No,* a narwhal is a large swimming mammal, like a whale.

_____ 7. The males *often* grow a single, long tusk.

_____ 8. *Gosh,* some tusks are almost nine feet long!

_____ 9. The narwhal doesn't use the tusk for fighting *or* digging.

_____10. People *once* thought the tusks were unicorn horns.

Chapter 15: The Parts of Speech

Review (Form B)

Exercise A   Decide whether each italicized verb is transitive or intransitive. On the line provided, write **T** for transitive or **I** for intransitive.

_____ 1. The dragon's breath *burned* the fence.

_____ 2. My sister *trains* police dogs.

_____ 3. A technician *is fixing* the keyboard now.

_____ 4. A fire *burned* in the fireplace, but no one was in the room.

_____ 5. Three different Pharaohs *built* those tombs.

Exercise B   Decide whether each italicized verb is an action verb or a linking verb. On the line provided, write **A** for action verb or **L** for linking verb.

_____ 1. During the operation, one nurse *looked* pale.

_____ 2. Margarita *grabbed* the horse by its mane.

_____ 3. Everyone *watched* the stunt parachutist.

_____ 4. Dr. Levine *handed* the woman her new glasses.

_____ 5. After raising the hood, the mechanic *checked* the wires.

_____ 6. Everyone *wore* a different kind of costume.

_____ 7. Your entire house *smells* spicy.

_____ 8. Latrice *is helping* me catalogue the books.

_____ 9. With one swift stroke, the chef *chopped* off the leaves.

_____10. The students at my new school *seem* friendly.

Exercise C   In each of the following sentences, underline the helping verb once and the main verb twice.

1. In science, we are studying vampire bats.

2. These bats are found in Central America and South America.

3. A vampire bat does not suck blood.

4. Instead, it will make a tiny cut on an animal's skin.

5. Usually, a bat will lap only a few drops of blood.

Chapter 15: The Parts of Speech

Review (Form B)

Exercise D In each of the following sentences, underline the prepositional phrase. Then underline the object of the preposition a second time.

1. The bottom of the ocean is very dark.

2. In most places, it is also cold.

3. However, in some places the ocean floor is warm.

4. One such place is near Ecuador.

5. Scientists discovered a crack in the ocean floor.

6. They found that heat poured from this crack.

7. The heat came from inside the earth.

8. Many plants and animals lived around this spot.

9. Tiny bacteria lived near giant worms.

10. These life forms lived eight thousand feet below the water's surface.

Exercise E Identify the italicized word or words in each of the following sentences as an adverb, conjunction, or interjection. On the line provided, write **ADV** for adverb, **C** for conjunction, or **I** for interjection.

_____ 1. One day in 1871, Gideon Merkel *and* John Gehret were working in a

quarry.

_____ 2. *Suddenly,* one of the men noticed a slit in one of the rocks.

_____ 3. Being curious, they crawled *inside.*

_____ 4. *Wow!* It was pitch black in there!

_____ 5. *Later,* they returned with lanterns.

_____ 6. The light allowed them to see *clearly.*

_____ 7. Weird shapes grew from *both* the floor *and* the roof.

_____ 8. Most surfaces *there* glittered brightly.

_____ 9. *Well,* they told many people about their find.

_____10. *Today* their discovery is called Crystal Cave.

Answer Key

Practice and Reinforcement (1)
Transitive and Intransitive Verbs

Exercise A

1. I
2. T
3. I
4. I
5. T
6. T

Exercise B: Expanding Sentences

(Answers will vary. Possible responses are given.)

1. Erin will not forget her lines.
2. Ernesto will recite his poem next.
3. Today we can draw portraits with charcoal.
4. While one partner works equations, the other watches the experiment.

Practice and Reinforcement (2)
Action Verbs and Linking Verbs

Exercise A

1. L—became
2. L—felt
3. A—resigned
4. A—practiced
5. L—seemed
6. A—fought
7. L—were
8. A—heard
9. A—died
10. L—was

Exercise B

1. The farm animals looked quite content.
2. The computerized voice sounds human.
3. After the storm, the islanders grew fearful of any dark clouds.
4. Some of the bristlecone pines are very old.
5. The huge diamond mine is now a museum.

Practice and Reinforcement (3)
Verb Phrases and Helping Verbs

Exercise A

1. Ancient Egyptians would sometimes buy birthday garlands.
2. The Persians would hold special feasts.
3. In nineteeth-century literature, birthdays were often described as sad affairs.
4. Some people do not like birthday celebrations.
5. Other people have celebrated in spectacular ways.
6. On one occasion, Julius Caesar had declared himself a god!
7. Perhaps we should copy certain Scandinavian celebrations.
8. On certain birthdays, the entire village will congratulate someone.
9. Festivities may include loud cannons and numerous speeches.
10. Maybe I will celebrate my birthday like that next year.

Exercise B

Scientists can explain the causes of thunder. Thunder is caused by the heat of lightning. A stroke of lightning can heat nearby air molecules. The heated air molecules will then expand. They will also move. Their movement can create sound waves. Because light can travel faster than sound, you will first see the lightning. The flash will occur almost immediately. Only afterwards will you hear the thunder.

Practice and Reinforcement (4)
The Adverb

Exercise A

1. daily—rides
2. always—has wanted
3. very—attractive
4. usually—cleans
5. Then—grooms
6. cheerfully—mounts
7. briskly—trots

Answer Key

8. especially—<u>enjoy</u>

9. successfully—<u>have competed</u>

10. always—<u>attend</u>

Exercise B: Revising

(Answers will vary. Possible responses are given.)

1. Many medieval castles were well protected by moats.

2. The moats were sometimes filled with water.

3. People safely crossed the moats on drawbridges.

4. These bridges could be raised quickly.

5. The gate to the castle was heavily covered with iron.

Practice and Reinforcement (5)
Prepositions and Prepositional Phrases

Exercise A:

1. along—<u>along the rotting log</u>

2. During—<u>During a crisis</u>

3. on—<u>on the ice</u>

4. above—<u>above the Gard River</u>

5. in—<u>in Ireland</u>

6. under—<u>under the shallow water</u>

Exercise B: Expanding Sentences

(Answers will vary. Possible responses are given.)

1. The frightened soldier hid inside a closet.

2. Canditha wore a beautiful scarf over her shoulders.

3. Suddenly, the prisoners heard a faint scratching noise behind the wall.

4. The creature had hideous, green tentacles between its horns.

Practice and Reinforcement (6)
Types of Conjunctions

Exercise A

1. <u>but</u>

2. <u>Either ... or</u>

3. <u>but</u>

4. <u>and</u>

5. <u>Neither ... nor</u>

6. <u>but</u>

7. <u>for</u>

8. <u>but</u>

9. <u>whether ... or</u>

10. <u>or</u>

Exercise B: Sentence Combining

(Answers will vary. Possible responses are given.)

1. Rudy plays either the trumpet or the trombone.

2. The horse bucked and reared.

3. Scott and Paco served the first course.

4. My sister does not speak or read Russian.

5. The building trembled but did not collapse.

Practice and Reinforcement (7)
The Interjection

Exercise A

1. <u>Ouch</u>

2. <u>Oh</u>

3. <u>Help</u>

4. <u>Well</u>

5. <u>Wow</u>

6. <u>Eureka</u>

7. <u>Gee</u>

8. <u>Hooray</u>

9. <u>Oops</u>

10. <u>Shucks</u>

Exercise B: Proofreading

You should try to come to the Harvest Festival our town holds each october. Oh it can get cold, but evryone bundles up. People bring in enormus pumpkins for one contest. Maybe you saw the picture in the newspaper last year. The winning pumpkin was bigger than the judge's young daughter. I tried to move it, but I couldn't. Wow That pumpkin was heavy!

Answer Key

Practice and Reinforcement (8)
Reviewing the Parts of Speech

Exercise A
1. ADJ
2. N
3. PRO
4. ADJ
5. PRO

Exercise B
1. ADV
2. V
3. C
4. ADV
5. PREP
6. I
7. PREP
8. PREP
9. C
10. V

Chapter Review
Form A

Exercise A
1. I
2. T
3. T
4. I
5. T

Exercise B
1. L
2. A
3. L
4. L
5. A
6. L
7. A
8. A
9. L
10. L

Exercise C
1. A chameleon's body <u>may grow</u> six inches long.
2. The animal's tongue <u>might be</u> even longer.
3. This long tongue <u>is kept</u> rolled up inside the animal's mouth.
4. The chameleon <u>can unroll</u> its tongue very quickly.
5. Chameleons <u>have caught</u> insects eight inches away.

Exercise D
1. Mildred Didrikson Zaharias came <u>from Texas.</u>
2. She was known <u>by her nickname</u>, Babe.
3. <u>During her teens</u>, she played basketball.
4. She scored more than one hundred points <u>in a single game.</u>
5. <u>At eighteen</u>, she set several track records.
6. <u>Before the year's end</u>, she won two Olympic medals.
7. Babe won one medal <u>for the javelin toss.</u>
8. She played baseball <u>with a professional team.</u>
9. <u>Until her early death</u>, she played golf.
10. She won more than fifty golf tournaments <u>in her life.</u>

Exercise E
1. ADV
2. C
3. ADV
4. ADV
5. ADV
6. I
7. ADV
8. I
9. C
10. ADV

Answer Key

Chapter Review
Form B

Exercise A

1. T
2. T
3. T
4. I
5. T

Exercise B

1. L
2. A
3. A
4. A
5. A
6. A
7. L
8. A
9. A
10. L

Exercise C

1. In science, we <u>are studying</u> vampire bats.
2. These bats <u>are found</u> in Central America and South America.
3. A vampire bat <u>does</u> not <u>suck</u> blood.
4. Instead, it <u>will make</u> a tiny cut on an animal's skin.
5. Usually, a bat <u>will lap</u> only a few drops of blood.

Exercise D

1. The bottom <u>of the ocean</u> is very dark.
2. In most <u>places</u>, it is also cold.
3. However, in some <u>places</u> the ocean floor is warm.
4. One such place is <u>near Ecuador</u>.
5. Scientists discovered a crack <u>in the ocean floor</u>.
6. They found that heat poured <u>from this crack</u>.
7. The heat came from <u>inside the earth</u>.
8. Many plants and animals lived <u>around this spot</u>.
9. Tiny bacteria lived <u>near giant worms</u>.
10. These life forms lived eight thousand feet <u>below the water's surface</u>.

Exercise E

1. C
2. ADV
3. ADV
4. I
5. ADV
6. ADV
7. C
8. ADV
9. I
10. ADV

Chapter 16: Complements

Direct Objects

Every sentence has a subject and a verb. In addition, many sentences have a **complement.** A complement is a word or a group of words that completes the meaning of a verb. One type of complement is a **direct object.** A direct object is a noun or a pronoun that receives the action of the verb or shows the result of that action. It answers the question *Whom?* or *What?* after a transitive verb.

> **Direct objects:** Ramón called *me* yesterday. (Whom did Ramón call?)
>
> Alexander Graham Bell invented the *telephone*. (What did Bell invent?)

A direct object may be a compound of two or more objects.

> **Compound:** Mia took *Brent* and *Lenise* to the play. (Whom did she take?)

A direct object can never follow a linking verb because a linking verb does not express action. Also, a direct object is never in a prepositional phrase.

> **Linking verb:** Bell *was* an inventor. (*Inventor* is not a direct object.)
>
> **Prepositional phrase:** He worked *in a laboratory*. (*Laboratory* is not a direct object.)

Exercise A   Underline the direct objects in the following sentences. One sentence contains a compound direct object. Some sentences do not contain direct objects.

1. Eli Whitney invented a machine for cotton farmers.

2. His machine was the cotton gin.

3. The machine separated seeds and small sticks from the cotton fibers.

4. It scratched the fibers with tiny, fine-toothed rakes.

5. Whitney's invention helped the South become a major cotton-growing region.

Exercise B   The following paragraph contains six single direct objects and two compound direct objects. Underline each one. Some sentences do not contain direct objects.

Thick plates of solid material form the earth's crust. Sometimes these plates move. The movement causes cracks in the earth's surface. One famous crack is the San Andreas fault in California. Sudden movements along this crack caused a terrible earthquake in 1906. It ruined many homes and other buildings in San Francisco. Several people lost their lives. Fallen buildings blocked many escape routes. Firefighters fought blazes throughout the city. But they didn't have enough water and equipment. The earthquake was very destructive. It was a terrible tragedy.

Chapter 16: Complements

Indirect Objects

An **indirect object** is a noun or pronoun that comes between the verb and the direct object. It tells *to whom* or *to what,* or *for whom* or *for what,* the action of the verb is done.

> **Indirect objects:** I gave *Hortensia* a gift. (To whom did I give a gift?)
>
> He gave the *chair* a coat of paint. (To what did he give a coat of paint?)

Like direct objects, indirect objects never follow linking verbs and never appear in prepositional phrases.

> **Indirect object:** He fed the *dog* a biscuit.
>
> **Prepositional phrase:** He fed a biscuit *to the dog*.

Like direct objects, indirect objects can be compounds, made up of two or more objects.

> **Compound**
> **indirect object:** I gave *Jaime* and *Alameda* their tickets.

Exercise A Each of the following sentences contains both a direct object and an indirect object. For each sentence, underline the direct object. On the line provided, write the indirect object. One sentence contains a compound indirect object.

_____ 1. The president gave the astronaut a medal.

_____ 2. The weather report promised us sunshine for the weekend.

_____ 3. After a long delay, the store sent Mr. Wong a refund.

_____ 4. Virgil and Mike sent Chim a birthday card.

_____ 5. María gave the carpenters and bricklayers clear directions.

Exercise B On the line provided, write **DO** if the underlined word is a direct object. Write **IO** if it is an indirect object. Write **N** if it is neither a direct object nor an indirect object.

_____ 1. The governor gave her staff a <u>party</u>.

_____ 2. Carlos showed Delia pictures from his <u>vacation.</u>

_____ 3. The witness gave the <u>jury</u> additional information about the crime scene.

_____ 4. Shizuo brought <u>sandwiches</u> to the picnic.

_____ 5. Felice threw the ball to <u>me</u>.

_____ 6. The scary movie gave <u>us</u> the shivers.

_____ 7. Melissa gave the waitress her <u>order</u>.

_____ 8. Please tell <u>me</u> a story, Arthur.

_____ 9. My friend Heather is the <u>secretary</u> of the Hiking Club.

_____10. Give the <u>speaker</u> your complete attention.

Chapter 16: Complements

Predicate Nominatives

A **subject complement** completes the meaning of a linking verb and identifies or describes the subject. Common linking verbs are forms of the verb *to be*. One kind of subject complement is a **predicate nominative**. A predicate nominative is a noun or a pronoun that follows a linking verb and explains or identifies the subject of the sentence.

	Subject	Linking verb			Predicate nominative	
A	*tiger*	*is*	a wild		*animal.*	(explains *tiger*)
My	*brother*	*may become*	a		*doctor.*	(identifies *brother*)

Sometimes people confuse a predicate nominative with a direct object. Remember that a predicate nominative always follows a linking verb. A direct object always follows an action verb.

> **Predicate nominative:** Masud is *captain* of our team.
> **Direct object:** The team elected *Masud*.

Remember that a predicate nominative is never part of a prepositional phrase.

> **Predicate nominative:** Anita became a great *runner*.
> **Prepositional phrase:** She is *in many races*.

A predicate nominative may be a compound.

> **Compound**
> **predicate nominative:** Carlos is my *friend* and *neighbor*.

Exercise A   Underline the linking verbs in the following sentences. Then write the predicate nominatives on the lines provided. One predicate nominative is compound.

_____ 1. Jacques-Yves Cousteau is a French underwater explorer.

_____ 2. His main interests are ocean life and conservation.

_____ 3. The fish and plants of the sea are his topics of study.

_____ 4. Underwater exploration can be a dangerous occupation.

_____ 5. Cousteau's explorations have become the subjects of films

and books.

Exercise B   On the line provided, write **PN** if the underlined word is a predicate nominative. Write **DO** if it is a direct object. Write **OP** if it is the object of a preposition.

_____ 1. Lyndon Johnson became our <u>president</u> in 1963.

_____ 2. That story is about the American <u>pioneers</u>.

_____ 3. Tomás Ortega is the best <u>student</u> in our class.

_____ 4. A leopard has <u>spots</u> on its coat.

_____ 5. A rake is a useful <u>tool</u> in a garden.

Chapter 16: Complements

Predicate Adjectives

A **predicate adjective** is one kind of subject complement. A predicate adjective follows a linking verb and describes the subject of the sentence.

	Subject	Linking verb		Predicate adjective
Your	*dog*	is	very	*big.*
The	*pizza*	tastes	too	*salty.*
Yesterday	*I*	felt		*sick.*

A predicate adjective may be compound.

Compound
predicate adjective: The cider was *cold* and *refreshing*.

Do not confuse predicate adjectives with predicate nominatives. A predicate adjective describes a subject. A predicate nominative is a noun or a pronoun that explains or identifies the subject of a sentence.

Predicate adjective: Yesterday was *sunny*.   (describes *Yesterday*)
Predicate nominative: Yesterday was my *birthday*.   (identifies *Yesterday*)

Exercise A   Underline the linking verbs in the following sentences. Then write the predicate adjectives on the lines provided. One predicate adjective is compound.

_____ 1. The ocean looks calm tonight.

_____ 2. The governor seemed pleased with the meeting.

_____ 3. After roller-skating, the children were hungry and tired.

_____ 4. Traffic on my street becomes quite heavy during rush hour.

_____ 5. The committee's plan is very complicated.

Exercise B   On the line before each sentence, write **PA** if the underlined word is a predicate adjective. Write **PN** if it is a predicate nominative.

_____ 1. Scott O'Dell is a fantastic <u>writer</u>.

_____ 2. His books have become <u>famous</u>.

_____ 3. *Island of the Blue Dolphins* is my <u>favorite</u>.

_____ 4. The main character is a Native American <u>girl</u>.

_____ 5. When she is left alone on a deserted island, she feels <u>lonely</u> and scared.

_____ 6. Fierce, wild dogs are her only <u>companions</u>.

_____ 7. They seem very <u>frightening</u> to her.

_____ 8. She becomes <u>determined</u> to leave the island in a canoe.

_____ 9. But her journey becomes <u>dangerous</u> when the canoe springs a leak.

_____10. She is a brave <u>person</u>, but she knows that she must turn back.

Chapter 16: Complements

Review (Form A)

Exercise A   On the line provided, write **DO** if the underlined word is a direct object. Write **IO** if it is an indirect object. Add **C** if it is part of a compound.

_____ 1. Pierre gave <u>me</u> a ticket to the opera *Madama Butterfly*.

_____ 2. We took a <u>bus</u> to the opera house.

_____ 3. An usher showed Pierre and <u>me</u> our seats.

_____ 4. The orchestra began the <u>overture</u>.

_____ 5. The opera tells a sad and touching <u>story</u>.

_____ 6. A woman marries a <u>man</u> who is in the navy.

_____ 7. Soon after their marriage, the man sails his <u>ship</u> to faraway places.

_____ 8. He leaves the woman and her little <u>child</u>.

_____ 9. She watches the <u>sea</u>, sadly hoping that he will return.

_____ 10. The performers tell <u>us</u> the entire story through their beautiful songs.

Exercise B   On the line provided, write **PN** if the underlined word is a predicate nominative. Write **PA** if it is a predicate adjective. Add **C** if it is part of a compound.

_____ 1. Fred Astaire was an actor and a <u>dancer</u>.

_____ 2. When he danced, he seemed very <u>light</u> on his feet.

_____ 3. Astaire's famous trademarks were his top hat and <u>cane</u>.

_____ 4. His dances often seem a <u>combination</u> of ballet, tap, and jazz.

_____ 5. In many movies, Ginger Rogers was his dancing <u>partner</u>.

_____ 6. The movies they made together became very famous and <u>popular</u>.

_____ 7. My two favorites are *Top Hat* and *Swing Time*.

_____ 8. Astaire's career was <u>long</u> and brilliant.

_____ 9. He became a movie <u>star</u> in 1933 and continued to make films until 1982.

_____ 10. He was always a modest <u>man</u>, who said, "I just dance."

Review (Form A)

Exercise C   On the line provided, write **DO** if the underlined word is a direct object, **IO** if it is an indirect object, **PN** if it is a predicate nominative, or **PA** if it is a predicate adjective. Add **C** if it is part of a compound.

_____ 1. Fred Gipson wrote a wonderful <u>book</u> called *Old Yeller*.

_____ 2. The main character and narrator is <u>Travis</u>, a teenage boy.

_____ 3. The setting is <u>Texas</u>, just after the Civil War.

_____ 4. Travis's father leaves their <u>home</u> to drive his cattle to market in Kansas.

_____ 5. Travis runs the <u>farm</u> during his father's absence.

_____ 6. One day, a stray dog steals some <u>meat</u>.

_____ 7. To Travis, the dog seems ugly and <u>useless</u>.

_____ 8. But over the next few weeks, the dog becomes a <u>companion</u> and a hero.

_____ 9. Quickly the dog gains the family's <u>affection</u> and gratitude.

_____10. I will lend <u>you</u> my copy of *Old Yeller* if you want to read a terrific book.

Exercise D   Circle the complement in each sentence. Then, on the line provided, write **DO** if it is a direct object, **PN** if it is a predicate nominative, or **PA** if it is a predicate adjective.

_____ 1. Rumpelstiltskin spun straw into gold for the miller's daughter.

_____ 2. Earth is not the only planet with a moon.

_____ 3. The bill of a pelican holds several quarts of water.

_____ 4. My older brother won a scholarship to Princeton.

_____ 5. Before the game, we attended a pep rally.

_____ 6. This apple tastes slightly sour.

_____ 7. Mark Twain's home in Hartford, Connecticut, has become a museum.

_____ 8. We read a ballad about John Henry.

_____ 9. Many of the magician's tricks were amazing.

_____10. Please send a postcard while you are in France.

Chapter 16: Complements

Review (Form B)

Exercise A   On the line provided, write **DO** if the underlined word is a direct object. Write **IO** if it is an indirect object. Add **C** if it is part of a compound.

_____ 1. My neighbor across the hall has an interesting <u>pet</u>.

_____ 2. The Stoneham Zoo gave <u>her</u> a chinchilla named Willy.

_____ 3. For years, the zoo featured the <u>chinchilla</u> in its Children's Zoo.

_____ 4. When Willy grew old, the zoo needed a new <u>home</u> for him.

_____ 5. Ms. Jefferson, my neighbor, wrote the <u>zoo</u> a letter.

_____ 6. She volunteered her <u>home</u> for Willy.

_____ 7. Ms. Jefferson leads programs and <u>workshops</u> at local hospitals.

_____ 8. She shows <u>patients</u> and staff members all kinds of animals and plants.

_____ 9. She told the zoo <u>staff</u> about this program.

_____10. Patients could hold <u>Willy</u> because he is so experienced with people.

Exercise B   On the line provided, write **PN** if the underlined word is a predicate nominative. Write **PA** if it is a predicate adjective. Add **C** if it is part of a compound.

_____ 1. Lawrence Kasdan is a skillful and clever <u>writer</u>.

_____ 2. His works are not books, <u>poems</u>, or articles.

_____ 3. Most of Kasdan's writing becomes exciting <u>films</u>.

_____ 4. One of the first movies that he wrote was *Raiders of the Lost Ark*.

_____ 5. To many people, that movie seemed <u>exciting</u> and funny.

_____ 6. Harrison Ford was <u>wonderful</u> as the leading man, Indiana Jones.

_____ 7. Kasdan's script for *Return of the Jedi* led to a film that is <u>full</u> of

adventure and colorful characters.

_____ 8. The western *Silverado* was another <u>film</u> by Kasdan.

_____ 9. The actor Kevin Kline is <u>one</u> of the stars of *Silverado*.

_____10. Kasdan was once a <u>student</u> at the University of Michigan.

Chapter 16: Complements

Review (Form B)

Exercise C   One the line provided, write **DO** if the underlined word is a direct object, **IO** if it is an indirect object, **PN** if it is a predicate nominative, or **PA** if it is a predicate adjective. Add **C** if it is part of a compound.

_____ 1. One of the United States' early pirates was <u>Dixie Bull</u>.

_____ 2. He attacked <u>ships</u> and stores in Bristol, Maine, in 1632.

_____ 3. Before he turned to piracy, Bull had been a farmer and a <u>fisherman</u>.

_____ 4. But French pirates stole <u>one</u> of his small fishing boats.

_____ 5. Angered at this, he became a <u>pirate</u> as well.

_____ 6. Key West, Florida, is <u>famous</u> for the pirates who once sailed in and out.

_____ 7. The ocean off Key West is often violent and <u>dangerous</u>.

_____ 8. The harsh waves and huge rocks gave <u>ships</u> a terrible beating.

_____ 9. Pirates would watch the <u>ships</u> as they passed through the rough waters.

_____ 10. They would give the <u>ships</u> aid, but they would also take the cargoes.

Exercise D   Circle the complement in each sentence. On the line provided, write **DO** if it is a direct object, **IO** if it is an indirect object, **PN** if it is a predicate nominative, or **PA** if it is a predicate adjective.

_____ 1. Henry David Thoreau wrote *Walden*.

_____ 2. It is a book about his experiences near Walden Pond in Massachusetts.

_____ 3. Thoreau was a teacher in Concord, Massachusetts.

_____ 4. In 1845, he left his home and went to the woods near Walden Pond.

_____ 5. He built a small cabin for himself and lived there for two years.

_____ 6. He was seeking a life of simplicity.

_____ 7. His life at Walden Pond was an experiment in quiet solitude.

_____ 8. For Thoreau, nature seemed a peaceful and instructive companion.

_____ 9. His daily journal about his life and thoughts became *Walden*.

_____ 10. The book is full of inspiring quotations about his search for personal freedom.

Answer Key

Practice and Reinforcement (1)
Direct Objects

Exercise A

1. Eli Whitney invented a <u>machine</u> for cotton farmers

2. His machine was the cotton gin.

3. The machine separated <u>seeds</u> and small <u>sticks</u> from the cotton fibers.

4. It scratched the <u>fibers</u> with tiny, fine-toothed rakes.

5. Whitney's invention helped the <u>South</u> become a major cotton-growing region.

Exercise B

Thick plates of solid material form the earth's <u>crust</u>. Sometimes these plates move. The movement causes <u>cracks</u> in the earth's surface. One famous crack is the San Andreas fault in California. Sudden movements along this crack caused a terrible <u>earthquake</u> in 1906. It ruined many <u>homes</u> and other <u>buildings</u> in San Francisco. Several people lost their <u>lives</u>. Fallen buildings blocked many escape <u>routes</u>. Firefighters fought <u>blazes</u> throughout the city. But they didn't have enough <u>water</u> and <u>equipment</u>. The earthquake was very destructive. It was a terrible tragedy.

Practice and Reinforcement (2)
Indirect Objects

Exercise A

1. astronaut — The president gave the astronaut a <u>medal</u>.

2. us — The weather report promised us <u>sunshine</u> for the weekend.

3. Mr. Wong — After a long delay, the store sent Mr. Wong a <u>refund</u>.

4. Chim — Virgil and Mike sent Chim a birthday <u>card</u>.

5. carpenters, bricklayers — María gave the carpenters and bricklayers clear <u>directions</u>.

Exercise B

1. DO
2. N
3. IO
4. DO
5. N
6. IO
7. DO
8. IO
9. N
10. IO

Practice and Reinforcement (3)
Predicate Nominatives

Exercise A

1. explorer — Jacques-Yves Cousteau <u>is</u> a French underwater explorer.

2. ocean life, conservation — His main interests <u>are</u> ocean life and conservation.

3. topics — The fish and plants of the sea <u>are</u> his topics of study.

4. occupation — Underwater exploration <u>can be</u> a dangerous occupation.

5. subjects — Cousteau's explorations <u>have become</u> the subjects of films and books.

Exercise B

1. PN
2. OP
3. PN
4. DO
5. PN

Answer Key

Practice and Reinforcement (4)
Predicate Adjectives

Exercise A

1. calm   The ocean <u>looks</u> calm tonight.
2. pleased   The governor <u>seemed</u> pleased with the meeting.
3. hungry, tired   After roller-skating, the children <u>were</u> hungry and tired.
4. heavy   Traffic on my street <u>becomes</u> quite heavy during rush hour.
5. complicated   The committee's plan <u>is</u> very complicated.

Exercise B

1. PN
2. PA
3. PN
4. PN
5. PA
6. PN
7. PA
8. PA
9. PA
10. PN

Chapter Review
Form A

Exercise A

1. IO
2. DO
3. IOC
4. DO
5. DO
6. DO
7. DO
8. DOC
9. DO
10. IO

Exercise B

1. PNC
2. PA
3. PNC
4. PN
5. PN
6. PAC
7. PNC
8. PAC
9. PN
10. PN

Exercise C

1. DO
2. PN
3. PN
4. DO
5. DO
6. DO
7. PAC
8. PNC
9. DOC
10. IO

Exercise D

1. DO   straw
2. PN   planet
3. DO   quarts
4. DO   scholarship
5. DO   pep rally
6. PA   sour
7. PN   museum
8. DO   ballad
9. PA   amazing
10. DO   postcard

Answer Key

Chapter Review
Form B

Exercise A

1. DO
2. IO
3. DO
4. DO
5. IO
6. DO
7. DOC
8. IOC
9. DO
10. DO

Exercise B

1. PN
2. PNC
3. PN
4. PN
5. PAC
6. PA
7. PA
8. PN
9. PN
10. PN

Exercise C

1. PN
2. DOC
3. PNC
4. DO
5. PN
6. PA
7. PAC
8. IO
9. DO
10. IO

Exercise D

1. DO   (Walden)
2. PN   (book)
3. PN   (teacher)
4. DO   (home)
5. DO   (cabin)
6. DO   (life)
7. PN   (experiment)
8. PN   (companion)
9. PN   (Walden)
10. PA   (full)

The Prepositional Phrase

A **prepositional phrase** includes a preposition, a noun or a pronoun called the **object of the preposition,** and any modifiers of that object.

during the days   with us

of noble deeds   about them

Notice that an article or another modifier often appears in a prepositional phrase. The first example above contains the article *the*. In the next example, the word *noble* modifies *deeds*.

The noun or pronoun that ends the prepositional phrase is called the **object of the preposition.** A prepositional phrase can have more than one object.

for the *parents* and their *children*

Exercise A   There are ten prepositional phrases in the following paragraph. Underline each prepositional phrase.

Many legends are told and retold about King Arthur and his knights. Through his strength, King Arthur proved his right to the British throne. He removed a great sword from a solid rock. Later, Arthur was given a sword with magical strength. The knights who gathered around King Arthur were known throughout the land for their courage and goodness. The knights of the Round Table led adventurous lives and fought many strong opponents. They dedicated themselves to honorable and noble ideals.

Exercise B: Expanding Sentences   The short blank in each sentence below shows where you can add a prepositional phrase. On the line following each sentence, write a prepositional phrase that can be added in the place where the short blank appears.

1. We are listening _____ on the radio.

_____

2. We're going home _____ .

_____

3. _____ was a pile of newspapers.

_____

4. Last week's game _____ ended in a tie.

_____

5. The oil painting _____ is priceless.

_____

The Adjective Phrase

A prepositional phrase that modifies a noun or a pronoun is called an **adjective phrase.**

Modifies a noun: The theme *of the story* is compassion. (The prepositional phrase *of the story* modifies the noun *theme.*)

Modifies a pronoun: One *of the scenes* shows the future. (The prepositional phrase *of the scenes* modifies the pronoun *One.*)

More than one adjective phrase may modify the same noun or pronoun.

The story *about Scrooge by Dickens* has become famous. (The two phrases, *about Scrooge* and *by Dickens,* both modify the noun *story.*)

An adjective phrase may also modify the object of another adjective phrase.

One *of the children in the class* was scared when the ghost appeared. (The adjective phrase *of the children* modifies the pronoun *One.* The adjective phrase *in the class* modifies the noun *children,* the object in the first phrase.)

Exercise A   Circle the adjective phrases in the following sentences. Draw an arrow from each adjective phrase to the noun or pronoun it modifies.

Example: Charles Dickens wrote many tales (about poverty.)

1. *A Christmas Carol* is the story of a rich man's repentance.

2. Ebenezer Scrooge was a man of wealth and property.

3. His clerk, Bob Cratchit, led a miserable life in poverty.

4. Spirits from the past, present, and future warned Scrooge.

5. One of them showed Scrooge the poor yet happy Cratchit family.

Exercise B   Each of the following sentences contains two adjectives phrases. On the lines provided, write the phrases and the words they modify.

Example: Microorganisms in the bodies of people and animals cause disease.

in the bodies—microorganisms; of people and animals—bodies

1. Louis Pasteur was a professor of chemistry at the University of Lille.

_____

2. The process of sterilization of milk is called pasteurization.

_____

3. Bacteria as the cause of disease was a new idea then.

_____

4. Pasteur's studies of infectious diseases in animals helped him formulate his germ theory.

_____

Chapter 17: The Phrase

The Adverb Phrase

A prepositional phrase that modifies a verb, an adjective, or another adverb is called an adverb phrase.

Modifies a verb: The assembly line method was invented *by Henry Ford.* (The adverb phrase *by Henry Ford* modifies the verb *was invented.*)

Modifies an adjective: People were ready *for a change.* (The adverb phrase *for a change* modifies the adjective *ready.*)

Modifies another adverb: Tasks were performed predictably *in the same order.* (The adverb phrase *in the same order* modifies the adverb *predictably.*)

Adverb phrases may appear at various places in sentences.

During the 1950s, the car became increasingly important.
The car became increasingly important *during the 1950s.*

More than one adverb phrase may modify the same word.

They worked *for hours on the assembly line.* (The adverb phrases *for hours* and *on the assembly line* modify the verb *worked.*)

Exercise A   Circle the adverb phrases in the following sentences. Draw an arrow from each adverb phrase to the verb, adjective, or adverb it modifies.

Example: (At one time,) cars were manufactured (by hand.)

1. Cars have not always been made in factories.

2. Through mass production, Henry Ford changed the world.

3. He put workers on assembly lines.

4. His employees worked repeatedly at the same individual tasks.

5. Early in the 1900s, low-priced cars were selling rapidly.

Exercise B   On the line provided, write the adverb phrases and the words they modify.

Example: This car could go for miles on a single cranking.
            for miles—go; on a single cranking—go

1. The moving assembly line was used in Ford's factories.

_____

2. Under his leadership, the company grew into an industrial giant.

_____

3. Throughout the world Henry Ford is known as a great inventor.

_____

4. By the late 1950s, millions sat proudly in the driver's seat.

_____

Participles and Participial Phrases

A **verbal** is a word that is formed from a verb but is used as a noun, an adjective, or an adverb.

A **participle** is a verb form that can be used as an adjective.

Present participles end in *-ing*.

> The *crying* child asked for his mother. (*Crying* is the present participle of the verb *cry*. The participle modifies the noun *child*.)

Past participles usually end in *-d* or *-ed*. Some past participles are irregularly formed.

> *Scattered* evidence was found in the house. (The past participle *Scattered* modifies the noun *evidence*.)

> Sheila needed a *written* excuse from her doctor. (The irregular past participle *written* modifies the noun *excuse*.)

A **participial phrase** consists of a participle and its modifiers and complements. The entire phrase is used as an adjective.

> *Waking slowly*, the dog stretched its legs. (The participle *Waking* is modified by the adverb *slowly*.)

> The record *broken by José Canseco* is impressive. (The participle *broken* is modified by the prepositional phrase *by José Canseco*.)

> *Hammering the nails*, Midori felt content. (The participle *Hammering* has the direct object *nails*.)

Exercise A   Draw a line under the participle in each of the following sentences. Then draw two lines under the word or words modified by the participle.

1. The baking bread smelled delicious.

2. From behind the tree came a screeching sound.

3. Under a pile of magazines lay the forgotten letter.

4. Frozen yogurt is his favorite dessert.

5. Devoted baseball fans are looking forward to the season.

Exercise B   Draw a line under the participial phrase in each of the following sentences. Then draw two lines under the word or words modified by the participial phrase.

1. Shaped like a flag, the sand sculpture won first prize.

2. The lion pacing in his cage looked angry.

3. Surrounded by the smell of apples, I walked through the orchard.

4. I heard something pounding against the windowpane.

5. Leaping into the air, the dancer thrilled the audience.

Infinitives and Infinitive Phrases

An **infinitive** is a verb form, usually preceded by *to*, that can be used as a noun, an adjective, or an adverb.

> **Infinitive used as a noun:** *To swim* is refreshing.
>
> **Infinitive used as an adjective:** The best place *to swim* is the local Y.
>
> **Infinitive used as an adverb:** Colleen goes to the local Y *to swim.*

An **infinitive phrase** consists of an infinitive and its modifiers and complements. It may be used as a noun, an adjective, or an adverb.

> *To write well* requires hard work. (The infinitive phrase is used as a noun. The infinitive *to write* is modified by the adverb *well.*)
>
> The time *to begin a paper* is long before the paper is due. (The infinitive phrase is used as an adjective modifying the noun *time.* The infinitive *to begin* has the direct object *paper.*)
>
> Elston went to the library *to write his paper.* (The infinitive phrase is used as an adverb modifying the verb *went.* The infinitive *to write* has the direct object *paper.*)

Exercise A   Underline the infinitives in the following sentences.

1. Pepita decided to join the track team.

2. Lamont wants to learn Spanish before fall.

3. Courtney is trying to sell more items than her classmates sell.

4. Robert Fulton tried to invent a practical submarine.

5. To learn about plants was George Washington Carver's goal.

6. The quartet tried to harmonize.

7. Elena offered to wash the car.

8. Justin was reluctant to try raw fish.

9. To fly was Wilbur Wright's dream.

10. Few astronauts have the opportunity to journey into space.

Exercise B   Underline the infinitive phrases in the following sentences.

1. Some satellites are designed to orbit the earth.

2. To stay in orbit, a satellite must move very fast.

3. Gravity causes objects to fall to the earth.

4. To escape gravity, satellites fly fast and far away.

5. To fall to earth at a rate of speed equal to the earth's curve is to be in orbit.

Chapter 17: The Phrase

Review (Form A)

Exercise A   Underline each prepositional phrase in the sentences that follow. Draw an arrow from the phrase to the word or words it modifies.

Example: A bath in warm water before bed relaxes your muscles.

1. Recently, scientists have been studying patterns of human sleep.

2. Our nightly rest is actually a series of short sleeps.

3. Some people sleep on their backs.

4. Other people rest quite comfortably on their sides.

5. The origin of dreams has always interested people.

6. One of the theories about dreams is that each of us writes our own script.

7. Most of our dreams appear as pictures in black and white.

8. The number of hours of sleep a person gets affects the number of dreams.

9. Some nightmares are caused by tension, worries, and nervousness.

10. People dream with greater regularity early in the morning than late at night.

Exercise B   On the line provided, identify the verbal phrase in each of the following sentences. Then tell whether it is a participial phrase or an infinitive phrase.

Example: The rain, falling gently, had a steady rhythm.

falling gently—participial phrase

1. To forecast the weather is not a simple process.

_____

2. Barometers, designed for measuring pressure, detect weather changes.

_____

3. The clouds forming in the sky also indicate weather conditions.

_____

4. To measure precipitation, gauges are used.

_____

5. Gauges indicating wind speed and direction are important tools.

_____

Chapter 17: The Phrase

Review (Form B)

Exercise A   Draw a line under each prepositional phrase and two lines under the word or words it modifies. On the line provided, write each phrase, and identify it as **ADV** if it is an adverb phrase or **ADJ** if it is an adjective phrase.

> **Example:** The submarine lies in wait deep beneath the sea.
> in wait—ADV; beneath the sea—ADV

1. Satellites bounce back information from distances high above the earth.

   _____

2. In the future, more and more information will be sent by satellite.

   _____

3. The news on television comes to us by satellite.

   _____

4. Cables under the ocean carry messages to our homes.

   _____

5. During the 1920s no one would have dreamed of such marvels in our own homes.

   _____

Exercise B   Circle the verbal phrase in each of the following sentences. On the line provided, identify the phrase by writing **PP** for participial phrase or **IP** for infinitive phrase.

_____ 1. Tennessee, named after a Cherokee village, is in the South.

_____ 2. He wrote a letter to the Chamber of Commerce asking for information.

_____ 3. The class wanted to visit Nashville.

_____ 4. They wished to see the Grand Ole Opry.

_____ 5. Others wanted to visit different places in Tennessee.

_____ 6. Gatlinburg, located at the gate of the Great Smoky Mountains National

   Park, was a favorite choice.

_____ 7. Topping the list of second choices, Memphis was a popular destination.

_____ 8. To hike in the mountains was the choice of just a few.

_____ 9. The choice finally agreed on by the class was Nashville.

_____ 10. They could not decide where to go in such an interesting state.

Answer Key

Practice and Reinforcement (1)
The Prepositional Phrase

Exercise A

Many legends are told and retold about King Arthur and his knights. Through his strength, King Arthur proved his right to the British throne. He removed a great sword from a solid rock. Later, Arthur was given a sword with magical strength. The knights who gathered around King Arthur were known throughout the land for their courage and goodness. The knights of the Round Table led adventurous lives and fought many strong opponents. They dedicated themselves to honorable and noble ideals.

Exercise B: Expanding Sentences

(Answers will vary. Possible responses are given.)

1. to the news
2. on the next plane
3. On the table
4. for the championship
5. in the museum

Practice and Reinforcement (2)
The Adjective Phrase

Exercise A

1. *A Christmas Carol* is the story (of a rich man's repentance.)
2. Ebenezer Scrooge was a man (of wealth and property.)
3. His clerk, Bob Cratchit, led a miserable life (in poverty.)
4. Spirits (from the past, present, and future) warned Scrooge.
5. One (of them) showed Scrooge the poor yet happy Cratchit family.

Exercise B

1. of chemistry—professor; at the University of Lille—professor
2. of sterilization—process; of milk—sterilization
3. as the cause—Bacteria; of disease—cause
4. of infectious diseases—studies; in animals—diseases

Practice and Reinforcement (3)
The Adverb Phrase

Exercise A

1. Cars have not always been made (in factories)
2. (Through mass production) Henry Ford changed the world.
3. He put workers (on assembly lines.)
4. His employees worked repeatedly (at the same individual tasks)
5. Early (in the 1900s) low-priced cars were selling rapidly.

Exercise B

1. in Ford's factories—was used
2. Under his leadership—grew; into an industrial giant—grew
3. Throughout the world—is known; as a great inventor—is known
4. By the late 1950s—sat; in the driver's seat—sat

Practice and Reinforcement (4)
Participles and Participial Phrases

Exercise A

1. The baking bread smelled delicious.
2. From behind the tree came a screeching sound.

Answer Key

3. Under a pile of magazines lay the forgotten letter.
4. Frozen yogurt is his favorite dessert.
5. Devoted baseball fans are looking forward to the season.

Exercise B

1. Shaped like a flag, the sand sculpture won first prize.
2. The lion pacing in his cage looked angry.
3. Surrounded by the smell of apples, I walked through the orchard.
4. I heard something pounding against the windowpane.
5. Leaping into the air, the dancer thrilled the audience.

Practice and Reinforcement (5)
Infinitives and Infinitive Phrases

Exercise A

1. Pepita decided to join the track team.
2. Lamont wants to learn Spanish before fall.
3. Courtney is trying to sell more items than her classmates sell.
4. Robert Fulton tried to invent a practical submarine.
5. To learn about plants was George Washington Carver's goal.
6. The quartet tried to harmonize.
7. Elena offered to wash the car.
8. Justin was reluctant to try raw fish.
9. To fly was Wilbur Wright's dream.
10. Few astronauts have the opportunity to journey into space.

Exercise B

1. Some satellites are designed to orbit the earth.
2. To stay in orbit, a satellite must move very fast.

3. Gravity causes objects to fall to the earth.
4. To escape gravity, satellites fly fast and far away.
5. To fall to earth at a rate of speed equal to the earth's curve is to be in orbit.

Chapter Review
Form A

Exercise A

1. Recently, scientists have been studying patterns of human sleep.
2. Our nightly rest is actually a series of short sleeps.
3. Some people sleep on their backs.
4. Other people rest quite comfortably on their sides.
5. The origin of dreams has always interested people.
6. One of the theories about dreams is that each of us writes our own script.
7. Most of our dreams appear as pictures in black and white.
8. The number of hours of sleep a person gets affects the number of dreams.
9. Some nightmares are caused by tension, worries, and nervousness.
10. People dream with greater regularity early in the morning than late at night.

Exercise B

1. To forecast the weather—infinitive phrase
2. designed for measuring pressure—participial phrase
3. forming in the sky—participial phrase
4. To measure precipitation—infinitive phrase
5. indicating wind speed and direction—participial phrase

Answer Key

Chapter Review
Form B

Exercise A

1. Satellites bounce <u>back</u> information <u>from</u> <u>distances</u> <u>high</u> <u>above the earth</u>.

   from distances—ADV; above the earth—ADV

2. <u>In the future</u>, more and more information <u>will be sent</u> by satellite.

   In the future—ADV; by satellite—ADV

3. The <u>news</u> <u>on television</u> <u>comes</u> to <u>us</u> by <u>satellite</u>.

   on television—ADJ; to us—ADV; by satellite—ADV

4. <u>Cables</u> <u>under the ocean</u> <u>carry</u> messages <u>to</u> <u>our homes</u>.

   under the ocean—ADJ; to our homes—ADV

5. <u>During the 1920s</u> no one <u>would have</u> <u>dreamed</u> of <u>such</u> <u>marvels</u> <u>in our own homes</u>.

   During the 1920s—ADV; of such marvels—ADV; in our own homes—ADJ

Exercise B

1. PP Tennessee, named after a Cherokee village, is in the South.

2. PP He wrote a letter to the Chamber of Commerce asking for information.

3. IF The class wanted to visit Nashville.

4. IF They wished to see the Grand Ole Opry

5. IF Others wanted to visit different places in Tennessee.

6. PP Gatlinburg, located at the gate of the Great Smoky Mountains National Park, was a favorite choice.

7. PP Topping the list of second choices, Memphis was a popular destination.

8. IF To hike in the mountains was the choice of just a few.

9. PP The choice finally agreed on by the class was Nashville.

10. IF They could not decide where to go in such an interesting state

Chapter 18: The Clause

Independent and Subordinate Clauses

A **clause** is a group of words that contains a verb and its subject. A clause is used as part of a sentence. An **independent** (or **main**) **clause** expresses a complete thought. It can stand alone as a sentence, or it can appear in a sentence that contains another clause.

> **Independent clause**
> **as a sentence:** *I will help.*

> **Independent clause**
> **within a sentence:** If you need me, *I will help.*

A **subordinate clause** does not express a complete thought and cannot stand alone as a sentence. A subordinate clause must be joined with at least one independent clause to make a sentence.

> **Subordinate clause:** *if you need me* (incomplete thought)

> **Subordinate clause**
> **joined with an**
> **independent clause:** *If you need me,* I will help.

Exercise A   On the line before each sentence, write **IC** if the italicized words form an independent clause. Write **SC** if the italicized words form a subordinate clause.

_____ 1. *When Jeremy came to visit,* I was not at home.

_____ 2. I know the woman *who owns that store.*

_____ 3. *I wonder* if the train will be late today.

_____ 4. Because it is hot today, *please water the garden.*

_____ 5. We hope *that he will finish his report on time.*

Exercise B: Expanding Sentences   On the lines provided, add independent clauses to these subordinate clauses to express complete thoughts.

1. When I graduate from high school, _____

_____

2. Because he surprised me, _____

_____

3. If you want to read a good book, _____

_____

4. Until Manchu moved to Chicago, _____

_____

5. After the game was over, _____

_____

The Adjective Clause

An **adjective clause** is a subordinate clause that modifies a noun or a pronoun. An adjective clause contains a verb and its subject. Look at the italicized words in the examples below.

> **Adjective:** a *striped* shirt
> **Adjective phrase:** a shirt *with stripes* (has no subject and verb)
> **Adjective clause:** a shirt *that has stripes* (has a subject and verb)

An adjective clause usually follows the noun or pronoun that it modifies. It tells *which one* or *what kind*. An adjective clause is usually introduced by a **relative pronoun.**

> **Relative pronouns:** *that   which   who   whom   whose*
> **Adjective clauses:** the book *that I read*; the man *who called*

Exercise A   Underline the adjective clause in each of the following sentences. Draw another line under the relative pronoun. Then circle the word or words that the adjective clause modifies.

1. Softball is a popular game that is played throughout the United States.

2. The game, whose origins are unknown, resembles baseball.

3. People who play softball are aware of slight differences in the two games.

4. The field that is used for softball is smaller than a baseball field.

5. The game, which lasts only seven innings, is shorter than a baseball game.

6. A softball is larger and softer than the ball that is used for baseball.

7. Players whom I especially envy can hit that big ball out of the park!

8. Kapok, which provides filling in sleeping bags, is also used in softballs.

9. Those who play softball do not need much protection from the ball.

10. Padded mitts are worn by only those whose positions require frequent catching.

Exercise B: Revising   Each of the following items is a noun or a pronoun modified by an adjective or an adjective phrase. Revise each item so that it is a noun or pronoun modified by an adjective clause. Write your revisions on the lines provided.

> **Example:** the boy with the torn jacket
> the boy whose jacket is torn

1. the player with the bat _____

2. the softball field at our school _____

3. the best team _____

4. the fastest runner _____

5. the player with the best batting average _____

Chapter 18: The Clause

The Adverb Clause

An **adverb clause** is a subordinate clause that is used as an adverb. An adverb clause may modify a verb, an adjective, or an adverb. An adverb clause contains a verb and its subject. An adverb clause answers one of these questions: *How? When? Where? Why? To what extent? How much? How long?* or *Under what condition?* Look at the italicized words in the examples below.

Adverb: Tomás ran the race *quickly.*

Adverb phrase: *With great speed,* Tomás ran the race.

Adverb clause: *Because Tomás ran the race with great speed,* he won.

(*Because Tomás ran the race with great speed* answers the question *Why he won.*)

An adverb clause is introduced by a word or a group of words called a **subordinating conjunction.** Some common subordinating conjunctions are *after, although, as if, as soon as, because, before, if, since, than, unless, until, when, wherever,* and *while.*

Exercise A   Underline the adverb clause in each of the following sentences. Draw another line under the word or group of words that is the subordinating conjunction.

1. I ate a bowl of popcorn while I did my homework.

2. We will have to hurry if we want to catch the 5:30 bus.

3. From the top of the hill, you can see trees wherever you look.

4. I need to borrow a pencil because I left mine at home.

5. The puppies act as if they are hungry.

6. A giraffe is taller than an elephant is.

7. Before we left for our vacation, we unplugged the refrigerator.

8. Since I love mystery stories, I enjoy the books by Agatha Christie.

9. They watch more television programs than I do.

10. Set the potted plants where they will get plenty of light.

Exercise B   For each sentence in Exercise A, write on the line below whether the adverb clause tells *how, when, where, why, how much,* or *under what condition.*

1. _____   6. _____

2. _____   7. _____

3. _____   8. _____

4. _____   9. _____

5. _____   10. _____

Review (Form A)

Exercise A   On the line provided, write **IC** if the italicized clause is an independent clause or **SC** if it is a subordinate clause.

_____ 1. The student *who owns the wallet* may claim it at the school office.

_____ 2. *This weekend we will wash the car,* which badly needs a good scrub.

_____ 3. The plant has small orange flowers *that open every morning.*

_____ 4. As soon as I finish my report, *let's go to the movies.*

_____ 5. *Although she had never taken piano lessons,* she could play very well.

_____ 6. Do you know the name of the boy *whom we saw on the train?*

_____ 7. *We stopped for a picnic,* which was very pleasant.

_____ 8. *Please accept this gift* that I made for you.

_____ 9. We practiced our roles in the play *until we were sure of our lines.*

_____ 10. *I wonder* whom the captain will select to represent the team.

Exercise B   Underline the adjective clause in each of the following sentences. Draw another line under the relative pronoun. Then circle the noun or pronoun that the clause modifies.

1. The concert that we'll hear tonight contains music by George Gershwin.

2. George Gershwin, who was a great composer, wrote *Porgy and Bess.*

3. This opera, which is set in South Carolina, features both jazz and ballet.

4. "Summertime," which is a beautiful song, is a highlight of the show.

5. Gershwin did not write the lyrics that went with his songs.

6. The lyricist whom Gershwin most respected was his brother, Ira.

7. Although George wrote the music, it was Ira who wrote the words.

8. Their musical play that I like the best is *An American in Paris.*

9. Gene Kelly stars in the movie that is based on this play.

10. Kelly, who sings and dances to Gershwin music in the film, is superb.

Chapter 18: The Clause

Review (Form A)

Exercise C   Underline the adverb clause in each sentence. Draw another line under the subordinating conjunction. On the line provided, write whether the clause tells *how, when, where, why, how much,* or *under what condition.*

_____ 1. Because I am in the high school band, I will march in the parade.

_____ 2. The parade will begin after all the bands and floats are in position.

_____ 3. Our band is larger than the band from Zavala High School is.

_____ 4. Since we are larger, we will play "The Star-Spangled Banner."

_____ 5. The parade will officially begin as soon as we finish the anthem.

_____ 6. After the parade, meet me where the band's buses are parked.

_____ 7. If it is raining, meet me in the lobby of City Hall.

_____ 8. The sky filled up with storm clouds as if it might rain.

_____ 9. Whenever I'm in a parade, the weather seems to work against me!

_____10. As soon as I start to play my horn, the weather becomes a music

                                          critic.

Exercise D   Underline the subordinate clause in each sentence. Then on the line provided, write **ADJ** if it is an adjective clause or **ADV** if it is an adverb clause.

_____ 1. Woody Allen, who has written many films, has also written plays.

_____ 2. *Play It Again, Sam,* a film that he made in 1972, was based on a play.

_____ 3. The play gained success on Broadway before he made it into a film.

_____ 4. The actor whom he chose for the leading role was Diane Keaton.

_____ 5. She went on to star in many other films that he wrote and directed.

_____ 6. After she appeared in *Play It Again, Sam,* she starred in *Sleeper* and then in

                 Annie Hall.

_____ 7. If you have never seen a Woody Allen film, you have missed some fun.

_____ 8. A scene that always makes me laugh is in *Take the Money and Run.*

_____ 9. Allen does not appear in all of the films that he writes.

_____10. However, the funniest moments in his films happen when he appears.

Chapter 18: The Clause

Review (Form B)

Exercise A   On the line provided, write **IC** if the italicized clause is an independent clause or **SC** if it is a subordinate clause.

_____ 1. The research report *that was assigned last month* is due tomorrow.

_____ 2. *Since the bicycle was on sale,* I bought it.

_____ 3. I voted for the candidate *who lost the election.*

_____ 4. I'll let you know *as soon as your package arrives.*

_____ 5. *Did you read the book* before you saw the movie?

_____ 6. The flag should be brought indoors *when the weather is bad.*

_____ 7. *After the final performance of the play,* the cast had a party.

_____ 8. *William Shakespeare is the best-known playwright in the world today.*

_____ 9. You may borrow my book overnight *if you'd like.*

_____10. *Please help me* when it is time to decorate the gym for the dance.

Exercise B   Underline the adjective clause in each of the following sentences. Draw another line under the relative pronoun. Then circle the noun or pronoun that the clause modifies.

1. What costume did you wear to the party that Juanita had?

2. My costume, which won a prize, was a chicken suit!

3. My cousin, whom I took to the party, went as a huge mosquito.

4. I couldn't recognize many of the people who were in costume.

5. Did you recognize Hillary, who came as a gorilla?

6. The person whom I didn't recognize was Mingan.

7. His costume, which was really original, was a large cardboard box.

8. The box, which was covered with clear plastic, was very shiny.

9. Mingan, who was hidden inside the box, kept saying, "I'm melting!"

10. The box that he wore was supposed to be an ice cube!

Chapter 18: The Clause

Review (Form B)

Exercise C   Underline the adverb clause in each sentence. Draw another line under the subordinating conjunction. On the line provided, write whether the clause tells *how, when, where, why, how much,* or *under what condition.*

_____ 1. As soon as the ground softens in the spring, plant your garden.

_____ 2. Some seeds take more time to sprout than others do.

_____ 3. If you want to grow morning glories, start the seeds under lights.

_____ 4. When the seeds sprout, you can transplant them into the garden.

_____ 5. Plant them near a fence or wall so that the plants can climb.

_____ 6. After the young plants grow strong, they will produce flowers.

_____ 7. The flowers will look as if they are big blue trumpets.

_____ 8. They're called morning glories because they open each morning.

_____ 9. When they are warmed by the morning sun, they open.

_____10. If the day is dark or stormy, they stay tightly shut, like umbrellas.

Exercise D   Underline the subordinate clause in each sentence. Then on the line provided, write **ADJ** if it is an adjective clause or **ADV** if it is an adverb clause.

_____ 1. Some words that are in the English language come from people's names.

_____ 2. Because Adolphe Sax invented the saxophone, it was named for him.

_____ 3. From *Caesar*, which was the title of Roman leaders, comes *czar*.

_____ 4. Trains had steam engines until Rudolf Diesel invented the diesel engine.

_____ 5. Theodore Roosevelt, who was president of the United States, was the

  inspiration for the term *teddy bear.*

_____ 6. We have the word *sideburns* because Ambrose Burnside had bushy whiskers.

_____ 7. Many words that we use every day are borrowed from other languages.

_____ 8. Native Americans who lived in the Northeast gave us the word *chipmunk.*

_____ 9. Although the French word *bureau* means "desk," we use it to mean "chest

  of drawers."

_____10. From Spanish comes the word *patio*, which means "an open courtyard."

Answer Key

Practice and Reinforcement (1)
Independent and Subordinate Clauses

Exercise A

1. SC
2. SC
3. IC
4. IC
5. SC

Exercise B: Expanding Sentences

(Answers will vary. Sample responses are given.)

1. When I graduate from high school, I will go to college.
2. Because he surprised me, I dropped my books.
3. If you want to read a good book, read *Jane Eyre*.
4. Until Manchu moved to Chicago, he had never ridden on an elevated train.
5. After the game was over, the members of both teams congratulated each other.

Practice and Reinforcement (2)
The Adjective Clause

Exercise A

1. Softball is a popular (game) that is played throughout the United States.
2. The (game,) whose origins are unknown, resembles baseball.
3. (People) who play softball are aware of slight differences in the two games.
4. The (field) that is used for softball is smaller than a baseball field.
5. The (game,) which lasts only seven innings, is shorter than a baseball game.
6. A softball is larger and softer than the (ball) that is used for baseball.
7. (Players) whom I especially envy can hit that big ball out of the park!

8. (Kapok) which provides filling in sleeping bags, is also used in softballs.
9. (Those) who play softball do not need much protection from the ball.
10. Padded mitts are worn by only (those) whose positions require frequent catching.

Exercise B: Revising

(Answers may vary. Sample responses are given.)

1. the player who has the bat
2. the softball field that is at our school
3. the team that is best
4. the runner who is fastest
5. the player whose batting average is the best

Practice and Reinforcement (3)
The Adverb Clause

Exercise A

1. I ate a bowl of popcorn <u>while I did my homework.</u>
2. We will have to hurry <u>if we want to catch the 5:30 bus.</u>
3. From the top of the hill, you can see trees <u>wherever you look.</u>
4. I need to borrow a pencil <u>because I left mine at home.</u>
5. The puppies act <u>as if they are hungry.</u>
6. A giraffe is taller <u>than an elephant is.</u>
7. <u>Before we left for our vacation,</u> we unplugged the refrigerator.
8. <u>Since I love mystery stories,</u> I enjoy the books by Agatha Christie.
9. They watch more television programs <u>than I do.</u>
10. Set the potted plants <u>where they will get plenty of light.</u>

Exercise B

1. when
2. under what condition
3. where
4. why
5. how
6. how much

Answer Key

7. when

8. why

9. how much

10. where

Chapter Review
Form A

Exercise A

1. SC

2. IC

3. SC

4. IC

5. SC

6. SC

7. IC

8. IC

9. SC

10. IC

Exercise B

1. The (concert) that we'll hear tonight contains music by George Gershwin.

2. (George Gershwin,) who was a great composer, wrote *Porgy and Bess*.

3. This (opera,) which is set in South Carolina, features both jazz and ballet.

4. ("Summertime,") which is a beautiful song, is a highlight of the show.

5. Gershwin did not write the (lyrics) that went with his songs.

6. The (lyricist) whom Gershwin most respected was his brother, Ira.

7. Although George wrote the music, it was (Ira) who wrote the words.

8. Their musical (play) that I like the best is *An American in Paris*.

9. Gene Kelly stars in the (movie) that is based on this play.

10. (Kelly,) who sings and dances to Gershwin music in the film, is superb.

Exercise C

1. why; Because I am in the high school band, I will march in the parade.

2. when; The parade will begin after all the bands and floats are in position.

3. how much; Our band is larger than the band from Zavala High School is.

4. why; Since we are larger, we will play "The Star-Spangled Banner."

5. when; The parade will officially begin as soon as we finish the anthem.

6. where; After the parade, meet me where the band's buses are parked.

7. under what condition; If it is raining, meet me in the lobby of City Hall.

8. how; The sky filled up with storm clouds as if it might rain.

9. when; Whenever I'm in a parade, the weather seems to work against me!

10. when; As soon as I start to play my horn, the weather becomes a music critic.

Exercise D

1. ADJ; Woody Allen, who has written many films, has also written plays.

2. ADJ; *Play It Again, Sam*, a film that he made in 1972, was based on a play.

3. ADV; The play gained success on Broadway before he made it into a film.

4. ADJ; The actor whom he chose for the leading role was Diane Keaton.

5. ADJ; She went on to star in many other films that he wrote and directed.

6. ADV; After she appeared in *Play It Again, Sam*, she starred in *Sleeper* and then in *Annie Hall*.

Answer Key

7. ADV;   If you have never seen a Woody Allen film, you have missed some fun.

8. ADJ;   A scene that always makes me laugh is in *Take the Money and Run*.

9. ADJ;   Allen does not appear in all of the films that he writes.

10. ADV;   However, the funniest moments in his films happen when he appears.

Chapter Review
Form B

Exercise A

1. SC
2. SC
3. SC
4. SC
5. IC
6. SC
7. SC
8. IC
9. SC
10. IC

Exercise B

1. What costume did you wear to the party that Juanita had?

2. My costume, which won a prize, was a chicken suit!

3. My cousin, whom I took to the party, went as a huge mosquito.

4. I couldn't recognize many of the people who were in costume.

5. Did you recognize Hillary who came as a gorilla?

6. The person whom I didn't recognize was Mingan.

7. His costume, which was really original, was a large cardboard box.

8. The box, which was covered with clear plastic, was very shiny.

9. Mingan, who was hidden inside the box, kept saying, "I'm melting!"

10. The box that he wore was supposed to be an ice cube!

Exercise C

1. when;   As soon as the ground softens in the spring, plant your garden.

2. how much;   Some seeds take more time to sprout than others do.

3. under what condition;   If you want to grow morning glories, start the seeds under lights.

4. when;   When the seeds sprout, you can transplant them into the garden.

5. why;   Plant them near a fence or wall so that the plants can climb.

6. when;   After the young plants grow strong, they will produce flowers.

7. how;   The flowers will look as if they are big blue trumpets.

8. why;   They're called morning glories because they open each morning.

9. when;   When they are warmed by the morning sun, they open.

10. under what condition;   If the day is dark or stormy, they stay tightly shut, like umbrellas.

Answer Key

Exercise D

1. ADJ; Some words that are in the English language come from people's names.

2. ADV; Because Adolphe Sax invented the saxophone, it was named for him.

3. ADJ; From *Caesar,* which was the title of Roman leaders, comes *czar.*

4. ADV; Trains had steam engines until Rudolf Diesel invented the diesel engine.

5. ADJ; Theodore Roosevelt, who was president of the United States, was the inspiration for the term *teddy bear.*

6. ADV; We have the word *sideburns* because Ambrose Burnside had bushy whiskers.

7. ADJ; Many words that we use every day are borrowed from other languages.

8. ADJ; Native Americans who lived in the Northeast gave us the word *chipmunk.*

9. ADV; Although the French word *bureau* means "desk," we use it to mean "chest of drawers."

10. ADJ; From Spanish comes the word *patio,* which means "an open courtyard."

Chapter 19: Kinds of Sentence Structure

The Simple Sentence

A **simple sentence** has one independent clause and no subordinate clauses. It may have a compound subject, a compound verb, or both.

Simple sentence *Thelma* and *Leo buy* and *sell* automobiles.

Exercise For the sentences below, circle each subject and underline each verb.

Example Claudia smiled sweetly and motioned the guests inside.

(Claudia) smiled sweetly and motioned the guests inside.

1. The pattern of every snowflake is unique.

2. Iris and Phil took a train to Chicago.

3. Carmen skated at the pond after school.

4. During the Renaissance, Italian women shaved the front part of their heads and kept the rest of their hair long.

5. Federico and Garth rowed over to the island last summer.

6. Emily Dickinson published only seven poems in her lifetime.

7. After the harvest, the workers have a dance in the barn.

8. Javier Pereira, a Zenu Indian from Colombia, died in 1955 at the age of 166.

9. Jupiter, Saturn, and Uranus have rings.

10. Christina played the guitar and sang songs from Chile.

Chapter 19: Kinds of Sentence Structure

The Compound Sentence

A **compound sentence** has two or more independent clauses and no subordinate clauses. The independent clauses are usually joined by a comma and one of the coordinating conjunctions: *and, but, or, nor, for, so,* or *yet.*

> **Independent clause:** Mark Twain wrote fiction
> **Independent clause:** T. S. Eliot wrote poetry.
> **Compound sentence:** Mark Twain wrote fiction**,** *and* T. S. Eliot wrote poetry.

Exercise A   Each of the following compound sentences contains two independent clauses joined by a conjunction. Underline the subject in each clause once and the verb twice. Draw a circle around the conjunction joining the clauses.

> **Example** Kiyo likes the beach, and she often goes there with her brothers.
>
> Kiyo <u>likes</u> the beach, (and) <u>she</u> often <u>goes</u> there with her brothers.

1. The ice-covered sidewalk was slippery, and several people fell down.

2. Some Brazil nuts come from Brazil, but others come from Peru, Venezuela, and Ecuador.

3. The talk show host was silly, but his show had a large audience.

4. A surfer must be careful, for one can fall off a surfboard quite easily.

5. Mr. Kumamoto showed us some great fossils, for he is an experienced fossil hunter.

6. We can go to a movie, or we can watch a videotape.

7. Angel wrote a poem about his father, for he loves his father very much.

8. Clouds gathered and rain fell.

9. The bears stole all our food, so we left the campground early.

10. Outside, a storm howled, yet we were warm inside the igloo.

Exercise B: Sentence Combining   Rewrite each pair of simple sentences as one compound sentence. Follow the directions in parentheses, and write your sentences on the lines provided.

1. Ants are small. They are powerful. (Combine with *but.*) _____

_____

2. Ants have strong legs. They can lift many times their own weight. (Combine with *and.*) _____

_____

Chapter 19: Kinds of Sentence Structure

Compound Sentences and Sentence Parts

A **compound sentence** has two or more independent clauses and no subordinate clauses. The independent clauses of compound sentences are usually joined by a comma and a coordinating conjunction (*and, but, for, nor, or, so,* or *yet*). However, the clauses may be connected by only a semicolon.

Compound sentences: The sky looked heavy and threatening, *and* we expected a storm.

The sky looked heavy and threatening; we expected a storm.

Exercise   Read each of the following sentences. Underline the independent clauses. On the line provided, write **S** if the sentence is simple. Write **C** is the sentence is compound.

Example: _____ Geronimo was an Apache; he struggled to preserve the Apache way of life.

___C___ <u>Geronimo was an Apache</u>; <u>he struggled to preserve the Apache way of life.</u>

_____ 1. Geronimo was born in No-doyohn Canyon, Arizona.

_____ 2. His mother named him Goyahkla; the name means "One Who Yawns."

_____ 3. Mexican bounty hunters killed his mother, his wife, and his children in 1850.

_____ 4. Geronimo wanted revenge, so he gathered a band of men.

_____ 5. He led thirty-nine Apaches in raids against Mexican and U.S. settlements

_____ 6. The Mexicans called him Geronimo; that name in English is Jerome.

_____ 7. The United States sent five thousand troops to capture Geronimo, but the Apache did not surrender for more than four months.

_____ 8. He was imprisoned in Florida and later in Oklahoma; he could never return to Arizona and to his Apache life.

_____ 9. He told his story to S. M. Barrett in 1905–1906, and Barrett wrote a book about it.

_____ 10. Geronimo died in 1909; he was a courageous man to the end.

Chapter 19: Kinds of Sentence Structure

The Complex Sentence

A **complex sentence** has one independent clause and at least one subordinate clause.

     Independent clause: I often go to the library.

     Subordinate clause: because I like to read

     Complex sentence: Because I like to read, I often go to the library.

The word *because* makes the second group of words a subordinate clause. A subordinate clause cannot stand alone as a sentence. The following words are often used to introduce subordinate clauses:

     who, whose, which, that

     after, as, because, if, since, before, when

Exercise A   Each of the following sentences is complex. For each sentence, underline the independent clause once and the subordinate clause twice.

1. Since I was five years old, I have read in bed at night.

2. For my twelfth birthday I received *A Light in the Attic*, which is a book of

    poems.

3. Before I go to sleep, I sometimes read my favorite poems to my little brother.

4. As he listens to me, he closes his eyes and falls asleep.

5. When he wakes up in the morning, he sometimes asks about the ending of a poem.

6. I may be a writer or an editor when I grow up.

7. My Aunt Sabrena, who lives in Dallas, is a copyeditor for a newspaper. (Hint:

    The independent clause in this sentence is in two parts.)

8. If I study hard, I can become an editor, too.

9. A job as an editor makes sense for me because I love words.

10. The books that I love most sit on a special shelf in my room. (Hint: The

    independent clause in this sentence is in two parts.)

Exercise B   The numbered sentences in the following paragraph are complex. For each numbered sentence, underline the independent clause once and the subordinate clause twice.

     Arachne is a character in a famous Greek myth. [1.] She can weave tapestries

that are very beautiful. [2.] When people see her work, they are really impressed.

Arachne becomes very proud. [3.] Because Arachne is so full of pride, the

goddess Athena turns her into a spider. [4.] The myth says that all spiders

descend from Arachne.

Chapter 19: Kinds of Sentence Structure

Review (Form A)

Exercise A   Read each of the following sentences. If the sentence is simple, write **S**. If the sentence is compound, write **C**.

_____ 1. A rodent's teeth never stop growing.

_____ 2. Rodents gnaw hard things, so their teeth don't get very long.

_____ 3. A mole is one kind of rodent.

_____ 4. Moles dig holes with their teeth.

_____ 5. A mole can dig a three-hundred foot tunnel, and it does so in a single night!

Exercise B   Read each of the following sentences. Write **C** if the sentence is compound or **Cx** if the sentence is complex.

_____ 1. When we have plumbing problems, we call Señor Rodríguez.

_____ 2. Sometimes Señor Rodríguez comes himself, and sometimes he sends one

     of his employees.

_____ 3. Elaine Blum, who lives across the street, is an electrician.

_____ 4. She has a pickup truck, which she uses to carry her tools and supplies.

_____ 5. We enjoy Elaine's company, and she is a helpful neighbor, too.

Exercise C   In the following sentences, underline each independent clause once and each subordinate clause twice. Then write **S** if the sentence is simple, **C** if the sentence is compound, or **Cx** if the sentence is complex.

_____ 1. David Atchison was the president of the United States for one day.

_____ 2. President Polk's term had ended on March 4, 1849, which was a Sunday.

_____ 3. Because it was a Sunday, the new president, Zachary Taylor, did not take the

     oath of office until March 5.

_____ 4. Under an old law, the president pro tempore of the Senate became the president

     of the United States if no one else held the office.

_____ 5. So Atchison was the president for a day, but he didn't realize the fact until later.

_____ 6. Here's another interesting fact.

_____ 7. Technically, George Washington was not the first president of the United States!

_____ 8. That honor belonged to a man who had been Maryland's representative at the

     Continental Congress.

Review (Form A)

_____ 9. The first president was John Hanson, and he was elected by the Congress on
November 5, 1781.

_____ 10. Hanson's title was "President of the United States in Congress Assembled,"
and he served for one year.

Exercise D Rewrite each of the following sentences. Follow the directions in
parentheses.

1. In the evenings we usually watch the news because we are interested in world
   events. (Rewrite as two simple sentences.) _____

   _____

2. It seems that we often have the world in our living room. (Cut three words.
   Rewrite as one simple sentence.) _____

   _____

3. Exciting events like the collapse of the Soviet Union sometimes occur. We watch
   the all-news channels. (Cut the word *sometimes* from the first sentence. Then
   combine the sentences to make one complex sentence. Begin the first clause
   with the word *When*.) _____

   _____

4. Television news is fascinating. Newspapers provide more in-depth coverage.
   (Combine the sentences to create one compound sentence. Use the conjunction
   but.) _____

   _____

Name _____ Date _____ Class _____

Review (Form B)

Exercise A   Read each of the following sentences. If the sentence is simple, write **S**. If the sentence is compound, write **C**.

_____ 1. The talented violinist asked for the audience's attention.

_____ 2. Pandas are rare, but they are not extinct.

_____ 3. We could make a booklet, or we could post our papers on the bulletin

board.

_____ 4. Elyssa came over and talked to me after the play.

_____ 5. We like our home, and we like our neighbors, too.

Exercise B   Read each of the following sentences. If the sentence is compound, write **C**. If the sentence is complex, write **Cx**.

_____ 1. When Abe Lincoln gave a stump speech, he stood on a real stump.

_____ 2. Trees lose their leaves in the fall, and they look cold and forlorn.

_____ 3. While we lived in southern Maryland, we visited Annapolis.

_____ 4. Brian has a bad temper, and he doesn't make friends easily.

_____ 5. If you move your knight to that square, I will capture him.

Exercise C   In the following sentences, underline each independent clause once and each subordinate clause twice. Then write **S** if the sentence is simple, **C** if the sentence is compound, or **Cx** if the sentence is complex.

_____ 1. *Inca* is the name that people associate with the Native Americans of Peru.

_____ 2. Actually, *Inca* means "emperor," and the Native American people used it

for only a few of their leaders.

_____ 3. The Native American people in Peru are called Quechuans.

_____ 4. Thor Heyerdahl was a Norwegian explorer.

_____ 5. He was also a scientist, and he had an idea about the Quechua people.

_____ 6. Heyerdahl had been to Polynesia, and he thought that the Quechua had

been the original settlers of those islands.

_____ 7. Polynesia is thousands of miles across the Pacific Ocean from Peru.

_____ 8. Heyerdahl believed that the Quechua had traveled to Polynesia from Peru.

_____ 9. He built a small raft out of balsa wood and named it *Kon-Tiki*.

_____10. Heyerdahl took five men with him on the perilous journey, and they did

eventually arrive in Peru.

Chapter 19: Kinds of Sentence Structure

Review (Form B)

Exercise D   Rewrite each of the following sentences on the lines provided. Follow the directions in parentheses.

1. After we found out about the shelter, Mona and I began helping the people there.

    (Rewrite as a compound sentence.) _____

    _____

2. We gathered our outgrown clothes and toys, and we put them neatly in boxes.

    (Rewrite as a complex sentence. Begin the first clause with *After*.) _____

    _____

3. My mother drove us to the shelter and helped us carry the boxes inside.

    (Rewrite as a compound sentence.) _____

    _____

4. When the shelter director saw our gifts, she seemed very happy. (Rewrite as

    two simple sentences.) _____

    _____

Answer Key

Practice and Reinforcement (1)
The Simple Sentence

Exercise

1. The (pattern) of every snowflake <u>is</u> unique.
2. (Iris) and (Phil) <u>took</u> a train to Chicago.
3. (Carmen) <u>skated</u> at the pond after school.
4. During the Renaissance, Italian (women) <u>shaved</u> the front part of their heads and <u>kept</u> the rest of their hair long.
5. (Federico) and (Garth) <u>rowed</u> over to the island last summer.
6. (Emily Dickinson) <u>published</u> only seven poems in her lifetime.
7. After the harvest, the (workers) <u>have</u> a dance in the barn.
8. (Javier Pereira) a Zenu Indian from Colombia, <u>died</u> in 1955 at the age of 166.
9. (Jupiter, Saturn,) and (Uranus) <u>have</u> rings.
10. (Christina) <u>played</u> the guitar and <u>sang</u> songs from Chile.

Practice and Reinforcement (2)
The Compound Sentence

Exercise A

1. The ice-covered <u>sidewalk</u> <u>was</u> slippery, (and) several <u>people</u> <u>fell</u> down.
2. Some Brazil <u>nuts</u> <u>come</u> from Brazil, (but) others <u>come</u> from Peru, Venezuela, and Ecuador.
3. The talk show <u>host</u> <u>was</u> silly, (but) his <u>show</u> <u>had</u> a large audience.
4. A <u>surfer</u> <u>must be</u> careful, (for) <u>one</u> <u>can fall</u> off a surfboard quite easily.
5. Mr. Kumamoto <u>showed</u> us some great fossils, (for) he <u>is</u> an experienced fossil hunter.

Exercise (right column)

6. We <u>can go</u> to a movie, (or) we <u>can watch</u> a videotape.
7. Angel <u>wrote</u> a poem about his father, (for) he <u>loves</u> his father very much.
8. Clouds <u>gathered</u> (and) rain <u>fell</u>.
9. The bears <u>stole</u> all our food, (so) we <u>left</u> the campground early.
10. Outside, a <u>storm</u> <u>howled</u>, (yet) we <u>were</u> warm inside the igloo.

Exercise B: Sentence Combining

1. Ants are small, but they are powerful.
2. Ants have strong legs, and they can lift many times their own weight.

Practice and Reinforcement (3)
Compound Sentences and Sentence Parts

Exercise

1. S Geronimo was born in No-doyohn Canyon, Arizona.
2. C His mother named him Goyahkla; the name means "One Who Yawns."
3. S Mexican bounty hunters killed his mother, his wife, and his children in 1850.
4. C Geronimo wanted revenge, so he gathered a band of men.
5. S He led thirty-nine Apaches in raids against Mexican and U.S. settlements.
6. C The Mexicans called him Geronimo; that name in English is Jerome.
7. C The United States sent five thousand troops to capture Geronimo, but the Apache did not surrender for more than four months.
8. C He was imprisoned in Florida and later in Oklahoma; he could never return to Arizona and to his Apache life.
9. C He told his story to S. M. Barrett in 1905–1906, and Barrett wrote a book about it.
10. C Geronimo died in 1909; he was a courageous man to the end.

Answer Key

Practice and Reinforcement (4)
The Complex Sentence

Exercise A

1. <u>Since I was five years old</u>, I have read in bed at night.
2. For my twelfth birthday I received *A Light in the Attic*, <u>which is a book of poems</u>.
3. <u>Before I go to sleep</u>, I sometimes read my favorite poems to my little brother.
4. <u>As he listens to me</u>, he closes his eyes and falls asleep.
5. <u>When he wakes up in the morning</u>, he sometimes asks about the ending of a poem.
6. I may be a writer or an editor <u>when I grow up</u>.
7. My Aunt Sabrena, <u>who lives in Dallas</u>, is a copyeditor for a newspaper.
8. <u>If I study hard</u>, I can become an editor, too.
9. A job as an editor makes sense for me <u>because I love words</u>.
10. The books <u>that I love most</u> sit on a special shelf in my room.

Exercise B

Arachne is a character in a famous Greek myth. [1.] She can weave tapestries <u>that are very beautiful</u>. [2.] <u>When people see her work</u>, they are really impressed. Arachne becomes very proud. [3.] <u>Because Arachne is so full of pride</u>, the goddess Athena turns her into a spider. [4.] The myth says <u>that all spiders descend from Arachne</u>.

Chapter Review
Form A

Exercise A

1. S
2. C
3. S
4. S
5. C

Exercise B

1. Cx
2. C
3. Cx
4. Cx
5. C

Exercise C

1. S; <u>David Atchison was the president of the United States for one day</u>.
2. Cx; President Polk's term had ended on March 4, 1849, <u>which was a Sunday</u>.
3. C; <u>Because it was a Sunday</u>, <u>the new president, Zachary Taylor, did not take the oath of office until March 5</u>.
4. C; <u>Under an old law, the president pro tempore of the Senate became the president of the United States</u> <u>if no one else held the office</u>.
5. C; <u>So Atchison was the president for a day</u>, <u>but he didn't realize the fact until later</u>.
6. S; <u>Here's another interesting fact</u>.
7. S; <u>Technically, George Washington was not the first president of the United States!</u>
8. Cx; <u>That honor belonged to a man</u> <u>who had been Maryland's representative at the Continental Congress</u>.
9. C; <u>The first president was John Hanson</u>, and <u>he was elected by the Congress on November 5, 1781</u>.
10. C; <u>Hanson's title was "President of the United States in Congress Assembled,"</u> and <u>he served for one year</u>.

Answer Key

Exercise D

1. In the evenings we usually watch the news. We are interested in world events.

2. We often have the world in our living room.

3. When exciting events like the collapse of the Soviet Union occur, we watch the all-news channels.

4. Television news is fascinating, but newspapers provide more in-depth coverage.

Chapter Review
Form B

Exercise A

1. S
2. C
3. C
4. S
5. C

Exercise B

1. Cx
2. C
3. Cx
4. C
5. Cx

Exercise C

1. Cx; *Inca* is the name that people associate with the Native Americans of Peru.

2. C; Actually, *Inca* means "emperor," and the Native American people used it for only a few of their leaders.

3. S; The Native American people in Peru are called Quechuans.

4. S; Thor Heyerdahl was a Norwegian explorer.

5. C; He was also a scientist, and he had an idea about the Quechua people.

6. Cx; Heyerdahl had been to Polynesia, and he thought that the Quechua had been the original settlers of those islands.

7. S; Polynesia is thousands of miles across the Pacific Ocean from Peru.

8. Cx; Heyerdahl believed that the Quechua had traveled to Polynesia from Peru.

9. S; He built a small raft out of balsa wood and named it *Kon-Tiki*.

10. C; Heyerdahl took five men with him on the perilous journey, and they did eventually arrive in Peru.

Exercise D

1. We found out about the shelter, and Mona and I began helping the people there.

2. After we gathered our outgrown clothes and toys, we put them neatly in boxes.

3. My mother drove us to the shelter, and she helped us carry the boxes inside.

4. The shelter director saw our gifts. She seemed very happy.

Assessment: Mastery Tests

Grammar Mastery Test (Form A)

Part 1   Decide whether each group of words is a sentence or a fragment. On the lines provided, write **S** for sentence or **F** for fragment. [2 points each]

_____ 1. Before we left on our camping trip.

_____ 2. Running around in all directions.

_____ 3. Finally, Mom and Dad took command.

_____ 4. Sent to the closet for the sleeping bags.

_____ 5. We will finish packing tomorrow.

Part 2   In each sentence, draw a line between the complete subject and the complete predicate. Underline each simple subject once and each simple predicate twice. [2 points each]

Example: The <u>tea</u> of that time | <u>was kept</u> in locked chests.

1. The owner casually walked through the store.

2. The editor heard about the flood and sent a reporter.

3. I run a mile every day.

4. Lola is not singing a solo at the concert.

5. On the floor were many large boxes.

6. The car in the driveway is ours.

7. Down the tree raced a baby squirrel.

8. The hikers gathered the wood and started a fire.

9. Seth and I will play basketball after school.

10. The first slice of fresh bread tastes best.

Part 3   On the line provided, write whether the sentence is declarative, interrogative, imperative, or exclamatory. Then write the last word of each sentence, and provide the appropriate end punctuation. [2 points each]

1. Do you know what a tigon is _____

2. A tigon is a cross between a tiger and a lion _____

3. I can hardly believe it _____

4. Explain why I've never heard of one _____

5. Tigons exist only in zoos _____

Assessment: Mastery Tests

Grammar Mastery Test (Form A)

Part 4   Each of the following sentences contains one word that is used twice in the sentence. On the line provided, indicate the part of speech of each italicized word. Write **N** for noun, **PRON** for pronoun, **V** for verb, **ADJ** for adjective, **ADV** for adverb, **PREP** for preposition, **CONJ** for conjunction, or **INTERJ** for interjection. Write the two answers in order. [1 point each]

Example: We hid in the *storm* shelter when the *storm* hit. __ADJ, N__

1. The *shade* on the lamp will *shade* your eyes. _____

2. We *still* remember looking at the *still* lake. _____

3. The *pencil* sharpener didn't sharpen my *pencil*. _____

4. Mother *set* the vase on the television *set*. _____

5. Do we take the *cross* street or *cross* the bridge? _____

6. *Well*, you washed the car *well*. _____

7. *That* was the proper dress for *that* occasion. _____

8. I was grounded *for* a week, *for* I was late again. _____

9. Rolf looked *up* and saw the cat climbing *up* the tree. _____

10. In the first *act*, Wenona will *act* sick. _____

Part 5   Underline the complement or complements in each of the following sentences. Then, on the line provided, identify each complement. Write **PA** for predicate adjective, **PN** for predicate nominative, **DO** for direct object, or **IO** for indirect object. [1 point each]

Example: __IO, DO__ Aunt Lucía sent us a picture.

_____ 1. Andy forgot his book this morning.

_____ 2. She is a fast reader.

_____ 3. The water in the cooler was lukewarm.

_____ 4. Noah told the teacher the correct answer.

_____ 5. I raked the lawn yesterday.

_____ 6. Someone gave my brother a tame snake.

_____ 7. My grandparents were all immigrants to this country.

_____ 8. By dinner time, we were all very hungry.

_____ 9. Matt's white sneakers look new.

_____10. That music is the national anthem of Canada.

Grammar Mastery Test (Form A)

Part 6 One phrase is italicized in each of the following sentences. Indicate what type of phrase each is. On the line provided, write **PREP** for prepositional phrase, **PART** for participial phrase, or **INF** for infinitive phrase. [1 point each]

_____ 1. My sister has a cage *of white mice*.

_____ 2. *Seeing a hole in the cage,* I called her.

_____ 3. *Worried about the mice,* we searched the house.

_____ 4. She and I looked *under the furniture*.

_____ 5. We thought we could hear them *squeaking somewhere*.

_____ 6. We wanted *to find them quickly*.

_____ 7. Suddenly our cat came *into the room*.

_____ 8. *Sensing the mice,* she ran to the closet.

_____ 9. My sister and I locked the cat *outside the room*.

_____10. The cat's good hearing allowed us *to locate the mice*.

Part 7 Decide whether the italicized clause in each of the following sentences is subordinate or independent. Then, on the line provided, write **SUB** for subordinate clause or **IND** for independent clause. [1 point each]

_____ 1. *After we run,* let's stop for lunch.

_____ 2. The man *who gave us directions* was a neighbor.

_____ 3. Nadene started to sing *since she gave up the piano*.

_____ 4. *This is the puppy* that I would like.

_____ 5. The motorcycle *that passed us* was loud.

_____ 6. Before you start your homework, *would you set the table?*

_____ 7. *When Inyet looked up,* he noticed the horseshoe on the wall.

_____ 8. *Coyotes now live in our town,* although they are not common.

_____ 9. When Virginia was first settled, *England sent over many prisoners*.

_____10. Thomas Edison, *who invented the phonograph,* was deaf.

Part 8 Decide what kind of sentence each is. On the line provided, write **S** for simple sentence, **CD** for compound sentence, or **CX** for complex sentence. [5 points each]

_____ 1. Simon asked for an apple and two oranges.

_____ 2. The apple trees are blooming this year, because we took care of them.

_____ 3. Mina and Nicole planned their social studies project.

_____ 4. Drew wanted a new radio, but he could not afford one.

Name _____ Date _____ Class _____ Score _____

Grammar Mastery Test (Form B)

Part 1   Decide whether each group of words is a sentence or a fragment. On the line provided, write **S** for sentence or **F** for fragment. [2 points each]

_____ 1. The French painter Henri Toulouse-Lautrec.

_____ 2. Two accidents crippled his legs.

_____ 3. His friends included many famous painters.

_____ 4. Produced hundreds of paintings and posters.

_____ 5. He died before the age of forty.

Part 2   In each sentence, draw a line between the complete subject and the complete predicate. Underline each simple subject once and each simple predicate twice.
[2 points each]

        Example: Lightning | struck the tree and split it in two.

1. U.S. voters elect a president every four years.

2. This is a wonderful collection of poems!

3. In the center of the island is a grove of pecan trees.

4. Dogs are trained as guides at the Seeing Eye Foundations.

5. Many books and magazines explain the space program and describe its projects.

6. The boots on the left are mine.

7. Under the back stairs is a small coat closet.

8. Homer's story about the Trojan War describes real places.

9. Judges and lawyers in Britain wear wigs in court.

10. Hermit crabs find and inhabit empty shells of other animals.

Part 3   On the line below each sentence, write whether it is declarative, interrogative, imperative, or exclamatory. Then, write the last word of each sentence, and provide the appropriate end punctuation. [2 points each]

        Example: I like to read

                declarative, read. _____

1. What a great book that is

_____

2. What do you like about it

_____

3. The book describes American frontier life

_____

Grammar Mastery Test (Form B)

4. Tell me about the book's author

_____

5. Laura Ingalls Wilder wrote it when she was over sixty

_____

Part 4   Each of the following sentences contains one word in italics. On the line provided, indicate the part of speech of each italicized word. Write **N** for noun, **PRON** for pronoun, **V** for verb, **ADJ** for adjective, **ADV** for adverb, **PREP** for preposition, **CONJ** for conjunction, or **INTERJ** for interjection. [1 point each]

Example: ADJ Apples are a *popular* fruit in this country.

_____ 1. Human beings have *only* four different kinds of taste buds.

_____ 2. Michelle *added* a bright red sun to her picture.

_____ 3. *Well,* maybe we can take a taxi instead.

_____ 4. Kwam jumped *into* the pool and swam.

_____ 5. With a *smile,* Kareem showed us his new cape.

_____ 6. Today, *neither* a nickle nor a dime is solid silver

_____ 7. Try one of *these,* which my brother cooked.

_____ 8. Let's listen to the tape *later,* when we have more time.

_____ 9. One woman *predicted* that the world would end on Friday.

_____ 10. In the *final* scene, all the characters appear onstage together.

Part 5   Underline the complement or complements in each of the following sentences. Then, on the lines provided, identify each complement. Write **PA** for predicate adjective, **PN** for predicate nominative, **DO** for direct object, or **IO** for indirect object. [1 point each]

Example: Aretha handed me her finished science paper.   IO, DO _____

1. The sculptor's mother was the model for the Statue of Liberty. _____

2. Julia Ward Howe wrote "The Battle Hymn of the Republic." _____

3. Jeff seems excited about something today. _____

4. Mrs. Golden always has a warm smile for everyone. _____

5. Mehmet looked very uncomfortable onstage. _____

6. The Durands showed us the slides from their vacation. _____

7. The colors and scents of the flowers attract bees. _____

8. My new video game is fun. _____

Assessment: Mastery Tests

Grammar Mastery Test (Form B)

9. The car of my dreams is a red convertible. _____

10. Some of the animals inside the cave have no eyes. _____

Part 6   One phrase is italicized in each of the following sentences. Indicate what type of phrase each is. On the line provided, write **PREP** for prepositional phrase, **PART** for participial phrase, or **INF** for infinitive phrase. [1 point each]

_____ 1. Last week our class went *to the county museum.*

_____ 2. The museum was established *to present the history of our county.*

_____ 3. *Arriving at the museum,* we were divided into smaller groups.

_____ 4. Each group, *accompanied by a guide,* toured the exhibits at its own pace.

_____ 5. My group liked the re-creation *of a nineteenth-century farm.*

_____ 6. For the first time, we realized the hardships *faced by the pioneers.*

_____ 7. *To earn a living in those days* required long hours of hard labor.

_____ 8. The guide told about a typical day in the life *of a pioneer farm family.*

_____ 9. She answered all our questions *in a patient manner.*

_____10. Afterwards, the class decided *to put on a play about farm life in the 1800's.*

Part 7   Decide whether the italicized clause in each of the following sentences is subordinate or independent. If a clause is a subordinate clause, decide whether it is an adjective or adverb clause. Then, on the line provided, write **SUB** for subordinate clause, **IND** for independent clause, **ADJ** for adjective clause, or **ADV** for adverb clause. [1 point each]

    Example: <u>SUB, ADV</u> I can't come over *until my mother gets home.*

_____ 1. On the vacation *that we took last year,* we traveled through three states.

_____ 2. From our home in Minneapolis, *we drove southward to Denver.*

_____ 3. The trip lasted only a week *because my parents had to return to work.*

_____ 4. We camped out along the way, and *we cooked many of our own meals.*

_____ 5. *As we drove,* my sister and I read the map.

_____ 6. We visited Mount Rushmore National Memorial, *which is in South Dakota.*

Assessment: Mastery Tests

Grammar Mastery Test (Form B)

_____ 7. *Although I had seen pictures of it,* Mount Rushmore still surprised me.

_____ 8. The huge carvings, *which show the heads of four U.S. Presidents,* impressed me.

_____ 9. My sister had a camera, and *she took some wonderful pictures.*

_____ 10. *When we returned home,* we decided to visit other historical landmarks.

Part 8   Decide what kind of sentence each of the following is. On the line provided, write **S** for simple sentence, **CD** for compound sentence, or **CX** for complex sentence. [2 points each]

_____ 1. Julio and I crossed the finish line together, and the race was declared a tie.

_____ 2. The school crossing guard, who is a volunteer, greets most students by name.

_____ 3. A walk through Old Hollywood will delight any movie fan.

_____ 4. No one was injured in the accident, but the car was badly damaged.

_____ 5. Antarctica is covered by ice, but it is as dry as a desert.

_____ 6. You can either walk the dog or take out the trash.

_____ 7. One tiny frog, which is half an inch long, lays one large egg.

_____ 8. During World War II, passenger pigeons carried many important messages.

_____ 9. Although I like animals, I don't have any pets.

_____ 10. Heather jumped over the net and shook my hand.

Assessment Tests

Grammar Mastery Test (Form A)

Part 1 [2 points each, 10 points total]

1. F
2. F
3. S
4. F
5. S

Part 2 [2 points each, 20 points total]

1. The <u>owner</u> I casually <u>walked</u> through the store.
2. The <u>editor</u> I <u>heard</u> about the flood and <u>sent</u> a reporter.
3. <u>I</u> I <u>run</u> a mile every day.
4. <u>Lola</u> I <u>is</u> not <u>singing</u> a solo at the concert.
5. On the floor <u>were</u> I many large <u>boxes</u>.
6. The <u>car</u> in the driveway I <u>is</u> ours.
7. Down the tree <u>raced</u> I a baby <u>squirrel</u>.
8. The <u>hikers</u> I <u>gathered</u> the wood and <u>started</u> a fire.
9. <u>Seth</u> and <u>I</u> I <u>will play</u> basketball after school.
10. The first <u>slice</u> of fresh bread I <u>tastes</u> best.

Part 3 [2 points each, 10 points total]

1. interrogative—is?
2. declarative—lion.
3. exclamatory—it!
4. imperative—one.
5. declarative—zoos.

Part 4 [1 point each, 10 points total]

1. N, V
2. ADV, ADJ
3. ADJ, N
4. V, N
5. ADJ, V
6. INTERJ, ADV
7. PRON, ADJ
8. PREP, CONJ
9. ADV, PREP
10. N, V

Part 5 [1 point each, 10 points total]

1. <u>book</u>—DO
2. <u>reader</u>—PN
3. <u>lukewarm</u>—PA
4. <u>teacher</u>, <u>answer</u>—IO, DO
5. <u>lawn</u>—DO
6. <u>brother</u>, <u>snake</u>—IO, DO
7. <u>immigrants</u>—PN
8. <u>hungry</u>—PA
9. <u>new</u>—PA
10. <u>anthem</u>—PN

Part 6 [1 point each, 10 points total]

1. PREP
2. PART
3. PART
4. PREP
5. PART
6. INF
7. PREP
8. PART
9. PREP
10. INF

Part 7 [1 point each, 10 points total]

1. SUB
2. SUB
3. SUB
4. IND
5. SUB
6. IND
7. SUB
8. IND
9. IND
10. SUB

Part 8 [5 points each, 10 points total]

1. S
2. CX
3. S
4. CD

Assessment Tests

Grammar Mastery Test (Form B)

Part 1 [2 points each, 10 points total]

1. F
2. S
3. S
4. F
5. S

Part 2 [2 points each, 20 points total]

1. U.S. <u>voters</u> | <u>elect</u> a president every four years.
2. <u>This</u> | <u>is</u> a wonderful collection of poems!
3. In the center of the island <u>is</u> | a <u>grove</u> of pecan trees.
4. <u>Dogs</u> | <u>are</u> <u>trained</u> as guides at the Seeing Eye Foundations.
5. Many <u>books</u> and <u>magazines</u> | <u>explain</u> the space program and <u>describe</u> its projects.
6. The <u>boots</u> on the left | <u>are</u> mine.
7. Under the back stairs <u>is</u> | a small coat <u>closet</u>.
8. Homer's <u>story</u> about the Trojan War | <u>describes</u> real places.
9. <u>Judges</u> and <u>lawyers</u> in Britain | <u>wear</u> wigs in court.
10. <u>Hermit crabs</u> | <u>find</u> and <u>inhabit</u> empty shells of other animals.

Part 3 [2 points each, 10 points total]

1. exclamatory—is!
2. interrogative—it?
3. declarative—life.
4. imperative—author.
5. declarative—sixty.

Part 4 [1 point each, 10 points total]

1. ADV
2. V
3. INTERJ
4. PREP
5. N
6. CONJ
7. PRON
8. ADV
9. V
10. ADJ

Part 5 [1 point each, 10 points total]

1. <u>model</u>—PN
2. <u>"The Battle Hymn of the Republic"</u>—DO
3. <u>excited</u>—PA
4. <u>smile</u>—DO
5. <u>uncomfortable</u>—PA
6. <u>us, slides</u>—IO, DO
7. <u>bees</u>—DO
8. <u>fun</u>—PA
9. <u>convertible</u>—PN
10. <u>eyes</u>—DO

Part 6 [1 point each, 10 points total]

1. PREP
2. INF
3. PART
4. PART
5. PREP
6. PART
7. INF
8. PREP
9. PREP
10. INF

Part 7 [1 point each, 10 points total]

1. SUB, ADJ
2. IND
3. SUB, ADV
4. IND
5. SUB, ADV
6. SUB, ADJ
7. SUB, ADV
8. SUB, ADJ
9. IND
10. SUB, ADV

Assessment Tests

Part 8 [2 points each, 20 points total]

1. CD
2. CX
3. S
4. CD
5. CD
6. S
7. CX
8. S
9. CX
10. S

Usage Pretests (Form A)

Pretest A   Two words appear in parentheses in each of the following sentences. Underline the correct word. [10 points each]

Example: Sandy and Judy (is, <u>are</u>) coming to dinner.

1. This news (was, were) just what Barb wanted to hear.

2. *Giants of Jazz* (is, are) an interesting book.

3. Everyone (is, are) expected to attend.

4. Most of our reading (was, were) done on weekends.

5. Neither Gordon nor Ruben (knows, know) the right answer.

6. In our yard (is, are) several oak trees.

7. She (doesn't, don't) know if she can go along.

8. Here (is, are) more books you will enjoy.

9. The students in the class (is, are) eager to meet you.

10. (Is, Are) the committee in the conference room?

Pretest B   Two pronoun choices appear in parentheses in each of the following sentences. Underline the correct choice. Then, underline the antecedent for that pronoun choice. Follow the rules for standard written English. [20 points each]

Example: <u>Riders</u> must fasten (her, <u>their</u>) seat belts.

1. Everyone put (his or her, their) sleeping bags on the bus.

2. Either Suki or Aolani will fix (their, her) costume.

3. Both Marc and Sue agreed with (her, their) counselor.

4. Several of my friends do (his or her, their) homework after school.

5. One of the boys used (his, their) bat in the game.

Pretest C   Each of the following sentences is missing a verb. Decide what form of the verb in parentheses will make the sentence clear and correct. Write the correct verb form on the line provided. [5 points each]

1. (lie)   Ben _____ on the couch all afternoon and read.

2. (set)   I thought I had _____ those packages on the table by the door.

3. (bring)   Minowa has _____ her radio, so we will have music.

4. (blow)   My brother had _____ out every candle with one deep breath.

5. (speak)   Dutch is the language that is _____ in Holland.

6. (choose)   Yesterday we _____ the new officers for our club.

7. (know)   Have you _____ Ms. Longstreet very long?

Usage Pretests (Form A)

8. (see)　　　How many people have ever _____ a UFO?

9. (wear)　　I wish José had _____ his lucky hat to the game.

10. (steal)　　Three runners _____ bases during the first inning.

11. (freeze)　We can skate only after the lake has _____ solid.

12. (lay)　　　Last night Lorraine _____ her homework on top of her books.

13. (rise)　　The Girl Scouts _____ early every morning last week.

14. (break)　The thunder _____ the silence.

15. (drink)　The runners have _____ at least a quart each since the race.

16. (ring)　　Who _____ the fire alarm so quickly?

17. (shrink)　Either my jeans have _____ or I've put on weight.

18. (throw)　That's the second time you've _____ the ball out of bounds.

19. (swim)　　After the boys had _____ for an hour, they rested.

20. (lead)　　Dudley _____ the parade last year, so now it's my turn.

Pretest D　　Each sentence below contains a pair of pronouns in parentheses. On the line provided, write the correct pronoun. [10 points each]

　　　　　　Example: __He__ (He, Him) and his cousin look alike.

_____ 1. Last Saturday Molly and (I, me) decided to see a movie.

_____ 2. Father suggested an afternoon movie to Molly and (I, me).

_____ 3. (We, Us) girls didn't like any of the afternoon movies.

_____ 4. "Between you and (I, me)," said Molly, " I'd rather go this evening."

_____ 5. The girls prepared (themselves, theirselfs) for the evening.

_____ 6. My little brother ran in and asked to go with (we, us).

_____ 7. Molly told (he, him) that this movie was not for little brothers.

_____ 8. My father took (he, him) and his friends to another movie.

_____ 9. Father and (them, they) left the house before we were ready to go.

_____10. Some friends met (we, us) girls just as we entered the theater.

Usage Pretests (Form A)

Pretest E   Each of the following sentences contains an adjective or adverb in parentheses. Decide what the correct form of that word should be. Then write the correct form on the line provided. [20 points each]

Example: The third truck is the (powerful). ___most powerful___

1. Rosalie's idea was (useful) than Merle's. _____

2. That is the (nice) compliment I've ever received. _____

3. We felt (bad) after losing the tournament game. _____

4. The wind is blowing (strongly) than it was blowing last night. _____

5. My sore throat feels (bad) today than it did yesterday. _____

Pretest F   Each sentence below contains a pair of answer choices in parentheses. Underline the choice that completes each sentence correctly. [20 points each]

1. The little boy (won't hardly, will hardly) look at anyone.

2. The blizzard ended even more (suddenly, suddener) than it had begun.

3. All of those computers are far (less, least) expensive than the ones in my country.

4. Each gymnast knew her routine (well, good).

5. This sweater is (more, most) colorful than the one I tried on earlier.

Pretest G   Each sentence below contains a misplaced modifying phrase or clause. Underline each misplaced modifier. Then, draw an arrow from the modifier to the place where it belongs. [20 points each]

Example: Hanging from the tree, Jesse saw a spiderweb.

1. The fruit was marked for quick sale bruised by the storm.

2. Those tapes came from the library that you heard.

3. That blue car is rented in the driveway.

4. Please put the dishes on the kitchen table for our breakfast.

5. We arrived just in time to see Heather jumping on her pony over the fence .

Usage Pretests (Form A)

Pretest H   Read each sentence below, and decide whether it contains an error in usage. If the sentence is correct, write **C** on the line provided. If the sentence contains an error in usage, underline the error, and write the correct form of the word or phrase on the line. [5 points each]

Example: I <u>can't hardly</u> see the signs in this fog.   <u>can hardly</u>

1. Try to be real quiet while you are inside the library. _____

2. We can't ride our bikes without it stops raining. _____

3. Be careful not to knock that lamp off of the table. _____

4. The cartoon page looks as if it got wet. _____

5. We brought the juice, but its still in the car. _____

6. Just do your best, and everything will be alright. _____

7. Robbie said that the lock on the back door is busted. _____

8. Andrea thought we should of turned right at the stop sign. _____

9. I think there are fewer chairs than there are people. _____

10. Divide the music between the three musicians. _____

11. Before 1920, farmers use to grow strawberries here. _____

12. My grandmother she worked in a factory at my age. _____

13. The rice will feed more people then the bread will. _____

14. Those game tickets are somewheres in this drawer. _____

15. Before our trip, we ought to buy a map. _____

16. Both cars had pin stripes painted on there hoods. _____

17. Who did you call about the leaky faucet? _____

18. The toll booth will except quarters and dimes but not pennies. _____

19. Chika is the woman whose going to be my math tutor. _____

20. By noon we were all ready to see Mr. Kerr's film. _____

Usage Pretests (Form B)

Pretest A   Choose the correct form of the verb given in parentheses in each of the following sentences. Write each answer in the blank provided. [5 points each]

   Example: _____are_____ Computers and robots (is, are) changing our
                            work habits.

_____ 1. Elephants (has, have) served people for centuries.

_____ 2. A blue vase (is, are) the only thing in the room.

_____ 3. (Doesn't, Don't) he come here every afternoon?

_____ 4. The exhibit of the drawings by John James Audubon (was, were) fascinating.

_____ 5. Civics (was, were) the only class that challenged me.

_____ 6. Since Mom fixed them, both of the radios (work, works).

_____ 7. Everyone (calls, call) Latisha by her nickname, Tish.

_____ 8. When (was, were) the steam engine invented?

_____ 9. Your doctor (knows, know) which vaccines you need.

_____10. (Is, Are) there any other blacksmiths in town?

_____11. I'm sorry, but somebody (has, have) checked out that book.

_____12. (Was, Were) the geese in the cornfield again?

_____13. All of the shells in my collection (was, were) displayed.

_____14. Neither Cindy nor David (knows, know) where to pan for gold.

_____15. Outside the back door (is, are) a few of your friends.

_____16. My brother (plays, play) shortstop for the church team.

_____17. He (doesn't, don't) ride his bicycle to school very often.

_____18. Here (is, are) several subjects for you to consider.

_____19. (Is, Are) all of the posters ready?

_____20. You (was, were) the only one to give the correct answer.

Pretest B   Each of the following sentences is missing a verb. Decide what form of the verb in parentheses will make the sentence clear and correct. Write the correct form on the line provided. [10 points each]

   Example: (fall)   After the storm, we saw that a tree had_____fallen_____.

1. (blow)   Unfortunately, a power surge has _____ the fuses.

2. (choose)   Sonia _____ to read the novel *The Learning Tree*, by Gordon Parks.

Usage Pretests (Form B)

3. (set)   Saul carefully _____ the eggs in the basket.

4. (know)   How long have they _____ the secret?

5. (speak)   After the movie, not a word was _____ .

6. (see)   We laughed gleefully when we _____ the clowns.

7. (wear)   All of my brothers have _____ this parka.

8. (steal)   Silently, we _____ into the forest.

9. (freeze)   The bottle that you put in the freezer has _____ .

10. (lay)   Your notebook is right where you _____ it last night.

Pretest C   For each of the following sentences, choose the correct pronoun given in parentheses. Write each answer in the blank provided. [5 points each]

      Example: _____He_____ (He, Him) doesn't like to dance.

_____ 1. One hot afternoon Mabel and (I, me) walked to the old icehouse.

_____ 2. Grandma sent a crate of apples to my family and (I, me).

_____ 3. (We, Us) were unable to find an economical solution.

_____ 4. Don't worry; my stepmother will take you and (I, me) home.

_____ 5. Mrs. Chávez sat between Kareem and (I, me) during the pep assembly.

_____ 6. It's a shame that the boys hurt (themselves, theirselves) last night.

_____ 7. Will you and (I, me) be able to reach them in time?

_____ 8. Mayor Petrakis asked my mom and (she, her) to help.

_____ 9. After I mailed the letter, Willie and (they, them) arrived.

_____10. Is this (she, her) to whom we spoke yesterday?

_____11. With their help (we, us) finished the jigsaw puzzle before dinner.

_____12. Roger and (I, me) are studying for our lifeguard certificates.

_____13. The fastest typists in class are Gene and (they, them).

_____14. Will you and (she, her) please come to my house this Wednesday?

_____15. While we were at the store, we saw my cousin and (she, her).

_____16. From where we were standing, we couldn't see them behind (we, us).

Assessment: Pretests

Usage Pretests (Form B)

_____ 17. Last night Dad told (he, him) the story of our dog Zip.

_____ 18. The nurse tested (he, him) for measles.

_____ 19. Mr. Knight and (they, them) left two hours ago for home.

_____ 20. (We, Us) scouts should be able to survive in the wild for two days.

Pretest D   Each of the following ten sentences contains a blank space that indicates a missing adjective or adverb form. Before each sentence is an adjective or adverb in parentheses. In the blank, write the from of the word in parentheses that correctly completes the sentence. [10 points each]

　　　　Example: (unhappy)   That is the ___unhappiest___ dog that I have ever seen.

 1. (useful)　　　Our new microwave oven is _____ than the old one.

 2. (nice)　　　Mr. Ricardo is the _____ person in town.

 3. (exciting)　　A circus is coming; what could be _____ ?

 4. (good)　　　Your balance is _____ than it was last summer.

 5. (difficult)　　What is the _____ thing that you've ever done?

 6. (easily)　　　The windmill is turning much _____ since Mr. Diego fixed it.

 7. (large)　　　We grew the _____ watermelon in the county.

 8. (bad)　　　When you are upset, your handwriting becomes _____ than it normally is.

 9. (white)　　　Her face turned _____ than a sheet.

 10. (well)　　　Of the five designs, which one do you like _____ ?

Pretest E   For each of the following sentences, choose the word in parentheses that will make the sentence correct. Write each answer in the blank provided. [5 points each]

　　　　Example: ____gently____ Lenise (gentle, gently) carried the ancient vase.

_____ 1. Run (quick, quickly) and call the fire department!

_____ 2. I've got to admit, my trumpet playing sounds (bad, badly).

_____ 3. Our setter came (shy, shyly) toward the new puppy.

_____ 4. Yoki was anxious, but she appeared (calm, calmly).

Usage Pretests (Form B)

_____ 5. Must the twins play so (noisy, noisily)!

_____ 6. I was so frightened that my knees felt (weak, weakly).

_____ 7. The spices and flower petals that I saved smell (fragrant, fragrantly).

_____ 8. We're pleased that you did so very (good, well).

_____ 9. After he came out of the office, Eric seemed (solemn, solemnly).

_____ 10. Its end was as (sudden, suddenly) as its beginning.

_____ 11. With a little oil, the engine turned (easy, easily).

_____ 12. Their performance is now (good, well) enough for any stage.

_____ 13. Eugenia glanced (quick, quickly) at the microscope.

_____ 14. It is (good, well) to be alive on a day like today.

_____ 15. Mrs. Bernstein seemed (excited, excitedly) when I saw her.

_____ 16. That painting appears (genuine, genuinely) to me.

_____ 17. José Canseco played (good, well).

_____ 18. The baby seems (restless, restlessly) tonight.

_____ 19. Uncle Pat's fresh peaches tasted (delicious, deliciously).

_____ 20. Janell has a (good, well) sense of color.

Pretest F   Each of the following sentences contains a misplaced modifier. Circle each misplaced modifier, and draw an arrow to show where the modifier should be placed. [20 points each]

> **Example:** A police car (carrying a bag of money) chased a thief.

1. The boy rode the pony with a brand-new pair of boots.

2. Sleeping on the porch, I almost stepped on the cat.

3. One cannot be small who is tall.

4. A package came for Marissa wrapped in tinfoil.

5. Tim looked wonderful at the rodeo wearing a ten-gallon hat.

Assessment Tests

Usage Pretests (Form A)

Pretest A [10 points each]

1. <u>was</u>
2. <u>is</u>
3. <u>is</u>
4. <u>was</u>
5. <u>knows</u>
6. <u>are</u>
7. <u>doesn't</u>
8. <u>are</u>
9. <u>are</u>
10. <u>Is</u>

Pretest B [20 points each]

1. <u>Everyone, his or her</u>
2. <u>Suki, Aolani, her</u>
3. <u>Marc, Sue, their</u>
4. <u>Several, their</u>
5. <u>One, his</u>

Pretest C [5 points each]

1. lay
2. set
3. brought
4. blown
5. spoken
6. chose
7. known
8. seen
9. worn
10. stole
11. frozen
12. laid
13. rose
14. broke
15. drunk
16. rang
17. shrunk
18. thrown
19. swum
20. led

Pretest D [10 points each]

1. I
2. me
3. We
4. me
5. themselves
6. us
7. him
8. him
9. they
10. us

Pretest E [20 points each]

1. more useful
2. nicest
3. bad
4. more strongly
5. worse

Pretest F [20 points each]

1. will hardly
2. suddenly
3. less
4. well
5. more

Pretest G [20 points each]

1. The fruit was marked for quick sale <u>bruised</u> by the storm.
2. Those tapes came from the library <u>that you</u> <u>heard</u>.
3. That blue car is rented <u>in the driveway</u>.
4. Please put the dishes on the kitchen table <u>for our breakfast</u>.
5. <u>We arrived just in time to see Heather jumping</u> <u>on her pony</u> over the fence.

Pretest H [5 points each]

1. <u>real</u>—really
2. <u>without</u>—unless
3. <u>off of</u>—off
4. C
5. <u>its</u>—it's
6. <u>alright</u>—all right
7. <u>busted</u>—broken
8. <u>should of</u>—should have
9. C
10. <u>between</u>—among
11. <u>use to</u>—used to
12. <u>grandmother she worked</u>—grandmother worked
13. <u>then</u>—than
14. <u>somewheres</u>—somewhere
15. C
16. <u>there</u>—their
17. <u>Who</u>—Whom

Assessment Tests

18. <u>except</u>—accept
19. <u>whose</u>—who's
20. C

Usage Pretests (Form B)

Pretest A [5 points each]

1. have	11. has
2. is	12. Were
3. Doesn't	13. were
4. was	14. knows
5. was	15. are
6. work	16. plays
7. calls	17. doesn't
8. was	18. are
9. knows	19. Are
10. Are	20. were

Pretest B [10 points each]

1. blown
2. chose
3. set
4. known
5. spoken
6. saw
7. worn
8. stole
9. frozen
10. laid

Pretest C [5 points each]

1. I	11. we
2. me	12. I
3. We	13. they
4. me	14. she
5. me	15. her
6. themselves	16. us
7. I	17. him
8. her	18. him
9. they	19. they
10. she	20. We

Pretest D [10 points each]

1. more useful
2. nicest
3. more exciting
4. better
5. most difficult
6. more easily
7. largest
8. worse
9. whiter
10. best

Pretest E [5 points each]

1. quickly	11. easily
2. bad	12. good
3. shyly	13. quickly
4. calm	14. good
5. noisily	15. excited
6. weak	16. genuine
7. fragrant	17. well
8. well	18. restless
9. solemn	19. delicious
10. sudden	20. good

Pretest F [20 points each]

1. The boy rode the pony with a brand-new pair of boots.
2. Sleeping on the porch, I almost stepped on the cat.
3. One cannot be small who is tall.
4. A package came for Marissa wrapped in tinfoil.
5. Tim looked wonderful at the rodeo wearing a ten-gallon hat.

Chapter 20: Agreement

Singular and Plural

When a word refers to one person, place, thing, or idea, it is **singular** in number. When a word refers to more than one, it is **plural** in number.

Singular:	circle	he	one	woman	loss
Plural:	circles	they	some	women	losses

Exercise A   For each of the following words, write **S** if the word is singular and **P** if the word is plural.

_____ 1. she

_____ 2. beach

_____ 3. we

_____ 4. men

_____ 5. mouse

_____ 6. cities

_____ 7. I

_____ 8. mouth

_____ 9. plateau

_____ 10. parentheses

_____ 11. shelves

_____ 12. people

_____ 13. many

_____ 14. guesses

_____ 15. geese

_____ 16. chickens

_____ 17. loaf

_____ 18. us

_____ 19. prophecies

_____ 20. citizen

Exercise B   For each of the following expressions, write **S** if the expression is singular and **P** if the expression is plural.

_____ 1. I look.

_____ 2. Ramiro enters.

_____ 3. He sings.

_____ 4. All dance.

_____ 5. Everyone smiles.

_____ 6. Each applauds.

_____ 7. They bow.

_____ 8. Nobody frowns.

_____ 9. Some curtsey.

_____ 10. Children laugh.

Name _____ Date _____ Class _____

Agreement of Subject and Verb

A verb agrees with its subject in number. Singular subjects take singular verbs. Plural subjects take plural verbs.

Mexican *art is* interesting. (The singular verb *is* agrees with the singular subject *art*.)

Mexican *holidays are celebrated* in the Southwest. (The plural verb *are* agrees with the plural subject *holidays*.)

When a sentence contains a verb phrase, the first helping verb in the verb phrase agrees with the subject.

Mr. Frank has been studying Mexican culture.

Exercise A   In each of the sentences below, two verbs appear in parentheses. Underline the verb that agrees with its subject.

1. The Fifth of May (is, are) an important Mexican holiday.

2. Many Mexican Americans (celebrate, celebrates) this holiday.

3. Some people (watch, watches) these celebrations in Los Angeles.

4. Others (see, sees) them in San Antonio.

5. The celebrations (include, includes) parades.

6. Bands (play, plays) traditional music.

7. Marchers (wear, wears) typical costumes.

8. Spectators (line, lines) the streets of the parade route.

9. The floats (seem, seems) lively and colorful.

10. Mexican Americans (view, views) parade with pride.

Exercise B   In each of the sentences below two helping verbs appear in parentheses. Underline the helping verb that agrees with its subject.

1. We (have, has) learned about Mexican traditions.

2. Immigrants (do, does) bring new traditions.

3. Mexican corridos (is, are) heard in the Southwest.

4. In English, corridos (is, are) called ballads.

5. What (do, does) these ballads describe?

6. In them, heroes' lives (has, have) been recorded.

7. Everyday people (do, does) appear in ballads, too.

8. One historian (has, have) begun to record these ballads.

9. They (is, are) trying to save these ballads.

10. (Do, Does) Horacio know any corridos?

Chapter 20: Agreement

Agreement of Prepositional Phrases

The number of a subject is not changed by a phrase following the subject.

The first two phases *of the moon* are the new moon and the waving crescent.
(The plural verb *are* agrees with the plural subject *phases*.)

Exercise A   In each of the sentences below, two verbs appear in parentheses.
Underline the verb that agrees with its subject.

1. The distance of the moon from the earth (is, are) 384,400 kilometers.

2. The features of the moon (is, are) seen through powerful telescopes.

3. The sun, like the earth, (influence, influences) the moon's motion.

4. The moon's orbit around the earth (take, takes) 27 days, 7 hours, and 43.2
   minutes.

5. The earth, at the same time, (move, moves) around the sun.

6. A full moon, on the average, (occur, occurs) every 29 days, 12 hours, and 44.1
   minutes.

7. Tides on the earth (rise, rises) according to the moon's gravitational pull.

8. Exploration by telescope and lunar landings (continue, continues).

9. Photography from lunar-orbiting vehicles (shows, show) spectacular features
   on the moon's surface.

10. People throughout history (have, has) studied the moon.

Exercise B   Underline the prepositional phrase in each of the sentences below. Then
underline the correct form of the verb in parentheses.

1. The history of Jewish Americans (begin, begins) in 1654.

2. New York at that time (was, were) a Dutch colony called New Amsterdam.

3. The governor of New Amsterdam (was, were) Peter Stuyvesant.

4. Jewish immigrants to our country (has, have) made many contributions.

5. The names of some Jewish American authors (is, are) well known.

6. A famous author of short stories (is, are) Bernard Malamud.

7. Jewish American writers of fiction (include, includes) Saul Bellow.

8. The winner of the Nobel Prize (was, were) Saul Bellow.

9. Another writer of Jewish descent (is, are) Philip Roth.

10. The contributions of immigrants (enrich, enriches) our country.

Chapter 20: Agreement

Agreement with Indefinite Pronouns

Personal pronouns refer to specific people, places, things, or ideas. A pronoun that does not refer to a definite person, place, thing, or idea is called an **indefinite pronoun.**

The following indefinite pronouns are singular: *each, either, neither, one, everyone, everybody, no one, nobody, anyone, anybody, someone, somebody.*

> **Singular:** *Nobody* on our street *grows* a better tomato than Otis.

The following indefinite pronouns are plural: *both, few, many, several.*

> **Plural:** *Many* of his tomatoes *taste* sweet and juicy.

The indefinite pronouns *all, any, most, none,* and *some* may be either singular or plural.

The number of the pronoun *all, any, most, none,* or *some* is determined by the number of the object in the prepositional phrase following the subject. If the subject refers to a singular object, the pronoun is singular. If the subject refers to a plural object, the pronoun is plural.

> **Singular:** *None* of his effort *is* wasted. (*None* is singular because it refers to one thing—*effort.* The singular verb *is* is used to agree with the subject *None.*)

> **Plural:** *Some* of his tomatoes *are* prize winners! (*Some* is plural because it refers to more than one thing—*tomatoes.* The plural verb *are* is used to agree with the subject *Some.*)

Exercise A Underline the indefinite pronoun in each of the sentences below. Then underline the correct form of the verb in parentheses.

1. One of my brothers (plants, plant) tomatoes every year.

2. No one on my block (believes, believe) his plants will grow.

3. Everyone in the neighborhood (say, says) the soil is not good enough.

4. Most of the plants (does, do) not do very well.

5. A few of them (reach, reaches) full size.

Exercise B Underline the indefinite pronoun in each of the sentences below. Then write **S** if the indefinite pronoun in the sentence is singular or **P** if it is plural. Then circle the correct form of the verb in parentheses.

_____ 1. All of my cousins (like, likes) mariachi bands.

_____ 2. Some of my classmates also (listen, listens) to them.

_____ 3. Any of the bands (play, plays) the music often.

_____ 4. None of our neighbors ever (complain, complains).

_____ 5. Most of our music (is, are) fun to listen to.

Chapter 20: Agreement

Agreement with Compound Subjects

Subjects joined by *and* usually take a plural verb.

Acids and bases are interesting.

A compound subject that names only one person or thing takes a singular verb.

Sweet and sour is a common style of food preparation. (One combination is meant.)

Singular subjects joined by *or* or *nor* take a singular verb.

Neither *Lucas nor Vo likes* lemonade.

Plural subjects joined by *or* or *nor* take a plural verb.

Strawberries or raspberries are in their backyard.

When a singular subject and a plural subject are joined by *or* or *nor*, the verb agrees with the subject nearer the verb.

Unripe *apples or* sour *milk makes* you sick. (The verb agrees with the nearer subject, *milk.*)

Melon or berries are usually on the dessert menu. (The verb agrees with the nearer subject, *berries.*)

Exercise A   Write **S** if the compound subject in each of the sentences below is singular or **P** if it is plural. Then underline the correct form of the verb in parentheses.

_____ 1. Vinegar and lemon juice (contain, contains) acids.

_____ 2. Neither lemons nor limes (is, are) bases.

_____ 3. Baking soda or soap (is, are) a salt.

_____ 4. Acids and bases (combines, combine) to make salts.

_____ 5. Acids and bases (is, are) one of our topics in science class.

_____ 6. Fats or oils (is, are) added to bases to make soap.

_____ 7. Plaster and cement (is, are) made with bases.

_____ 8. Some food and common household items (contain, contains) acids.

_____ 9. (Do, Does) macaroni and cheese contain acids?

_____10. Litmus paper or strong tea (is, are) used as an indicator of the presence of an acid or a base.

Exercise B: Proofreading   The following paragraph contains three errors in agreement between compound subjects and verbs. It also contains two spelling errors. Can you find these errors? Proofread the paragraph to correct all the errors you can find.

Amy and Bethany have learned that spaghetti and meatballs are the best-known Italian dish. Lasagna and pizza is also well known. But macarroni or tomato sause is not in every Italian dish. Meat juices or marinade are sometimes used for flavor.

Chapter 20: Agreement
Other Problems in Agreement

A **collective noun,** like *flock* or *class,* names a group. It takes a singular verb when it refers to the whole group. It takes a plural verb when it refers to the parts of the group.

The *family is* closely knit. (The family as a unit is closely knit.)

The *family are meeting* in Rochester. (The parts, or individual members, of the family are meeting.)

The subject usually follows the verb in questions and in sentences beginning with *here* or *there.* Make sure the subject and verb agree in such sentences.

There *is* the *house.* (The singular subject *house* follows the singular verb *is.*)

The contractions *here's, there's,* and *where's* contain the verb *is* and should be used only with singular subjects.

Here**'**s the *bill* for the *party.* (The subject *bill* is singular.)

Words stating amounts are usually singular.

Five dollars is a good price for that football.

A title is singular, even when plural in form.

Beauty and the Beast is a scary but fun movie.

The words *don't* and *doesn't* are contractions of *do not* and *does not.* Use *don't* with all plural subjects and with the pronouns *I* and *you.* Use *doesn't* with all singular subjects except *I* and *you.*

Plaids don't match with stripes.
Brown doesn't go well with purple.

Exercise   In each sentence below, underline the subject and the correct verb.

1. Civics (is, are) his favorite subject.

2. The class (is, are) working on their science project.

3. You (doesn't, don't) have enough money.

4. The family (is, are) discussing their vacation plans.

5. (Has, Have) the jury reached a verdict?

6. Here (is, are) the canned goods for the food drive.

7. A machine (don't, doesn't) work properly unless it is oiled.

8. Ten pounds (is, are) a lot of weight to lose.

9. *The Magnificent Ambersons* (is, are) a famous movie.

10. (Doesn't, Don't) Thelma look healthy?

Chapter 20: Agreement

Agreement of Pronoun and Antecedent

A pronoun usually refers to a noun or another pronoun, called its **antecedent.** Whenever you use a pronoun, make sure that it agrees with its antecedent.

A pronoun agrees with its antecedent in number and gender. Some singular personal pronouns have forms that indicate gender. Masculine pronouns (*he, him, his*) refer to males. Feminine pronouns (*she, her, hers*) refer to females. Neuter pronouns (*it, its*) refer to things (neither male nor female) and sometimes to animals.

> *Dolores* lost *her* scarf.

The antecedent of a personal pronoun can be another kind of pronoun, such as *each, neither,* or *none.* In such cases, you need to look in the phrase that follows the antecedent to determine which personal pronoun to use.

> *Each* of the *men* put *his* keys on the conveyer belt.

Some antecedents may be either masculine or feminine. When referring to such antecedents, use both the masculine and the feminine forms.

> *Everybody* in the group wanted *his or her* own invitation.

Use a singular pronoun to refer to *each, either, neither, one, everyone, everybody, no one, nobody, anyone, anybody, someone,* or *somebody.*

> *No one* in the league wanted *his or her* team to lose.

Use a singular pronoun to refer to two or more singular antecedents joined by *or.*

> *Either Talasi or Wilma* will share *her* room.

Use a plural pronoun to refer to two or more antecedents joined by *and.*

> *Bill and Buddy* will lend *their* microscope to the class.

Exercise: Proofreading   The following paragraph contains five errors in agreement between pronouns and their antecedents. It also contains five spelling errors. Can you find these errors? Proofread the paragraph to correct all the errors you can find.

Dairy products are a rich sourse of protein. They are also good sources of calcium and various vitamens. Unfortunately, many dairy products are high in fat. Almost everyone should include some dairy products in their diet. Yet, no one should do so without thinking about his fat intake. For example, Ms. Wittimer chooses low-fat dairy products such as yogert in her diet. Mr. and Mrs. Rubin include low-fat cottage cheese in their diet. The Ramirez sisters use skim milk with her breakfast sereals. Each of these individuals is making a sensable decision about their dairy products. By doing so, each is contributing to their own well-being.

Chapter 20: Agreement

Review (Form A)

Exercise A   For each of the following sentences, write **C** if the italicized verb agrees with its subject. If the italicized verb does not agree with its subject, write the correct form of the verb on the line.

_____ 1. Where *is* the Mason-Dixon line?

_____ 2. The highest peak in the United States *are* Mount McKinley.

_____ 3. The Senate *are* in session now.

_____ 4. Several of the legends *are* about Hercules.

_____ 5. None of the symphony players *listens* to rock-and-roll.

_____ 6. Fifteen ounces *are* the total weight of the package.

_____ 7. *Are* Adrianne or Suki going to the party?

_____ 8. There *is* the tickets to tonight's game.

_____ 9. In the mailbox *were* both letters from Vicente.

_____ 10. The Pickwick Papers *are* a novel by Dickens.

Exercise B   For each of the following sentences, write **C** if the italicized pronoun agrees with its antecedent. If the italicized pronoun does not agree with its antecedent, write the correct form of the pronoun.

_____ 1. Either of the two sisters will bring *her* notebook.

_____ 2. Either a hamster or a gerbil shows affection for *their* owner.

_____ 3. I hope everyone remembers *their* lunch.

_____ 4. Each of the children will need *his* own permission slip.

_____ 5. Some of the girls have opened *their* gifts already.

_____ 6. Neither Earl nor Fred has opened *their* mail yet.

_____ 7. A few of the teachers want *their* students to type their papers.

_____ 8. One of the coaches is going to put those boys on *his* team.

_____ 9. Many of the boys lost *their* flashcards.

_____ 10. Each of the contestants will do *their* best.

Chapter 20: Agreement

Review (Form B)

Exercise A   In each of the following sentences, underline the subject once and the verb twice. If the subject and verb agree, write *Correct* on the line below. If the subject and verb do not agree, correct the sentence as you rewrite it on the line below.

1. Twenty gallons are a good size for an aquarium.

_____

2. *Tropical Fishes* is a handy guidebook to own.

_____

3. Neither Doyle nor Ana know how to set up an aquarium.

_____

4. Plants in an aquarium doesn't have to be real to look good.

_____

5. The tropical fish club is holding a meeting next Wednesday.

_____

Exercise B   In each of the following sentences, underline the pronoun that refers to each italicized antecedent. If the pronoun and antecedent agree, write *Correct* on the line below. If the pronoun and antecedent do not agree, correct the sentence as you rewrite it on the line below.

1. *One* of my sisters thinks they will be a firefighter.

_____

2. *Each* of my sisters has had plenty of time to decide on their future.

_____

3. A *person* can change their career several times over a lifetime.

_____

4. If *anybody* asked me, I would tell them I hope to be a doctor one day.

_____

5. *Hector* or *Mateo* will write his report on careers of the future.

_____

Answer Key

Practice and Reinforcement (1)
Singular and Plural

Exercise A

1. S
2. S
3. P
4. P
5. S
6. P
7. S
8. S
9. S
10. P
11. P
12. P
13. P
14. P
15. P
16. P
17. S
18. P
19. P
20. S

Exercise B

1. S
2. S
3. S
4. P
5. S
6. S
7. P
8. S
9. P
10. P

Practice and Reinforcement (2)
Agreement of Subject and Verb

Exercise A

1. The Fifth of May (is, are) an important Mexican holiday.
2. Many Mexican Americans (celebrate, celebrates) this holiday.
3. Some people (watch, watches) these celebration in Los Angeles.
4. Others (see, sees) them in San Antonio.
5. The celebrations (include, includes) parades.
6. Bands (play, plays) traditional music.
7. Marchers (wear, wears) typical costumes.
8. Spectators (line, lines) the streets of the parade route.
9. The floats (seem, seems) lively and colorful.
10. Mexican Americans (view, views) parade with pride.

Exercise B

1. We (have, has) learned about Mexican traditions.
2. Immigrants (do, does) bring new traditions.
3. Mexican corridos (is, are) heard in the Southwest.
4. In English, corridos (is, are) called ballads.
5. What (do, does) these ballads describe?
6. In them, heroes' lives (has, have) been recorded.
7. Everyday people (do, does) appear in ballads, too.
8. One historian (has, have) begun to record these ballads.
9. They (is, are) trying to save these ballads.
10. (Do, Does) Horacio know any corridos?

Answer Key

Practice and Reinforcement (3)
Agreement and Prepositional Phrases

Exercise A

1. The distance of the moon from the earth (is, are) 384,400 kilometers.

2. The features of the moon (is, are) seen through powerful telescopes.

3. The sun, like the earth, (influence, influences) the moon's motion.

4. The moon's orbit around the earth (take, takes) 27 days, 7 hours, and 43.2 minutes.

5. The earth, at the same time, (move, moves) around the sun

6. A full moon, on the average, (occur, occurs) every 29 days, 12 hours, and 44.1 minutes.

7. Tides on the earth (rise, rises) according to the moon's gravitational pull.

8. Exploration by telescope and lunar landings (continue, continues).

9. Photography from lunar-orbiting vehicles (shows, show) spectacular features on the moon's surface.

10. People throughout history (have, has) studied the moon.

Exercise B

1. The history of Jewish Americans (begin, begins) in 1654.

2. New York at that time (was, were) a Dutch colony called New Amsterdam.

3. The governor of New Amsterdam (was, were) Peter Stuyvesant.

4. Jewish immigrants to our country (has, have) made many contributions.

5. The names of some Jewish American authors (is, are) well known.

6. A famous author of short stories (is, are) Bernard Malamud.

7. Jewish American writers of fiction (include, includes) Saul Bellow.

8. The winner of the Nobel prize (was, were) Saul Bellow.

9. Another writer of Jewish descent (is, are) Philip Roth.

10. The contributions of immigrants (enrich, enriches) our country.

Practice and Reinforcement (4)
Agreement with Indefinite Pronouns

Exercise A

1. One of my brothers (plants, plant) tomatoes every year.

2. No one on my block (believes, believe) his plants will grow.

3. Everyone in the neighborhood (say, says) the soil is not good enough.

4. Most of the plants (does, do) not do very well.

5. A few of them (reach, reaches) full size.

Exercise B

1. P All of my cousins (like, likes) mariachi bands.

2. P Some of my classmates also (listen, listens) to them.

3. P Any of the bands (play, plays) the music often.

4. P None of our neighbors ever (complain, complains).

5. S Most of our music (is, are) fun to listen to.

Practice and Reinforcement (5)
Agreement with Compound Subjects

Exercise A

1. P Vinegar and lemon juice (contain, contains) acids.

2. P Neither lemons nor limes (is, are) bases.

3. S Baking soda or soap (is, are) a salt.

4. P Acids and bases (combines, combine) to make salts.

5. S Acids and bases (is, are) one of our topics in science class.

Answer Key

6. P Fats or oils (is, <u>are</u>) added to bases to make soap.

7. P Plaster and cement (is, <u>are</u>) made with bases.

8. P Some food or common household items (<u>contain</u>, contains) acids.

9. S (Do, <u>Does</u>) macaroni and cheese contain acids?

10. S Litmus paper or strong tea (<u>is</u>, are) used as an indicator of the presence of an acid or a base.

Exercise B: Proofreading

Amy and Bethany have learned that spaghetti and meatballs ~~are~~ *is* the best-known Italian dish. Lasagna and pizza ~~is~~ *are* also well known. But macaroni or tomato sauce *is* not in every Italian dish. Meat juices or marinade ~~are~~ *is* sometimes used for flavor.

Practice and Reinforcement (6)
Other Problems in Agreement

Exercise

1. <u>Civics</u> (<u>is</u>, are) his favorite subject.

2. The <u>class</u> (is, <u>are</u>) working on their science projects.

3. <u>You</u> (doesn't, <u>don't</u>) have enough money.

4. The <u>family</u> (<u>is</u>, are) discussing their vacation plans.

5. (<u>Has</u>, Have) the <u>jury</u> reached a verdict?

6. Here (is, <u>are</u>) the canned <u>goods</u> for the food drive.

7. A <u>machine</u> (<u>doesn't</u>, don't) work properly unless it is oiled.

8. Ten <u>pounds</u> (<u>is</u>, are) a lot of weight to lose.

9. *The Magnificent Ambersons* (<u>is</u>, are) a famous movie.

10. (<u>Doesn't</u>, Don't) Thelma look healthy?

Practice and Reinforcement (7)
Agreement of Pronoun and Antecedent

Exercise: Proofreading

Dairy products are a rich source of protein. They are also good sources of calcium and various vitamins. Unfortunately, many dairy products are high in fat. Almost everyone should include some dairy products in *his or her* ~~their~~ diet. Yet, no one should do so without thinking about his *or her* fat intake. For example, Ms. Wittimer chooses low-fat dairy products such as yogurt in her diet. Mr. and Mrs. Rubin include low-fat cottage cheese in their diet. The Ramirez sisters use skim milk with *their* ~~her~~ breakfast cereals. Each of these individuals is making a sensible decision about *his or her* ~~their~~ dairy products. By doing so, each is contributing to *his or her* ~~their~~ own well-being.

Chapter Review
Form A

Exercise A

1. C
2. is
3. is
4. C
5. listen
6. is
7. Is
8. are
9. C
10. is

Exercise B

1. C
2. its
3. his or her
4. his or her
5. C

Answer Key

6. his

7. C

8. his or her

9. C

10. his or her

Chapter Review
Form B

Exercise A

1. <u>Twenty gallons</u> <u>are</u> a good size for an aquarium.

   Twenty gallons is a good size for an aquarium.

2. *Tropical Fishes* <u>is</u> a handy guidebook to own.

   Correct

3. Neither <u>Doyle</u> nor <u>Ana</u> <u>know</u> how to set up an aquarium.

   Neither Doyle nor Ana knows how to set up an aquarium.

4. <u>Plants</u> in an aquarium <u>doesn't</u> have to be real to look good.

   Plants in an aquarium don't have to be real to look good.

5. The tropical fish <u>club</u> <u>is</u> holding a meeting next Wednesday.

   Correct

Exercise B

1. *One* of my sisters thinks <u>they</u> will be a firefighter.

   One of my sisters thinks she will be a firefighter.

2. *Each* of my sisters has had plenty of time to decide on <u>their</u> future.

   Each of my sisters has had plenty of time to decide on her future.

3. A *person* can change <u>their</u> career several times over a lifetime.

   A person can change his or her career several times over a lifetime.

4. If *anybody* asked me, I would tell <u>them</u> I hope to be a doctor one day.

   If anybody asked me, I would tell him or her I hope to be a doctor one day.

5. *Hector* or *Mateo* will write <u>his</u> report on careers of the future.

   Correct

Chapter 21: Using Verbs Correctly

Principal Parts of Regular Verbs

The four basic forms of a verb are called the **principal parts** of the verb. The principal parts of a verb are the **base** (*or* infinitive) the present participle, the past, and the past participle.

Base (*or* Infinitive)	Present Participle	Past	Past Participle
wish	(is) wishing	wished	(have) wished

A **regular verb** forms its past and past participle by adding *-d* or *-ed* to the base form. The present participle and the past participle require helping verbs (forms of *be* and *have*).

When forming the past or the past participle of a regular verb, avoid the error of leaving off the *-d* or *-ed* ending.

Incorrect: The grocery store *use* to be closed on Sundays.

Correct: The grocery store *used* to be closed on Sundays.

Exercise A   For each sentence below, write the correct form (present participle, past or past participle) of the verb in parentheses.

1. Today, many people are (look) _____ for ways to improve their health.

2. I have (start) _____ to walk to school every day.

3. Walking is (suppose) _____ to be good for a person's health.

4. Last year Shane (decide) _____ to do something to improve his health.

5. He (use) _____ to eat junk food and spent most of his free time

   watching television.

6. His mother had (notice) _____ that he had very little energy.

7. He also was (gain) _____ weight rapidly.

8. Now Shane is (exercise) _____ and eating well.

9. He has (start) _____ an aerobics class that meets three times a week.

10. Aerobics are (suppose) _____ to improve the function of the heart and lungs.

Exercise B   All but one of the sentences below contain errors in verb usage. On the line provided, rewrite each sentence, correcting the error. Write C if the sentence is correct.

1. Last week we watch several videos about health and safety in science class.

   _____

2. From one video we learned a great deal of information about first aid.

   _____

3. The narrator in the video demonstrate the Heimlich maneuver.

   _____

4. You are suppose to use the Heimlich maneuver on someone who is choking.

   _____

Chapter 21: Using Verbs Correctly

Principal Parts of Irregular Verbs

The principal parts of a verb are the **base** (*or* infinitive), the **present participle**, the **past**, and the **past participle**.

Base (*or* Infinitive)	Present Participle	Past	Past Participle
eat	(is) eating	ate	(have) eaten
do	(is) doing	did	(have) done
hurt	(is) hurting	hurt	(have) hurt

An **irregular verb** forms its past and past participle in some other way than by adding *-d* or *-ed* to the base form. Notice that as with regular verbs, the past participle requires a helping verb that is a form of *have*.

Exercise A   For each of the following sentences, underline the correct verb in parentheses.

1. Calinda (took, taken) her sister to the rain forest exhibit at the museum.

2. Do you know what year the *Lusitania* (sank, sunk)?

3. Claudia has (drew, drawn) a picture of the meadow behind the cottage.

4. The camels have (drank, drunk) an enormous amount of water and are ready to being their journey across the desert.

5. The three boys (ran, run) as if they were being chased.

6. On Tuesday, Alfonso (wore, worn) the sweater that his mother gave him for his birthday.

7. Ms. Shapiro (drove, driven) the school bus home and parked it in her driveway.

8. Pieces of a meteor have (fell, fallen) on an island off the coast of Florida.

9. The teacher (rang, rung) the bell to get the students back to their desks.

10. In the last race, gusts of wind (blew, blown) a sailboat off its course.

Exercise B   For each sentence below, write the correct form (past or past participle) of the verb in parentheses.

1. The truck drive (make) _____ her last delivery at six o'clock.

2. Have you ever (hurt) _____ yourself playing soccer?

3. When you have (do) _____ the last problem on the test, you may leave.

4. Scott (build) _____ the house himself and is very proud of his work.

5. Our family has (know) _____ the Vierlings for more than twenty years.

Chapter 21: Using Verbs Correctly

Verb Tense

The **tense** of a verb indicates the time of the action or of the state of being expressed by the verb. Every verb has six tenses: *present, past, future, present perfect, past perfect,* and *future perfect.*

Present: The bird sings.   **Present perfect:** The bird has sung.

Past: The bird sang.   **Past perfect:** The bird had sung.

Future: The bird will sing.   **Future perfect:** The bird will have sung.

When writing, do not change needlessly from one tense to another.

Inconsistent: We *sat* on the porch and *gaze* at the stars. [*Sat* is in the past tense, and *gaze* is in the present tense.]

Consistent: We *sat* on the porch and *gazed* at the stars. [Both *sat* and *gazed* are in the past tense.]

Exercise A   Underline the verb in each of the following sentences. Then on the line provided, write its tense.

1. Alex smelled the aroma of barbecued chicken. _____

2. The cook, my uncle Rosco, will mix more of his special sauce. _____

3. Trays of salads and fruit line the picnic tables. _____

4. Some corn on the cob has disappeared from the platter. _____

5. Everyone at the picnic had awaited the signal for lunch. _____

Exercise B   Each of the following sentences contains an error in consistency of verb tense. On the line provided, rewrite each sentence, correcting the error.

1. By the time the frontier had closed in 1890, thousands of hardy pioneers have traveled across the country in Conestoga wagons.

_____

2. After the president of the United States threw out the first ball, the baseball game begins.

_____

3. The hungry child will eat some crackers and drank a cup of milk.

_____

4. Eduardo was working in the garden when he hears the strange sound.

_____

Chapter 21: Using Verbs Correctly

Troublesome Verbs

Three pairs of verbs that can be troublesome are *sit* and *set*, *rise* and *raise*, and *lie* and *lay*.

sit, set   *Sit* is a verb that means "to be seated" or "to rest." *Sit* seldom takes an object. *Set* is a verb that means "to place" or "to put (something)." *Set* usually takes an object.

rise, raise   *Rise* is a verb that means "to move upward" or "to go up." *Rise* never takes an object. *Raise* is a verb that means "to lift (something) up." *Raise* usually takes an object.

lie, lay   *Lie* is a verb that means "to recline," "to be in a place," or "to remain lying down." *Lie* never takes an object. *Lay* is a verb that means "to put (something) down" or "to place (something)." *Lay* usually takes an object.

Exercise A   For each of the following sentences, underline the correct verb in parentheses.

1. The rickety elevator was slowly (rising, raising) to the third floor.

2. The teacher asked the students to (sit, set) up straight in their chairs.

3. Rosa is (lying, laying) in her bed, dreaming about her future as an actor.

4. It took a great deal of planning, time, and energy to (lie, lay) the track for the transcontinental railroad.

5. His expectations and goals have (risen, raised) with every success.

6. Chan has (set, sat) in that chair since noon, reading a book about dolphins.

7. Mr. Buckman's car has (lain, laid) in a ditch since the snowstorm last week.

8. (Raise, rise) your voice so that I can hear you over all this noise.

9. Darcy is (sitting, setting) the alarm for seven o'clock.

10. The travelers (lay, laid) their weary heads on their pillows and fell asleep.

Exercise B: Proofreading   The following paragraph contains three errors in verb usage, one error in spelling, and one error in capitalization. Can you find these errors? Proofread the paragraph to correct all the errors that you find.

The audience stood at attension while the flag was risen. then everyone

joined in the singing of the national anthem. When the crowd had sat down once

again, the game began. The ball was sat at the forty-yard line for the kickoff.

Soon, football players were laying in a tangled heap in the middle of the field.

What an exciting game this was going to be!

Chapter 21: Using Verbs Correctly

Review (Form A)

Exercise A   For each sentence below, write the correct form (present participle, past, or past participle) of the verb in parentheses.

1. Tia is (hope) _____ for a chance to skate in the Olympic games.

2. The plane (soar) _____ into the clouds and out of sight.

3. The town has (approve) _____ the mayor's plan to build a homeless shelter.

4. Are you (suppose) _____ to be out so soon after having the flu?

5. I have (promise) _____ my brother that I will read him a story.

6. The principal is (place) _____ the trophy in the case where it will remain until the next competition.

7. Babe Ruth, the famous baseball player, always (want) _____ to manage a baseball team.

8. Many Europeans (use) _____ to believe that America's streets were paved with gold.

9. President Lyndon Johnson (decide) _____ not to seek reelection in 1968.

10. Lola is (help) _____ me with my writing assignment.

Exercise B   For each of the following sentences, write the correct form (past or past participle) of the verb in parentheses.

1. Alex Haley (write) _____ *Roots*, a book about his family history.

2. The clever detective (know) _____ just where to look for the evidence.

3. The children (sing) _____ as they marched up and over the hill.

4. Mrs. Alvarez has (go) _____ to San Salvador to visit her granddaughter.

5. Many fruits and vegetables from the garden have been (freeze) _____ for winter meals.

6. The tennis coach (make) _____ Delbert his assistant.

7. It's a terrible feeling to realize you have (break) _____ a family heirloom.

8. We (see) _____ a murder mystery play in which the audience helped to solve the crime.

9. The police officer (begin) _____ to question all the witnesses to the accident.

10. I can't remember where I (put) _____ my notebook.

Chapter 21: Using Verbs Correctly

Review (Form A)

Exercise C Underline the verb in each of the following sentences. Then identify its tense by writing **P** if the verb is present, **T** if it is past, or **F** if it is future.

_____ 1. The chorus will sing a medley of Stevie Wonder's hits.

_____ 2. Many singers participated in last year's concert.

_____ 3. Ms. Das leads the chorus as well as the orchestra.

_____ 4. Mika will play a solo on the trumpet in tonight's concert.

_____ 5. She practiced for the performance all weekend.

Exercise D For each of the following sentences, write the form of the verb described in parentheses.

1. By the time the people arrive, Teresa and Anne (future perfect tense of *do*)

   _____ their homework.

2. The bells in the tower (past tense of *ring*) _____ every hour on the hour.

3. Carlos (present perfect tense of *begin*) _____ to play the drums like a pro.

4. We (past perfect tense of *see*) _____ what happens when people are careless with the environment.

5. Tula (present perfect tense of *speak*) _____ about this topic many times.

Exercise E For each of the following sentences, underline the correct verb in parentheses.

1. The colorful balloons (raised, rose) high up into the sky and disappeared.

2. We (sat, set) and waited all day for the package to arrive, but it never did.

3. (Lie, Lay) your clothes out the night before, and you will have a head start in the morning.

4. Mother is (setting, sitting) the bouquet of flowers on the table.

5. The cost of living seems to (raise, rise) every month.

Chapter 21: Using Verbs Correctly

Review (Form B)

Exercise A   For each sentence below, write the correct form (present participle, past, or past participle) of the verb in parentheses.

1. The children (comb) _____ their hair and brushed their teeth before they left for school.

2. Many of the vegetable plants in our garden have (die) _____ because of an early frost.

3. I am (look) _____ for a book about the American Revolution.

4. Yoko is (suppose) _____ to meet me in the cafeteria to go over the plans for the annual charity fun run.

5. More than one hundred years ago, the people of the United States (elect) _____ Ulysses S. Grant president.

6. Cletha has (decide) _____ that she will make a model of the Alamo.

7. There (use) _____ to be a petting zoo where that high-rise apartment building is.

8. You have (arrive) _____ just in time to join us for dinner.

9. Carl is (figure) _____ out exactly how many days he has been alive.

10. Do you know who (cook) _____ the arroz con pollo?

Exercise B   For each of the following sentences write the correct form (past or past participle) of the verb in parentheses.

1. I have (lose) _____ my team jacket.

2. My favorite pair of jeans (shrink) _____ in the wash.

3. Martin (hurt) _____ his back when he tried to lift that heavy carton alone.

4. Tanya has (do) _____ so well in math this year she has been placed in an advanced class for next year.

5. The pitcher (catch) _____ the ball barehanded.

6. My parents have (show) _____ us how to handle money responsibly.

7. The balloon (burst) _____ and startled everyone in the room.

8. The main character has not (see) _____ his brother for seven years.

9. This morning, we (swim) _____ across the lake and back.

10. The rancher has (ride) _____ out to find his lost cattle.

Review (Form B)

Exercise C   Underline the verb in each of the following sentences. Then identify its tense by writing **P** if the verb is present, **T** if it is past, or **F** if it is future.

_____ 1. Lionel accidentally spilled his milk all over my paper.

_____ 2. There will be an assembly in the cafeteria after lunch today.

_____ 3. The child sang with a sweet, gentle voice.

_____ 4. The principal knows the names of all the students in the school.

_____ 5. The man sold his antique watch for cash.

Exercise D   For each of the sentences below, write the form of the verb described in parentheses.

1. Mr. Diaz (past perfect tense of *send*) _____ his manuscript to the publisher.

2. He (future perfect tense of *hear*) _____ something from his publisher by March.

3. Many people (present perfect tense of *write*) _____ books that will never be published.

4. Other writers (past perfect tense of *tell*) _____ him how difficult it was to get published.

5. In spite of many disappointments, he (past tense of *say*) _____ he will keep working to see his words in print.

Exercise E   For each of the sentences below, underline the correct verb in parentheses.

1. Whose bicycle is (laying, lying) in the driveway?

2. My parents are thrilled because all my grades have (raised, risen) this term.

3. The meat has been (sitting, setting) on the counter all day and is probably spoiled.

4. If there are any questions after the speech, please (rise, raise) your hand.

5. The artist had (laid, lain) his paintings on the sidewalk for passersby to admire.

Answer Key

Practice and Reinforcement (1)
Principal Parts of Regular Verbs

Exercise A

1. looking
2. started
3. supposed
4. decided
5. used
6. noticed
7. gaining
8. exercising
9. started
10. supposed

Exercise B

1. Last week we watched several videos about health and safety in science class.
2. C
3. The narrator in the video demonstrated the Heimlich maneuver.
4. You are supposed to use the Heimlich maneuver on someone who is choking.

Practice and Reinforcement (2)
Principal Parts of Irregular Verbs

Exercise A

1. took
2. sank
3. drawn
4. drunk
5. ran
6. wore
7. drove
8. fallen
9. rang
10. blew

Exercise B

1. made
2. hurt
3. done
4. built
5. known

Practice and Reinforcement (3)
Verb Tense

Exercise A

1. smelled/past
2. will mix/future
3. line/present
4. has disappeared/present perfect
5. had awaited/past perfect

Exercise B

(Answers will vary. Possible responses are given.)

1. By the time the frontier had closed in 1890, thousands of hardy pioneers had traveled across the country in Conestoga wagons.
2. After the president of the United States threw out the first ball, the baseball game began.
3. The hungry child will eat some crackers and will drink a cup of milk.
4. Eduardo was working in the garden when he heard the strange sound.

Practice and Reinforcement (4)
Troublesome Verbs

Exercise A

1. rising
2. sit
3. lying
4. lay
5. risen

Answer Key

6. sat
7. lain
8. Raise
9. setting
10. laid

Exercise B: Proofreading

    The audience stood at atten*t*ion while the flag
was ~~risen~~ *raised* then everyone joined in the singing of
the national anthem. When the crowd had sat
down once again, the game began. The ball was
s*e*t at the forty-yard line for the kickoff. Soon,
football players were ~~laying~~ *lying* in a tangled heap in
the middle of the field. What an exciting game this
was going to be!

Chapter Review
Form A

Exercise A

1. hoping
2. soared
3. approved
4. supposed
5. promised
6. placing
7. wanted
8. used
9. decided
10. helping

Exercise B

1. wrote
2. knew
3. sang
4 gone
5. frozen
6. made
7. broken
8. saw
9. began
10. put

Exercise C

1. will sing/F
2. participated/T
3. leads/P
4. will play/F
5. practiced/T

Exercise D

1. will have done
2. rang
3. has begun
4. had seen
5. has spoken

Exercise E

1. rose
2. sat
3. Lay
4. setting
5. rise

Chapter Review
Form B

Exercise A

1. combed
2. died
3. looking
4. supposed
5. elected
6. decided
7. used
8. arrived
9. figuring
10. cooked

Exercise B

1. lost
2. shrank
3. hurt
4. done

Answer Key

5. caught

6. shown

7. burst

8. seen

9. swam

10. ridden

Exercise C

1. spilled/T

2. will be/F

3. sang/T

4. knows/P

5. sold/T

Exercise D

1. had sent

2. will have heard

3. have written

4. had told

5. said

Exercise E

1. lying

2. risen

3. sitting

4. raise

5. laid

Chapter 22: Using Pronouns Correctly

The Nominative Case

Case is the form of a noun or pronoun that shows its use in a sentence. The **nominative case** forms of personal pronouns are *I, you, he, she, it, we,* and *they*.

The subject of a verb is in the nominative case. The subject of a verb may be compound.

> **Simple subject:** *We* locked the door.
>
> **Compound subject:** *Sarah* and *I* painted the scenery.
>
> **Compound subject:** *You* and *they* can ride in the blue van.

A **predicate nominative** is in the nominative case. A predicate nominative follows a linking verb and identifies or explains the subject of a verb.

> The last person to board the airplane was *he*.
>
> Our best friends in the first grade were Lester and *she*.

Exercise A   Read each sentence below and decide which pronoun in parentheses is correct. Write the correct pronoun on the line provided.

1. You and (her, she) need to discuss the rules.

2. Amy and (I, me) climbed into the ship's hold.

3. Yesterday (us, we) began reading *Nisei Daughter*.

4. Find out if the Mystery Man is really (he, him)

5. Peter and (them, they) are practicing skateboard tricks.

6. The membership committee will be Cesar, Akela, and (me, I).

Exercise B: Revising   Revise each of the following sentences by replacing the italicized word or words with a pronoun. Write the revised sentences on the lines provided.

> **Example:** Bruce and *Maria* will marry in September.
>
> Bruce and she will marry in September.

1. The sky divers and *Aunt Bea* checked the time.

_____

2. The best people for the job are Kelly and *Rico*.

_____

3. The clowns and *the dogs* performed tricks in the center ring.

_____

4. Cleon and *Loretta and I* will be the only solo singers.

_____

Chapter 22: Using Pronouns Correctly

The Objective Case

The **objective case** forms of personal pronouns are *me, you, him, her, it, us,* and *them.*

Direct objects and **indirect objects** of verbs are in the objective case. A direct object follows an action verb and tells *whom* or *what.* An indirect object comes between an action verb and a direct object and tells *to whom* or *to what* or *for whom* or *for what.* A direct object or an indirect object may be compound.

> **Direct object:** The seagull attacked *me.* [*Me* tells whom the seagull attacked.]
>
> **Indirect object:** The catcher gave Amy and *him* a signal. [*Him* is part of a compound indirect object. *Amy* and *him* tells to whom the catcher gave the signal.]

The **object of a preposition** is in the objective case. The object of the preposition is a noun or pronoun that follows a preposition. Together with any of the object's modifiers, the preposition and its object make a **prepositional phrase.** An object of a preposition may be a compound.

> **Object of a preposition:** Standing between *him* and *her* is Mario. (*Him* and *her* are objects of the preposition *between.*)

Exercise A   Read each sentence below and decide whether the italicized pronoun is a direct object, an indirect object, or an object of a preposition. Then, on the line provided, write **DO** for direct object, **IO** for indirect object, or **OP** for object of a preposition.

_____ 1. The magician gave *her* the blindfold.

_____ 2. Toshiro photographed *me* in front of the state capitol.

_____ 3. With a wink, Father handed *us* the car keys.

_____ 4. The dog ran right by *them.*

_____ 5. Behind Dr. Haddad and *her* stood the new patient.

Exercise B: Revising   Revise each of the following sentences by replacing the italicized word or words with a pronoun. Write the revised sentences on the lines provided.

> **Example:** The tiger looked straight at Vince and *Bertha.*
> The tiger looked straight at Vince and her.

1. Uncle Hugo explained the fable to *Doyle and me.*

_____

2. The author describes *the main character* as fearful.

_____

3. The train thundered past *Justin and Clara.*

_____

4. A nurse quickly handed *Koko* the scissors.

_____

Chapter 22: Using Pronouns Correctly

Nominative or Objective?

Before you can choose the correct pronoun, you have to know how it is used in the sentence. Choosing the correct pronoun may be confusing, especially if the pronoun is part of a compound subject, predicate nominative, or object. To help you choose the correct pronoun in a compound sentence part, try each form of the pronoun separately.

Compound Subject: The police officer and (her, she) led the cow off the highway.

(*Her* led the cow off the highway.)

(*She* led the cow off the highway.)

Correct Form: The police officer and *she* led the cow off the highway.

Compound Object: We've been waiting for you and (him, he) for half an hour.

(We've been waiting for *him* for half an hour.)

(We've been waiting for *he* for half an hour.)

Correct Form: We've been waiting for you and *him* for half an hour.

Exercise A   Underline the pronoun in each of the following sentences and decide how it is used. Then, on the lines provided, write **S** for subject, **PN** for predicate nominative, **DO** for direct object, **IO** for indirect object, or **OP** for object of a preposition.

_____ 1. The special effects impressed me.

_____ 2. Could the spies possibly be they?

_____ 3. Mother and we posed for a family portrait.

_____ 4. Una borrowed the tools from the Lincolns and us.

_____ 5. The manager offered him a part-time job.

Exercise B   Decide whether the form of the italicized pronoun in each of the following sentences is correct. If it is, write **C** in the space provided. If the pronoun form is incorrect, write the correct form in the space.

_____ 1. Suddenly everyone was talking about *us.*

_____ 2. The most exciting match was between Tipley and *he.*

_____ 3. In June, you and *him* should go to San Juan.

_____ 4. Now the person without a partner is *me.*

_____ 5. The package was for Herlis and *she.*

_____ 6. My grandfather and *her* operate a small inn in Vermont.

_____ 7. The coach praised Manuel and *he.*

_____ 8. No one gave Mu Lan or *I* the message.

_____ 9. I felt certain that the man in the superhero costume was *he.*

_____ 10. The crowd cheered when the principal gave Stacy and *she* the trophies.

Chapter 22: Using Pronouns Correctly

Who *and* Whom

The pronoun *who* has different forms in the nominative and objective cases. *Who* is the nominative form. *Whom* is the objective form.

When you are choosing between *who* or *whom* in a question, follow these steps.

> **Step 1:** Rephrase the question as a statement.
>
> **Step 2:** Decide how the pronoun is used in the statement—as subject, predicate nominative, object of a verb, or object of a preposition.
>
> **Step 3:** Determine the case of the pronoun according to the rules of standard English.
>
> **Step 4:** Select the correct form of the pronoun.
>
> **Choices:** (Who, Whom) shall I invite?
>
> I shall invite (who, whom).
> [The pronoun is the object of the verb *invite*. The pronoun should be in the objective case.]
>
> *Whom* shall I invite?

Exercise A   Underline the correct pronoun in the following sentences.

1. (Who, Whom) did you beat in the first race?

2. To (who, whom) shall I send the application?

3. (Who, Whom) called so early this morning?

4. With (who, whom) did you go to the fiesta?

5. (Who, Whom) was the actor in the mask?

6. (Who, Whom) did Kathy give it to?

7. After dinner, (who, whom) will wash the dishes?

8. (Who, Whom) did Trevor imitate?

9. (Who, Whom) seemed the fastest runner?

10. For (who, whom) did you make that card?

Exercise B: Proofreading   The following paragraph contains three pronoun errors, one spelling error, and one error in capitalization. Can you find all five errors? Proofread the paragraph to correct all the errors you find.

At the track meet, Sami and me were given the same numbers. The coach

gave them to us by accident. first, she gave me number 23. Then, she gave the

same number to him. To who should the number be given? The coach ansered

the question herself. She asked, "Was Sami or him number 23 last time? Who

wore the number? Give it to him again."

Other Pronoun Problems

Sometimes a pronoun is followed directly by a noun that identifies the pronoun. Such a noun is called an **appositive**. To choose which pronoun to use before an appositive, try each form of the pronoun without the appositive.

    Sentence with appositive: The crowd cheered (*us, we*) rodeo clowns.

    Sentence with The crowd cheered *us*. [*Us* is correct, because it is the
    appositive omitted: object of *cheered*.]

    Correct pronoun: The crowd cheered *us* rodeo clowns.

The reflexive pronouns *himself* and *themselves* can be used as objects. Do not use the nonstandard form *hisself* and *theirselfs* or *theirselves* in place of *himself* or *themselves*.

    Nonstandard: Ron saw *hisself* reflected in the huge window.

    Standard: Ron saw *himself* reflected in the huge window.

Exercise A   Underline the correct form of the pronoun in each sentence.

1. (We, Us) athletes watch our diets.

2. Mr. Red Cloud told (we, us) Eagle Scouts what to do.

3. The owner always gives (we, us) clerks overtime on Saturdays.

4. The present treasurer took (hisself, himself) out of the contest.

5. Before the next show, (we, us) stagehands should get better props.

6. The best choice would be (we, us) skaters.

7. Ian described (himself, hisself) as patient and dependable.

8. For the past three years, one of (us, we) Monteros has won first place in the county spelling bee.

9. The chaperones talked among (theirselves, themselves) most of the evening.

10. Maybe Kale will ask (we, us) photographers to judge the show.

Exercise B: Revising   Revise each sentence to correct the pronoun error. Write your revised sentences on the lines provided.

1. The Broncos lost to we Tornadoes.

_____

2. Us computer types enjoy this game.

_____

3. The students who raised the most money were us seventh graders.

_____

4. Did you see Reed put hisself in front of the goal?

_____

5. Danielle read the letter to we girls.

_____

Chapter 22: Using Pronouns Correctly

Review (Form A)

Exercise A   Decide whether the italicized pronoun in each sentence is a subject or a predicate nominative. Then, on the line provided, write **S** for subject or **PN** for predicate nominative.

_____ 1. Harry and *I* both liked the movie.

_____ 2. After lunch, perhaps Klaus and *she* will help us paint.

_____ 3. The two finalists were Fatima and *I*.

_____ 4. The only people to speak had been *they*.

_____ 5. Without warning, *he* jumped up and pointed to the witness.

Exercise B   Decide whether the italicized pronoun in each sentence is the object of a verb or the object of a preposition. Then, on the line provided, write **OV** for object of a verb or **OP** for object of a preposition.

_____ 1. A sudden storm took *me* by surprise.

_____ 2. The visitor saw a signal pass between the king and *him*.

_____ 3. The firefighter showed *us* how to save someone from choking.

_____ 4. My uncle always gives my cousin and *her* newspaper clippings.

_____ 5. Unfortunately, the bus left without *him*.

Exercise C   Each of the following sentences contains two pronouns in parentheses. Underline the correct pronoun.

1. Last week (me, I) read about the Molasses Flood of 1919.

2. The school librarian showed (we, us) books of newspaper stories.

3. Some of (they, them) were about the Molasses Flood in Boston.

4. (They, Them) told about the explosion of a huge tank of molasses.

5. The story about the dangerous flood of molasses was news to (me, I).

6. (I, Me) read that people were killed and buildings were destroyed.

7. (They, Them) were buried under millions of gallons of molasses.

8. Residents said that the smell of molasses bothered (they, them) for months.

9. This month, (we, us) are supposed to write reports about Massachusetts.

10. The person with the most interesting report may be (me, I).

Chapter 22: Using Pronouns Correctly

Review (Form A)

Exercise D   Decide whether the italicized pronoun in each sentence is correct. If it is correct, write **C** on the line provided. If it is not correct, write the correct pronoun on the line.

_____ 1. *Who* knows what instrument Van Cliburn plays?

_____ 2. For *who* was this library named?

_____ 3. *Who* can I call for the notes?

_____ 4. Now, *whom* recorded the song originally?

_____ 5. *Whom* will you sit with?

_____ 6. *Whom* is that ice skater?

_____ 7. To *who* shall I address this letter?

_____ 8. *Who* remembers Barbara Jordan's speech?

_____ 9. *Who* will you choose as your running mate?

_____10. *Who* did you replace on the team?

Exercise E   Each sentence below has a pronoun error. Rewrite each sentence correctly on the line provided.

1. She showed we students how someone cuts a diamond.

_____

2. The doctor first tried the new medicine on hisself.

_____

3. Us left-handed people have trouble using most scissors.

_____

4. The mayor congratulated we lifeguards.

_____

5. Finally, the detectives asked theirselfs the right question.

_____

Review (Form B)

Exercise A   Decide whether the italicized pronoun in each sentence is a subject or a predicate nominative. Then, on the line provided, write **S** for subject or **PN** for predicate nominative.

_____ 1. Then *she* showed me how the computer worked.

_____ 2. The only judges were Mrs. Okana and *he.*

_____ 3. Susana and *we* may be late.

_____ 4. The two finalists could be Elmore and *I.*

_____ 5. At the curtain call, *they* took another bow.

Exercise B   Decide whether the italicized pronoun in each sentence is the object of a verb or the object of a preposition. Then, on the line provided, write **OV** for object of a verb or **OP** for object of a preposition.

_____ 1. The horse under *him* felt strong.

_____ 2. The gate banged against *her* when it closed.

_____ 3. Please pass *me* the atlas.

_____ 4. Melba told *us* about her day at the Bluegrass Music Festival.

_____ 5. Did they ask Eliot or *him* to join?

Exercise C   Each of the following sentences contains two pronouns in parentheses. Underline the correct pronoun.

 1. Yesterday (me, I) read about James C. Boyle.

 2. A little-known inventor was (he, him).

 3. (He, Him) invented the derby tipper in the 1890s.

 4. This invention tipped a man's hat for (he, him).

 5. When Boyle greeted a woman, he always tipped his hat at (she, her).

 6. A woman of that time expected (he, him) to do this.

 7. The derby tipper tipped Boyle's hat as he approached (she, her).

 8. To make the tipper work, (he, him) just nodded his head slightly.

 9. The patent office gave (he, him) a patent for the invention.

10. However, the invention never made (he, him) rich.

Chapter 22: Using Pronouns Correctly

Review (Form B)

Exercise D   Decide whether the italicized pronoun in each sentence is correct. If it is correct, write **C** on the line provided. If it is not correct, write the correct pronoun on the line.

_____ 1. To *who* should we give the money?

_____ 2. *Who* wants vanilla yogurt?

_____ 3. With *whom* can Red share a room?

_____ 4. *Who* has Alicia asked to help her?

_____ 5. Of all the speakers, *whom* did you like the most?

_____ 6. *Whom* understands how this computer program works?

_____ 7. *Who* did you vote for?

_____ 8. Before Andrew Johnson, *who* was the president?

_____ 9. *Who* is this package meant for?

_____ 10. *Whom* can show us where Mexico City is?

Exercise E   Each sentence below has a pronoun error. Rewrite each sentence correctly on the line provided.

1. As he worked, Octave talked to hisself.

_____

2. Now us pilots can land at night.

_____

3. The team was surprised when the fans applauded we players.

_____

4. The bears helped theirselves to the campers' food.

_____

5. Us dancers practice two hours every day.

_____

Answer Key

Practice and Reinforcement (1)
The Nominative Case

Exercise A

1. she
2. I
3. we
4. he
5. they
6. I

Exercise B: Revising

1. The sky divers and she checked the time.
2. The best people for the job are Kelly and he.
3. The clowns and they performed tricks in the center ring.
4. Cleon and we will be the only solo singers.

Practice and Reinforcement (2)
The Objective Case

Exercise A

1. IO
2. DO
3. IO
4. OP
5. OP

Exercise B: Revising

1. Uncle Hugo explained the fable to us.
2. The author describes him (*or* her) as fearful.
3. The train thundered past them.
4. A nurse quickly handed her the scissors.

Practice and Reinforcement (3)
Nominative or Objective?

Exercise A

1. me—DO
2. they—PN
3. we—S

4. us—OP
5. him —IO

Exercise B

1. C
2. him
3. he
4. I
5. her
6. she
7. him
8. me
9. C
10. her

Practice and Reinforcement (4)
Who *and* Whom

Exercise A

1. Whom
2. whom
3. Who
4. whom
5. Who
6. Whom
7. who
8. Whom
9. Who
10. whom

Exercise B: Proofreading

At the track meet, Sami and ~~me~~ *I* were given the same numbers. The coach gave them to us by accident. ~~f~~First, she gave me number 23. Then, she gave the same number to him. To who*m* should the number be given? The coach an*w*sered the question herself. She asked, "Was Sami or ~~him~~ *he* number 23 last time? Who wore the number? Give it to him again."

Answer Key

Practice and Reinforcement (5)
Other Pronoun Problems

Exercise A

1. We
2. us
3. us
4. himself
5. we
6. we
7. himself
8. us
9. themselves
10. us

Exercise B: Revising

1. The Broncos lost to us Tornadoes.
2. We computer types enjoy this game.
3. The students who raised the most money were we seventh graders.
4. Did you see Reed put himself in front of the goal?
5. Danielle read the letter to us girls.

Chapter Review
Form A

Exercise A

1. S
2. S
3. PN
4. PN
5. S

Exercise B

1. OV
2. OP
3. OV
4. OV
5. OP

Exercise C

1. I
2. us
3. them
4. They
5. me
6. I
7. They
8. them
9. we
10. I

Exercise D

1. C
2. whom
3. Whom
4. who
5. C
6. Who
7. whom
8. C
9. Whom
10. Whom

Exercise E

1. She showed us students how someone cuts a diamond.
2. The doctor first tried the new medicine on himself.
3. We left-handed people have trouble using most scissors.
4. The mayor congratulated us lifeguards.
5. Finally, the detectives asked themselves the right question.

Chapter Review
Form B

Exercise A

1. S
2. PN

Answer Key

3. S
4. PN
5. S

Exercise B
1. OP
2. OP
3. OV
4. OV
5. OV

Exercise C
1. I
2. he
3. He
4. him
5. her
6. him
7. her
8. he
9. him
10. him

Exercise D
1. whom
2. C
3. C
4. Whom
5. C
6. Who
7. Whom
8. C
9. Whom
10. Who

Exercise E
1. As he worked, Octave talked to himself.
2. Now we pilots can land at night.
3. The team was surprised when the fans applauded us players.
4. The bears helped themselves to the campers' food.
5. We dancers practice two hours every day.

Chapter 23: Using Modifiers Correctly

Degrees of Comparison

In making comparisons, adjectives and adverbs take different forms. These forms are called **degrees of comparison.** The **positive degree** is used when only one thing is being described. The **comparative degree** is used when two things are being compared. The **superlative degree** is used when three or more things are being compared.

Adjectives

Positive degree: A boxer is a *big* dog. (1)

Comparative degree: A mastiff is *bigger* than a boxer. (2)

Superlative degree: A Great Dane is the *biggest* dog of all. (3 or more)

Adverbs

Positive degree: Juan works *carefully*. (1)

Comparative degree: Julia works *more carefully* than Juan. (2)

Superlative degree: Of all my friends, Albert works *most carefully*. (3 or more)

Exercise A   On the lines, write **P** if the italicized modifier is in the positive degree. Write **C** if it is in the comparative degree. Write **S** if it is in the superlative degree. Then write **1, 2,** or **3 or more** to tell how many things are being described or compared.

Example: Who is the *tallest* basketball player on the team?

S—3 or more

_____ 1. Which is *heavier*—a pound of feathers or a pound of nails?

_____ 2. Of the lion, tiger, and cheetah, the cheetah can run *most rapidly*.

_____ 3. Maura is the *most qualified* candidate who ever ran for president.

_____ 4. Bernise dances *more gracefully* than I do.

_____ 5. This math problem seems extremely *difficult*.

Exercise B   On the line provided before each sentence, write the correct form of the modifier shown in parentheses.

_____ 1. It rained (hard, harder) yesterday than it did today.

_____ 2. Please pat the cat (more gently, most gently) than that.

_____ 3. The Yukon River is (longer, longest) than the Rio Grande.

_____ 4. Of all the players, Peder kicks the ball (more forcefully, most

forcefully).

_____ 5. Of the six department stores in the mall, this one is the (larger,

largest).

Chapter 23: Using Modifiers Correctly

Regular Comparison

Most one-syllable modifiers form their comparative and superlative degrees by adding *-er* and *-est*. Some two-syllable modifiers form their comparative and superlative degrees by adding *-er* and *-est*. Other two-syllable modifiers use *more* and *most*. Modifiers that have three or more syllables form their comparative and superlative degrees by using *more* and *most*.

	Positive	Comparative	Superlative
One syllable	*fast*	*faster*	*fastest*
Two syllables	*simple*	*simpler*	*simplest*
	cheaply	*more cheaply*	*most cheaply*
Three or more	*beautiful*	*more beautiful*	*most beautiful*
syllables	*foolishly*	*more foolishly*	*most foolishly*

To show decreasing comparisons, all modifiers form their comparative and superlative degrees with *less* and *least*.

bright	*less bright*	*least bright*
proudly	*less proudly*	*least proudly*

Exercise A   On the lines provided, write the comparative and superlative degrees of the following modifiers.

Positive	Comparative	Superlative
1. importantly	_____	_____
2. possible	_____	_____
3. loud	_____	_____
4. bravely	_____	_____
5. brilliantly	_____	_____

Exercise B   On the line before each sentence, write the correct comparative or superlative form of the modifier shown in parentheses.

Example: __taller__ Homer is (taller, more tall) than any other boy in the class.

_____ 1. This pail is (less full, least full) than that one.

_____ 2. That is one of the (funnier, funniest) jokes I have ever heard.

_____ 3. A rabbit runs (rapidlier, more rapidly) than a skunk does.

_____ 4. This piece of pie seems (smaller, more small) than that one.

_____ 5. Of all school subjects, I think math is (less difficult, least difficult).

Irregular Comparison

Some adjectives and adverbs do not form their comparative and superlative degrees by using the regular methods.

Positive	Comparative	Superlative
bad	worse	worst
far	farther	farthest
good	better	best
well	better	best
many	more	most
much	more	most

Exercise A   Choose the correct form of the modifier in parentheses, and write it on the line provided before each sentence.

_____ 1. Carlos likes science fiction stories (better, best) than mysteries.

_____ 2. I think Friday is the (better, best) day in the whole week.

_____ 3. (Many, More) people came to the meeting than we had expected.

_____ 4. Of all the members of the team, Inez bats (more well, best).

_____ 5. My cousin was able to save (much, more) money than I.

_____ 6. Of my four brothers, Chet has delivered the (more, most)

newspapers.

_____ 7. After supper, I felt (worse, worst) than I had felt in the afternoon.

_____ 8. We hiked (more far, farther) today than we hiked yesterday.

_____ 9. Dad plays the (better, best) game of tennis in the family.

_____10. This is the (worse, worst) cold I've ever had.

Exercise B   On the line provided write an adjective or adverb that completes the sentence.

1. In my opinion, that was a _____ movie.

2. Which of the four theaters is _____ from your house?

3. Lita is the _____ speller of the three contestants.

4. Georgia plays _____ in all sports.

5. My tennis serve is _____ than it was last year.

Chapter 23: Using Modifiers Correctly

Special Problems with Modifiers

Use *good* as an adjective to modify a noun or a pronoun. Use *well* as an adverb to modify a verb.

> Barbara is a *good* artist. (*Good* modifies the noun *artist*.)

> Barbara paints *well*. (*Well* modifies the verb *paints*.)

Although *well* is usually an adverb, *well* may also be used as an adjective meaning "in good health" or "pleasing in appearance."

> I was sick, but now I am *well*. (*Well* modifies the pronoun *I*.)

Use adjectives, not adverbs, after linking verbs.

> I feel *bad* (not *badly*) about my mistake.

> The homemade bread tastes *good* (not *well*).

Exercise A   Choose the correct modifier in parentheses and write it on the line provided.

_____ 1. The orchestra sounds (good, well) tonight.

_____ 2. Did the team play (bad, badly) in the final quarter?

_____ 3. The Chang twins play the piano very (good, well).

_____ 4. The milk smelled (bad, badly).

_____ 5. You look (good, well) now that your cold is gone.

_____ 6. The mariachis strolled (slow, slowly) through the crowd.

_____ 7. How (good, well) did you do on the spelling test?

_____ 8. Eduardo was (quick, quickly) in solving problems.

_____ 9. Because she has the flu, she doesn't feel (good, well) today.

_____10. Unfortunately, the actor performed (bad, badly) in the last act.

Exercise B: Expanding Sentences   Add an adjective or an adverb to complete each of the following sentences.

> **Example:** In class, Jonah acted <u>strangely.</u>_____

1. Lanelle spoke _____

2. That song sounds _____

3. Yesterday you seemed _____

4. Karen whispered _____

5. All afternoon, Mario worked _____

Chapter 23: Using Modifiers Correctly

Double Comparisons and Double Negatives

A **double comparison** is the use of both -er and more (less) -est and most (least), to form a comparison. When you make a comparison, use only one form, not both.

> **Nonstandard:** I have just read Carl Sagan's *most latest* book.
>
> **Standard:** I have just read Carl Sagan's *latest* book.

A **double negative** is the use of two negative words to express one negative idea. Common negative words include *barely, hardly, neither, never, no, nobody, not, nothing,* and *scarcely.* To express a negative idea, use only one of these words, not two.

> **Nonstandard:** I *haven't never* read a book by Carl Sagan.
>
> **Standard:** I *have never* read a book by Carl Sagan.
>
> **Standard:** I *haven't ever* read a book by Carl Sagan.

Exercise A   Circle the correct choice to complete each of the following sentences.

1. I am (busy, busier, more busier, busiest) today than I was yesterday.

2. It's the (scarier, more scarier, scariest, most scariest) book I've ever read.

3. No fish (were, weren't) biting in the stream this morning.

4. Nobody (was, wasn't) disappointed with the results of the fund-raiser.

5. This salsa tastes (less spicy, less spicier, least spiciest) than the salsa I make.

6. The fable didn't mean (nothing, anything) to him.

7. He is (more smart, more smarter, smarter, smartest) than he thinks.

8. It is (easier, more easier, easiest) to jump than it is to dive.

9. You (can, can't) hardly find this type of pen in the stores.

10. This is the (most short, more short, shorter, shortest) song on the album.

Exercise B: Proofreading   The following paragraph contains two errors in double comparisons, two errors in double negatives, and one error in spelling. Can you find these errors? Proofread the paragraph to correct all the errors you can find.

Nobody never taught me how to play the piano. Therefore, I wasn't prepared

for the surprise. At first, I played a few notes very softly. When I felt more

confidenter, I played less softly. The notes didn't make no song, but they seemed

to go together well. I practiced the notes over and over again. Then my

grandmother called to me. "What song are you playing?" she asked. "I don't

recognize it, but it is one of the most prettiest songs I've ever heard. It reminds

me of a love song I herd many years ago."

Chapter 23: Using Modifiers Correctly

Misplaced Prepositional Phrases

Place a **prepositional phrase** used as an **adjective** directly after the word it modifies.

          Misplaced: The dog belongs to that man *with the black spots.*

          Clear: The dog *with the black spots* belongs to that man.

Place a **prepositional phrase** used as an **adverb** near the word it modifies.

          Misplaced: We talked about the football game *in the locker room.*

          Clear: *In the locker room,* we talked about the football game.

Avoid placing a prepositional phrase so that it seems to modify either of two words.

          Misplaced: We decided *on Tuesday* we would visit you. (Does the phrase modify *decided* or *would visit?*)

          Clear: *On Tuesday,* we decided we would visit you. (The phrase clearly modifies *decided.*)

          Clear: We decided we would visit you *on Tuesday.* (The phrase clearly modifies *would visit.*)

Exercise A   Underline the prepositional phrase in each sentence. Then circle the word that the phrase modifies.

1. The woman in the red car is Ms. Prasad, my principal.

2. I found your bracelet under the sofa.

3. With a map, we found our way home.

4. We used glue to repair the chair with the broken leg.

5. On Monday afternoon he told us that he scored the game's winning goal.

Exercise B: Revising   Each of the following sentences contains a misplaced prepositional phrase. On the line provided, rewrite each sentence to make its meaning clear. Place each prepositional phrase next to, or near to, the word that it modifies.

1. The parrot spoke three words to my mother in the brass cage. _____

_____

2. We sat at the table and talked about our fishing trip in the kitchen. _____

_____

3. In the game I scored two points at the high point. _____

_____

4. I read about the lost puppy that was found in today's newspaper. _____

_____

5. The runner twisted his ankle with the blue T-shirt. _____

_____

Chapter 23: Using Modifiers Correctly

Misplaced and Dangling Participial Phrases

A **participial phrase** consists of a verb form—either a present participle or a past participle—and its related words. A participial phrase modifies a noun or a pronoun. A participial phrase should be placed near the word it modifies.

<table>
<tr><td align="right">Participial phrase
with present participle:</td><td>*Walking home,* I saw a robin. (The phrase modifies the pronoun *I.*)</td></tr>
<tr><td align="right">Participial phrase
with past participle:</td><td>*Built of twigs,* the nest is sturdy. (The phrase modifies the noun *nest.*)</td></tr>
</table>

A participial phrase that is not placed next to the noun or pronoun that it modifies is called a **misplaced modifier.**

Misplaced modifier: I saw a robin *walking home.* (Was the robin walking home?)

A participial phrase that does not clearly and sensibly modify another word in a sentence is called a **dangling modifier.**

Dangling: *Walking to school,* the experience was exciting.
Correct: *Walking to school,* I had an exciting experience. (The phrase clearly modifies *I.*)

Exercise A: Revising   Each of these sentences contains a misplaced or dangling modifier. On the lines provided, revise the sentences so that they are clear.

1. Modene did not hear the ringing telephone taking a shower. _____

_____

2. The missing baseball card was found cleaning my closet. _____

_____

3. Making the bed, my pet gerbil burrowed under the pillows. _____

_____

4. Sitting on its nest, I saw a bluebird. _____

_____

5. Running to catch the bus, a dog barked at me. _____

_____

Exercise B: Proofreading   The following paragraph contains one misplaced modifier, two errors in spelling, and one error in capitalization. Can you find these errors? Proofread the paragraph to correct all the errors you can find.

   I spoke softly to the house sitting in the saddle. Trotting gently, the horse seemed to understand that I was slightly scared. As I went around a corner, a fallen tree was seen on the path. Suprised, i dropped the reins. I was lucky that the horse stopped so gentley. Walking slowly around the fallen tree, the horse saved me from a bad fall.

Chapter 23: Using Modifiers Correctly

Misplaced Adjective Clauses

An **adjective clause** modifies a noun or a pronoun. Most adjective clauses begin with a relative pronoun—*that, which, who, whom,* or *whose.* An adjective clause should be placed directly after the words they modify.

     Misplaced: We walked on the grass in our bare feet which was wet.
                 (Were the feet wet?)
       Correct: We walked on the grass which was wet in our bare feet.
     Misplaced: The book was about insects that we read.
                 (Did you read the insects?)
       Correct: The book that we read was about insects.

Exercise A   Underline the adjective clause in each of the following sentences. Then circle the noun or pronoun that the clause modifies.

1. The president whom I respect the most is Thomas Jefferson.

2. I would like to hike up a mountain that has a snow-covered peak.

3. The player who scores the most goals will be elected Most Valuable Player.

4. We drove to Springfield, which is about an hour away from Columbus.

5. My best friend is Elbert, whose father was in the army with my father.

Exercise B: Revising   Each of these sentences contains a misplaced adjective clause. On the lines provided, rewrite the sentences so that they are clear.

1. I served the food to the athletes that they were planning to eat for lunch. _____
   _____

2. Mom chose the puppy as a gift for my little brother that has brown fur. _____
   _____

3. The actor gave me his autograph, who starred in the film. _____
   _____

4. I put the camera in the closet that my uncle gave me. _____
   _____

5. My cousin gave me a parakeet who goes to college in Alabama. _____
   _____

Chapter 23: Using Modifiers Correctly

Review (Form A)

Exercise A   On the line provided before each sentence, write the correct form of the modifier shown in parentheses.

_____ 1. Trains can travel (faster, more fast, fastest) than buses.

_____ 2. I think football is (excitinger, more exciting, most exciting)

than baseball.

_____ 3. Gino is the (smart, smarter, smartest) boy that I know.

_____ 4. That was the (better, best, gooder, goodest) movie that we've

ever seen.

_____ 5. I feel (bad, badly, more badly) about Rhonda's lost dog.

Exercise B   On the lines provided, complete the following chart. For each modifier in the positive degree, write the corresponding modifiers in the comparative and superlative degrees.

Positive	Comparative	Superlative
1. far	_____	_____
2. many	_____	_____
3. terrific	_____	_____
4. safe	_____	_____
5. silently	_____	_____

Exercise C   In each of these sentences, a modifier is used incorrectly. The mistake may result from the use of (1) a double comparison or (2) a double negative. On the lines provided, rewrite the sentences so that they are correct.

1. Nobody doesn't like to be late for school. _____

_____

2. That's the most silliest story I've ever heard. _____

_____

Chapter 23: Using Modifiers Correctly

Review (Form A)

3. Joanna worked more harder than I did. _____

_____

4. I couldn't recognize Georgio in his costume. _____

_____

5. The people who live in that house aren't never home. _____

_____

Exercise D   Each sentence contains a misplaced prepositional phrase. Underline the phrase. Then draw a caret (^) to show where the phrase should appear in the sentence.

1. Elena called while you were taking a shower from Texas.

2. My uncle made a table for my aunt with carved legs.

3. In the soup, Maryam ate all the noodles.

4. On the day, Rosa was sick of her birthday party.

5. I stood under the table and watched the cat chase a ball.

Exercise E   Each sentence contains a misplaced or dangling participial phrase. Rewrite the sentences to make them clear and correct.

1. Overgrown and full of weeds, I found the garden. _____

_____

2. I was interrupted by a visitor eating my lunch. _____

_____

3. Howin was reading a book about bears relaxing in his bathtub. ____

_____

4. Backing up, a wall was hit by the truck. _____

_____

5. Hidden in the wall, the inspector found a clue. _____

_____

Chapter 23: Using Modifiers Correctly

Review (Form A)

Exercise F   Each sentence contains a misplaced or dangling modifier. Rewrite the sentences to make them clear and correct.

1. The house is about a mile from Dunbar High School that my parents want to buy. _____

    _____

2. My pen pal wants a dog who lives in Kansas. _____

    _____

3. That dog needs a bath covered with dirt. _____

    _____

4. Tired and sleepy, the bed seemed very comfortable. _____

    _____

5. The horse, who is Angelo's teacher, belongs to Ms. Fernandez. _____

    _____

Chapter 23: Using Modifiers Correctly

Review (Form B)

Exercise A On the line provided before each sentence, write the correct form of the modifier shown in parentheses.

_____ 1. Rats are (larger, more large, largest) than mice.

_____ 2. Of all the trees in the forest, the pines are the (beautiful, more beautiful, most beautiful).

_____ 3. This book is (interesting, interestinger, more interesting) than that one.

_____ 4. Hector felt (bad, badly, more badly), so he went to see a doctor.

_____ 5. This is the (better, best, gooder, goodest) cheese that I've ever eaten.

Exercise B On the lines provided, complete the following chart. For each modifier in the positive degree, write the corresponding modifiers in the comparative and superlative degrees.

Positive	Comparative	Superlative
1. bad	_____	_____
2. much	_____	_____
3. suddenly	_____	_____
4. intelligent	_____	_____
5. safe	_____	_____

Exercise C In each of these sentences, a modifier is used incorrectly. The mistake may result from the use of (1) a double comparison or (2) a double negative. On the lines provided, rewrite the sentences so that they are correct.

1. Of all the roads leading into the canyon, this one is the most dangerousest. _____

_____

2. I think Toshi is more braver than Sid. _____

_____

Chapter 23: Using Modifiers Correctly

Review (Form B)

3. We didn't have nothing to do. _____

_____

4. I've never heard a more sadder song. _____

_____

5. I couldn't hardly move the heavy carton. _____

_____

Exercise D   Each sentence contains a misplaced prepositional phrase. Underline the phrase. Then draw a caret (^) to show where the phrase should appear in the sentence.

1. Vernon gave a fish to his friend with purple fins.

2. On the outside he wrote her name of the envelope.

3. Stormy wants the bike for her birthday in the store window.

4. Elia in the frying pan scrambled some eggs.

5. In my report, I wrote about hurricanes for my science class.

Exercise E   Each sentence contains a misplaced or dangling participial phrase. Rewrite the sentences to make them clear and correct.

1. Sitting in the bathtub, the telephone rang. _____

_____

2. Chopped into small pieces, Muhammad put onions in the stew. _____

_____

3. The artist painted a picture of lions standing in his studio. _____

_____

Chapter 23: Using Modifiers Correctly

Review (Form B)

4. Turning around quickly, a fire engine was seen. _____

_____

5. Falling from the cliff, she saw a boulder. _____

_____

Exercise F   Each sentence contains a misplaced or dangling modifier. Rewrite the sentences to make them clear and correct.

1. My neighbor who lives on Mars wrote a play about a strange creature. _____

_____

2. Stuck in a scrapbook, my uncle has several old photographs. _____

_____

3. I'm wearing my new boots at the store that I bought. _____

_____

4. Your friend that you toasted ate the sandwich. _____

_____

5. Kicking hard, the soccer ball shot into the goal. _____

_____

Answer Key

Practice and Reinforcement (1)
Degrees of Comparison

Exercise A

1. C—2
2. S—3 or more
3. S—3 or more
4. C—2
5. P—1

Exercise B

1. harder
2. more gently
3. longer
4. most forcefully
5. largest

Practice and Reinforcement (2)
Regular Comparison

Exercise A

	Comparative	Superlative
1.	more importantly	most importantly
2.	more possible	most possible
3.	louder	loudest
4.	more bravely	most bravely
5.	more brilliantly	most brilliantly

Exercise B

1. less full
2. funniest
3. more rapidly
4. smaller
5. least difficult

Practice and Reinforcement (3)
Irregular Comparison

Exercise A

1. better
2. best
3. More
4. best
5. more
6. most
7. worse
8. farther
9. best
10. worst

Exercise B

(Answers will vary. Possible responses are given.)

1. bad
2. farthest
3. best
4. well
5. better

Practice and Reinforcement (4)
Special Problems with Modifiers

Exercise A

1. good
2. badly
3. well
4. bad
5. well
6. slowly
7. well
8. quick
9. well
10. badly

Answer Key

Exercise B: Expanding Sentences

(Answers will vary. Possible responses are given.)

1. Lanelle spoke softly. (adverb)
2. That song sounds beautiful. (adjective)
3. Yesterday you seemed sad. (adjective)
4. Karen whispered frantically. (adverb)
5. All afternoon, Mario worked diligently. (adverb)

Practice and Reinforcement (5)
Double Comparisons and Double Negatives

Exercise A

1. I am (busy, busier) more busier, busiest) today than I was yesterday.
2. It's the (scarier, more scarier, scariest) most scariest) book I've ever read.
3. No fish (were) weren't) biting in the stream this morning.
4. Nobody (was) wasn't) disappointed with the results of the fund-raiser.
5. The salsa tastes (less spicy,) less spicier, least spiciest) than the salsa I make.
6. The fable didn't mean (nothing, anything) to him.
7. He is (more smart, more smarter, smarter) smartest) than he thinks.
8. It is (easier) more easier, easiest) to jump than it is to dive.
9. You (can) can't) hardly find this type of pen in the stores.
10. This is the (most short, more shorter, shortest) song on the album.

Exercise B: Proofreading

Nobody ever taught me how to play the piano. Therefore, I wasn't prepared for the surprise. At first, I played a few notes very softly. When I felt more confident, I played less softly. The notes didn't make a song, but they seemed to go together well. I practiced the notes over and over again. Then my grandmother called to me. "What song are you playing?" she asked. "I don't recognize it, but it is one of the prettiest songs I've ever heard. It reminds me of a love song I heard many years ago."

Practice and Reinforcement (6)
Misplaced Prepositional Phrases

Exercise A

1. The (woman) in the red car is Ms. Prasad, my principal.
2. I (found) your bracelet under the sofa.
3. With a map, we (found) our way home.
4. We used glue to repair the (chair) with the broken leg.
5. On Monday afternoon he (told) us that he scored the game's winning goal.

Exercise B: Revising

(Answers may vary. Possible responses are given.)

1. The parrot in the brass cage spoke three words to my mother.
2. We sat at the table in the kitchen and talked about our fishing trip.
3. At the high point in the game, I scored two points.
4. In today's newspaper, I read about the lost puppy that was found.
5. The runner with the blue T-shirt twisted his ankle.

Practice and Reinforcement (7)
Misplaced and Dangling Participial Phrases

Exercise A: Revising

(Answers may vary. Possible responses are given.)

1. Taking a shower, Modene did not hear the ringing telephone.
2. Cleaning my closet, I found the missing baseball card.
3. While I was making the bed, my pet gerbil burrowed under the pillows.
4. I saw a bluebird sitting on its nest.
5. While I was running to catch the bus, a dog barked at me.

Answer Key

Exercise B: Proofreading

<u>Sitting in the saddle,</u> I spoke softly to the horse. Trotting gently, the horse seemed to understand that I was slightly scared. As I went around a corner, <u>I saw</u> a fallen tree on the path. <u>Surprised,</u> I dropped the reins. I was lucky that the horse stopped <u>gently.</u> Walking slowly around the fallen tree, the horse saved me from a bad fall.

Practice and Reinforcement (8)
Misplaced Adjective Clauses

Exercise A

1. The (president) whom I respect the most is Thomas Jefferson.
2. I would like to hike up a (mountain) that has a snow-covered peak.
3. The (player) who scores the most goals will be elected Most Valuable Player.
4. We drove to (Springfield) which is about an hour away from Columbus.
5. My best friend is (Elbert,) whose father was in the army with my father.

Exercise B: Revising

(Answers may vary. Possible responses are given.)

1. I served the food that they were planning to eat for lunch to the athletes.
2. Mom chose the puppy that has brown fur as a gift for my little brother.
3. The actor who starred in the film gave me his autograph.
4. I put the camera that my uncle gave me in the closet.
5. My cousin who goes to college in Alabama gave me a parakeet.

Chapter Review
Form A

Exercise A

1. faster
2. more exciting

3. smartest
4. best
5. bad

Exercise B

1. farther, farthest
2. more, most
3. more terrific, most terrific
4. safer, safest
5. more silently, most silently

Exercise C

1. Nobody likes to be late for school.
2. That's the silliest story I've ever heard.
3. Joanna worked harder than I did.
4. I could hardly recognize Georgio in his costume.
5. The people who live in that house are never (or aren't ever) home.

Exercise D

(Answers may vary. Possible responses are given.)

1. Elena called ∧ while you were taking a shower <u>from Texas.</u>
2. My uncle made a table ∧ for my aunt <u>with carved legs.</u>
3. <u>In the soup,</u> Maryam ate all the noodles ∧ .
4. On the day ∧ , Rosa was sick <u>of her birthday party.</u>
5. I stood <u>under the table</u> and watched the cat chase a ball ∧ .

Exercise E

1. I found the garden overgrown and full of weeds.
2. Eating my lunch, I was interrupted by a visitor.

Answer Key

3. Relaxing in his bathtub, Howin was reading a book about bears.

4. Backing up, the truck hit a wall.

5. The inspector found a clue hidden in the wall.

Exercise F

(Some answers may vary. Sample responses are given.)

1. The house that my parents want to buy is about a mile from Dunbar High School.

2. My pen pal, who lives in Kansas, wants a dog.

3. That dog covered with dirt needs a bath.

4. Because I was tired and sleepy, the bed seemed very comfortable.

5. The horse belongs to Ms. Fernandez, who is Angelo's teacher.

Chapter Review
Form B

Exercise A

1. larger

2. most beautiful

3. more interesting

4. bad

5. best

Exercise B

1. worse, worst

2. more, most

3. more suddenly, most suddenly

4. more intelligent, most intelligent

5. safer, safest

Exercise C

1. Of all the roads leading into the canyon, this one is the most dangerous.

2. I think Toshi is braver than Sid.

3. We didn't have anything to do.

4. I've never heard a sadder song.

5. I could hardly move the heavy carton.

Exercise D

(Answers may vary. Possible responses are given.)

1. Vernon gave a fish ∧ to his friend <u>with purple fins.</u>

2. On the outside ∧ he wrote her name <u>of the envelope.</u>

3. Stormy wants the bike ∧ for her birthday <u>in the store window.</u>

4. Elia <u>in the frying pan</u> scrambled some eggs∧.

5. In my report ∧ , I wrote about hurricanes <u>for my science class.</u>

Exercise E

(Some answers may vary. Sample responses are given.)

1. While I was sitting in the bathtub, the telephone rang.

2. In the stew, Muhammad put onions chopped into small pieces.

3. Standing in his studio, the artist painted a picture of lions.

4. Turning around quickly, we saw a fire engine.

5. She saw a boulder falling from the cliff.

Answer Key

Exercise F

(Answers may vary. Sample responses are given.)

1. My neighbor wrote a play about a strange creature who lives on Mars.

2. My uncle has several old photographs stuck in a scrapbook.

3. I'm wearing my new boots that I bought at the store.

4. Your friend ate the sandwich that you toasted.

5. Kicking hard, Raoul shot the soccer ball into the goal.

Common Usage Problems A

Study the following guidelines for usage:

accept, except   *Accept* is a verb that means "to receive." *Except* may be either a verb or a preposition. As a verb, it means "to leave out" or "to exclude"; as a preposition, *except* means "other than" or "excluding."

all ready, already   *All ready* means "completely prepared." *Already* means "previously."

bad, badly   *Bad* is an adjective. *Badly* is an adverb.

fewer, less   *Fewer* is used with plural words and tells "how many." *Less* is used with singular words and tells "how much."

Exercise   Two words or phrases appear in parentheses in each of the following sentences. Underline the correct word or phrase.

1. We have all the ingredients (accept, except) cream of tartar.

2. We need to get Crissy (all ready, already) by the time Dad gets home with the camping gear.

3. Adeola didn't do (bad, badly) at all the first time she was on ice skates.

4. We have (fewer, less) sopranos in the chorus than we did last year.

5. Jana was (already, all ready) in college by the time her sister was born.

6. I don't (except, accept) criticism very well, but I do listen when someone is praising me!

7. To me blue cheese tastes (bad, badly), but Bobby Dale really likes it.

8. Jacques has (less, fewer) money than Canditha does today, so she will buy the popcorn for the movie.

9. Carmen gladly (accepted, excepted) the warm sweater from her father.

10. Let's surprise Mr. Singh and be (already, all ready) when he gets back from the office.

Chapter 24: A Glossary of Usage

Common Usage Problems B

Study the following guidelines for usage:

its, it's   *Its* is the possessive form of the personal pronoun *it*. *It's* is a contraction of *it is* or *it has*.

kind of, sort of   The words *kind of* and *sort of* are sometimes used in place of *somewhat* or *rather*. In formal English, *somewhat* or *rather* is preferred.

learn, teach   *Learn* means "to acquire knowledge." *Teach* means "to instruct or to show how."

like, as   *Like* is a preposition. It introduces a prepositional phrase. *As* is a conjunction. It introduces an adverb clause. In informal English, *like* is often used as a conjunction meaning "as." In formal English, *as* is always preferred.

Exercise A   Two words or phrases appear in parentheses in each of the following sentences. Underline the correct word or phrase.

1. The baby is (kind of, rather) cranky today because she hasn't had a nap.

2. My skating instructor can (teach, learn) me how to skate backward on one foot.

3. I'd like to learn how to use a calculator (like, as) my math teacher does.

4. The kitten has been chasing (it's, its) tail, and now the poor little cat is dizzy.

5. In cold weather, we all become (sort of, rather) irritable if we stay inside for several days.

6. When spring comes, (it's, its) time to plan our town's May parade of flowers.

7. If you practice (like, as) we do, you'll learn to dance in no time.

8. My sister will (learn, teach) me how to do a back flip at the pool this afternoon.

9. I can tell the cake is done because (its, it's) top springs back when I press it.

10. Jaime is (kind of, rather) scared of dogs, so we keep Buster tied up when Jaime comes over.

Exercise B: Proofreading   The following paragraph contains three errors in usage and two spelling errors. Can you find these errors? Proofread the paragraph to correct all the errors you can find.

When its my turn to wash the dishes, I allways wash them the same way. I

rinse and stack them like my sister does. Then I scrub and rinse them thurrowly.

Then I hand them to my brother to dry. Washing dishes is kind of fun now that

I'm so good at it.

Chapter 24: A Glossary of Usage

Common Usage Problems C

Study the following guidelines for usage:

use to, used to Be sure to add the –d to use. *Used to* is in the past form.

way, ways Use *way*, not *ways*, in referring to a distance.

when, where Try not to use *when* or *where* incorrectly in writing a definition.
>   **Nonstandard:** A mallard is a when a duck is wild.
>   **Standard:** A mallard is a wild duck.

without, unless *Without* is a preposition. It introduces a phrase. *Unless* is a conjunction. It introduces a clause.

Exercise A Two words or groups of words appear in parentheses in each of the following sentences. Underline the correct word or word group.

1. Never cross the street (unless, without) you look both ways first.

2. When I was nine or ten, I (use, used) to need help ironing my blouses.

3. Carlos travelled a long (way, ways) to get to this country.

4. A square dance is (when you dance, a dance) with four couples grouped

    in a square.

Exercise B: Revising Revise the following sentences to correct errors in usage. Write your corrected sentences on the lines provided.

>   **Example:** It's a long ways from Texas to Alaska.
>   It's a long way from Texas to Alaska. _____

1. The produce market is only a short ways from my house. _____

_____

2. Clara Barton use to stress the importance of cleanliness to her nurses. _____

_____

3. I can't stay over at your house without I get my mother's permission. _____

_____

4. Watercolor painting is when you use water-based paint on paper or fabric. _____

_____

5. Carissa can run a long ways without getting tired. _____

_____

6. I use to be clumsy at all sports, but now I'm fairly good at baseball. _____

_____

Chapter 24: A Glossary of Usage

Review (Form A)

Exercise A   Two words or phrases appear in parentheses in each of the following sentences. Underline the correct word or phrase.

1. For a few days, the student could not (accept, except) being cut from the soccer team.

2. Last winter, I skated (bad, badly), but now I hardly ever fall.

3. There are (less, fewer) people in the café now than there were an hour ago.

4. We were (already, all ready) sitting on the train when Corinne raced up to the ticket counter.

5. (Except, Accept) for Ira, no one in our class has travelled outside the country.

Exercise B   Rewrite each of the following sentences to correct the error in usage.

1. All the players accept Melba were on the team last year. _____

_____

2. The gumbo is already to be served. _____

_____

3. The violin is one instrument that sounds really badly until you know how to

   play it. _____

_____

4. There is fewer snow on the mountain this year than there was last year. _____

_____

5. If you have all ready painted a watercolor, why don't you try oil painting for

   your next project? _____

Exercise C   Two words or phrases appear in parentheses in each of the following sentences. Underline the correct word or phrase.

1. (It's, Its) too cold to play miniature golf.

2. When Maryam tries to dress (like, as) her older sister does, she looks a little silly.

3. José is trying to (learn, teach) his sister Gloria to swim.

4. Squid is (kind of, somewhat) tough, so I usually pound it with a meat tenderizer before I cook it.

5. A lioness has to leave (its, it's) young to hunt for food.

Chapter 24: A Glossary of Usage

Review (Form A)

Exercise D   Rewrite each of the following sentences to correct the error in usage.

1. The shark flicked it's tail fin as it swam toward the reef. _____

_____

2. Helen Marie will learn me how to ride horses next summer. _____

_____

3. Hana can make pottery like her father does. _____

_____

4. Although we were sort of nervous, we knocked on the door of the senator's

office. _____

_____

5. The bird can't fly because one of it's wings is broken. _____

_____

_____

Exercise E   Two words or groups of words appear in parentheses in each of the following sentences. Underline the correct word or word group.

1. Skimming is (when you read, reading) quickly to get a general idea of what a piece of writing is about.

2. Kendra and Alex walked a long (way, ways) to get to school from their parents' farm.

3. Most of the speeches were interesting, but a few were (kind of, rather) boring.

4. Before the car was invented, people (use to, used to) travel by horse and carriage.

5. Never eat a wild mushroom (without, unless) you know that it was picked by someone who is an expert on mushrooms.

Chapter 24: A Glossary of Usage

Review (Form B)

Exercise A   Two words or phrases appear in parentheses in each of the following sentences. Underline the correct word or phrase.

1. The queen decided that she would never (accept, except) any man's offer of marriage.

2. The milk smelled (bad, badly), so we had to throw it away.

3. If you take (less, fewer) money to the store, maybe you'll keep more in the bank.

4. The bully looked (already, all ready) for a fight, but we simply ignored him.

5. I have (already, all ready) done my homework, and now I'd like to go to Niyatee's house.

Exercise B   Rewrite each of the following sentences to correct the error in usage.

1. Luckily, the sheep were all ready in the high pasture when the flood started. _____

_____

_____

2. All the foliage accept the pine needles was gone from our trees by December. _____

_____

_____

3. My sister's casserole tasted badly, but I ate some of it because I didn't want to hurt her

feelings. _____

_____

4. Lions have less babies than domestic cats have. _____

_____

5. If you won't except my apology, then I guess we can't be friends right now. _____

_____

_____

Exercise C   Two words or phrases appear in parentheses in each of the following sentences. Underline the correct word or phrase.

1. The cat is licking (its, it's) paw because it has a splinter.

2. The figure skater was (kind of, somewhat) disappointed with her performance in the final round.

Chapter 24: A Glossary of Usage

Review (Form B)

3. Hold your head high (as, like) a swan does, and your back will be straight.

4. Books cannot (teach, learn) you kindness; that virtue comes from experience.

5. After the slumber party last night, the girls were (kind of, rather) tired.

Exercise D   Rewrite each of the following sentences to correct the error in usage.

1. A snake sheds it's skin as it grows. _____

_____

2. If you learn me how to knit, I will show you how to crochet. _____

_____

_____

3. In the ballet that our teacher planned, some of the dancers move like fish in water. _____

_____

_____

4. Now that Russia flies it's own flag, the communist flag has been taken down. _____

_____

_____

5. A song played in a minor key sounds kind of sad. _____

_____

Exercise E   Two words or groups of words appear in parentheses in each of the following sentences. Underline the correct word or word group.

1. A dictator is (when a ruler has, a ruler with) complete authority over a group of people.

2. A marathon is a twenty-six mile run; that is a long (way, ways) to run.

3. Never play under a pile of leaves (without, unless) the leaves are off the street.

4. When we lived in New Hampshire, we (use, used) to cross-country ski in the winter.

5. A patent is (when you have a right to, a right to) an invention.

Answer Key

Practice and Reinforcement (1)
Common Usage Problems A

Exercise

1. We have all the ingredients (accept, except) cream of tartar.

2. We need to get Crissy (all ready, already) by the time Dad gets home with the camping gear.

3. Adeola didn't do (bad, badly) at all the first time she was on ice skates.

4. We have (fewer, less) sopranos in the chorus than we did last year.

5. Jana was (already, all ready) in college by the time her sister was born.

6. I don't (except, accept) criticism very well, but I do listen when someone is praising me!

7. To me blue cheese tastes (bad, badly), but Bobby Dale really likes it.

8. Jacques has (less, fewer) money than Canditha does today, so she will buy the popcorn for the movie.

9. Carmen gladly (accepted, excepted) the warm sweater from her father.

10. Let's surprise Mr. Singh and be (already, all ready) when he gets back from the office.

Practice and Reinforcement (2)
Common Usage Problems B

Exercise A

1. The baby is (kind of, rather) cranky today because she hasn't had a nap.

2. My skating instructor can (teach, learn) me how to skate backward on one foot.

3. I'd like to learn how to use a calculator (like, as) my math teacher does.

4. The kitten has been chasing (it's, its) tail, and now the poor little cat is dizzy.

5. In cold weather, we all become (sort of, rather) irritable if we stay inside for several days.

6. When spring comes, (it's, its) time to plan our town's May parade of flowers.

7. If you practice (like, as) we do, you'll learn to dance in no time.

8. My sister will (learn, teach) me how to do a back flip at the pool this afternoon.

9. I can tell the cake is done because (its, it's) top springs back when I press it.

10. Jaime is (kind of, rather) scared of dogs, so we keep Buster tied up when Jaime comes over.

Exercise B: Proofreading

When it's my turn to wash the dishes, I always wash them the same way. I rinse and stack them as my sister does. Then I scrub and rinse them thoroughly. Then I hand them to my brother to dry. Washing dishes is rather fun now that I'm so good at it.

Practice and Reinforcement (3)
Common Usage Problems C

Exercise A

1. Never cross the street (unless, without) you look both ways first.

2. When I was nine or ten, I (use, used) to need help ironing my blouses.

3. Carlos travelled a long (way, ways) to get to this country.

4. A square dance is (when you dance, a dance) with four couples grouped in a square.

Exercise B: Revising

1. The produce market is only a short way from my house.

2. Clara Barton used to stress the importance of cleanliness to her nurses.

3. I can't stay over at your house unless I get my mother's permission.

4. Watercolor painting is using water-based paint on paper or fabric.

5. Carissa can run a long way without getting tired.

6. I used to be clumsy at all sports, but now I'm fairly good at baseball.

Chapter Review
Form A

Exercise A

1. For a few days, the student could not (accept, except) being cut from the soccer team.

2. Last winter, I skated (bad, badly), but now I hardly ever fall.

3. There are (less, fewer) people in the café now than there were an hour ago.

4. We were (already, all ready) sitting on the train when Corinne raced up to the ticket counter.

5. (Except, Accept) for Ira, no one in our class has travelled outside the country.

Exercise B

1. All the players except Melba were on the team last year.

2. The gumbo is all ready to be served.

3. The violin is one instrument that sounds really bad until you know how to play it.

4. There is less snow on the mountain this year than there was last year.

5. If you have already painted a watercolor, why don't you try oil painting for your next project?

Exercise C

1. (It's, Its) too cold to play miniature golf.

2. When Maryam tries to dress (like, as) her older sister does, she looks a little silly.

3. José is trying to (learn, teach) his sister Gloria to swim.

4. Squid is (kind of, somewhat) tough, so I usually pound it with a meat tenderizer before I cook it.

5. A lioness has to leave (its, it's) young to hunt for food.

Exercise D

1. The shark flicked its tail fin as it swam toward the reef.

2. Helen Marie will teach me how to ride horses next summer.

3. Hana can make pottery as her father does.

4. Although we were rather nervous, we knocked on the door of the senator's office.

5. The bird can't fly because one of its wings is broken.

Exercise E

1. Skimming is (when you read, reading) quickly to get a general idea of what a piece of writing is about.

2. Kendra and Alex walked a long (way, ways) to get to school from their parents' farm.

3. Most of the speeches were interesting, but a few were (kind of, rather) boring.

4. Before the car was invented, people (use to, used to) travel by horse and carriage.

5. Never eat a wild mushroom (without, unless) you know that it was picked by someone who is an expert on mushrooms.

Chapter Review
Form B

Exercise A

1. The queen decided that she would never (accept, except) any man's offer of marriage.

2. The milk smelled (bad, badly), so we had to throw it away.

3. If you take (less, fewer) money to the store, maybe you'll keep more in the bank.

4. The bully looked (already, all ready) for a fight, but we simply ignored him.

5. I have (already, all ready) done my homework, and now I'd like to go to Niyatee's house.

Exercise B

1. Luckily, the sheep were already in the high pasture when the flood started.

2. All the foliage except the pine needles was gone from our trees by December.

3. My sister's casserole tasted bad, but I ate some of it because I didn't want to hurt her feelings.

4. Lions have fewer babies than domestic cats have.

5. If you won't accept my apology, then I guess we can't be friends right now.

Exercise C

1. The cat is licking (<u>its</u>, it's) paw because it has a splinter.

2. The figure skater was (kind of, <u>somewhat</u>) disappointed with her performance in the final round.

3. Hold your head high (<u>as</u>, like) a swan does, and your back will be straight.

4. Books cannot (<u>teach</u>, learn) you kindness; that virtue comes from experience.

5. After the slumber party last night, the girls were (kind of, <u>rather</u>) tired.

Exercise D

1. A snake sheds its skin as it grows.

2. If you teach me how to knit, I will show you how to crochet.

3. In the ballet that our teacher planned, some of the dancers move as fish move.

4. Now that Russia flies its own flag, the communist flag has been taken down.

5. A song played in a minor key sounds rather sad.

Exercise E

1. A dictator is (when a ruler has, <u>a ruler with</u>) complete authority over a group of people.

2. A marathon is a twenty-six mile run; that is a long (<u>way</u>, ways) to run.

3. Never play under a pile of leaves (without, <u>unless</u>) the leaves are off the street.

4. When we lived in New Hampshire, we (use, <u>used</u>) to cross-country ski in the winter.

5. A patent is (when you have a right to, <u>a right to</u>) an invention.

Name _____ Date _____ Class _____ Score _____

Usage Mastery Test (Form A)

Part 1   Read each of the following sentences. On the line provided, write **C** if the verb agrees with its subject. Write the correct verb form if the verb does not agree with its subject. [1 point each]

_____ 1. Either the box or the papers has disappeared.

_____ 2. She don't think that's good enough.

_____ 3. A book by Jade Snow Wong lies on the table.

_____ 4. Is there enough costumes for everyone?

_____ 5. Neither the trains nor the bus ever arrive on time.

_____ 6. Two balls of yarn was left over after I finished.

_____ 7. Ninety-five cents were the amount I could spend.

_____ 8. The town of Pompton Lakes are in northern New Jersey.

_____ 9. That don't ring a bell.

_____ 10. The United Nations have its headquarters in New York.

_____ 11. Nobody in my class speak Mandarin.

_____ 12. Where were your family at that time?

_____ 13. Thirteen muffins makes a baker's dozen.

_____ 14. Several books on my shelf was written by my uncle.

_____ 15. The news of the world is on at ten.

Part 2   Each of the following sentences is missing a pronoun. On the line provided, write a pronoun that will complete the meaning of the sentence. [2 points each]

1. Lena and Rich invited me to _____ house.

2. Each of my uncles will bring _____ own racket.

3. My class moved into a new room, and _____ was happy to move.

4. One of the women had brought along _____ pet parrot.

5. Either Rafael or Hubert will let us use _____ scissors.

Part 3   Each of the following sentences is missing a verb. Decide what form of the verb in parentheses will make the sentence clear and correct. On the line provided, write the correct verb form. [1 point each]

1. (lay)   I _____ my knife on a high shelf.

2. (lie)   My cat has _____ in its bed all day.

Usage Mastery Test (Form A)

3. (give)   My parents had _____ me the blue jacket as a birthday present.

4. (eat)   Have you ever _____ goat cheese?

5. (break)   I _____ the hurdling record last summer

6. (fall)   High winds made all the apples _____ off the tree.

7. (go)   Delsin may have _____ to work early.

8. (know)   We _____ we looked silly in our clown costumes.

9. (rise)   When I _____ to answer the phone, I hit my elbow.

10. (swim)   When we stayed at the shore, we _____ every day.

11. (chose) Carrie has _____ Stephanie as her science partner.

12. (rise)   Pang had _____ early because of the trip.

13. (burst) Only two balloons _____ before the party started.

14. (freeze) The skiers almost _____ on the mountain.

15. (lead)   Before the show, the trainer _____ the horses around the ring.

Part 4   For each sentence below, underline the correct pronoun in parentheses. [1 point each]

1. Yesterday my friend and (I, me) had an argument.

2. (She, Her) and I usually find ways to solve our problems.

3. Our brothers and sisters found (theirselfs, themselves) in agreement.

4. Usually, one of us says, "Between you and (I, me), I'm tired of this."

5. (Us, We) Polivkas rarely argue.

6. In school, my friends rarely argue with (I, me).

7. Of course, our principal might put (we, us) on probation.

8. "Too many of (us, we) Americans fight instead of think," he said.

9. My father is easygoing, and my mother and (he, him) seldom disagree.

10. It is easy for (they, them) to resolve disagreements.

Assessment: Mastery Tests

Usage Mastery Test (Form A)

Part 5   In many of the following sentences, a modifier is used incorrectly. On the lines provided, write those sentences correctly. Write **C** if a sentence is correct. [2 points each]

1. One of the worse experiences I had was in fifth grade.

_____

2. The first game was our most easiest win of the season.

_____

3. Of the two shirts, this one is least expensive.

_____

4. By half time, our team was playing beautifully.

_____

5. He didn't have no money left for popcorn.

_____

Part 6   For each sentence below, underline the correct form of the modifier in parentheses. [1 point each]

1. After we received our typhoid shots, we felt (feverish, feverishly).

2. Ms. Yen's dog barks (vigorous, vigorously) at strangers.

3. I could not sleep (good, well) because of the noise at night.

4. The Suwannee River flows (slow, slowly) through the swamps of Georgia.

5. I (sure, surely) agree that Martin Luther King, Jr. deserved a Nobel Prize.

6. My room looks (beautiful, beautifully) with its new curtains.

7. Dad checks the traffic (careful, carefully) before backing up the car.

8. The cocker spaniel was the (bigger, biggest) of the two dogs.

9. I can finish my math homework more (quicker, quickly) than my French homework.

10. On this slide, you can (easy, easily) see the form of the cells.

Part 7   Most of the sentences below contain misplaced modifiers. Circle each misplaced modifier. Then, draw an arrow from the modifier to the place where it belongs. If a sentence is correct, write **C** in the space provided. [1 point each]

> **Example:** (Hanging from the back of the chair,) I saw my coat.

1. The castanets belong to my sister that I lent you.

2. Juggling oranges, we were impressed by the performer.

Usage Mastery Test (Form A)

3. Reba lent the magazine to her sister that she had bought.

4. Hearne noticed his broken shoelace climbing onto the bus.

5. The alarm clock in the guest room is unplugged.

6. Wood ducks live in trees with their mates.

7. Mr. Eng noticed the advertisement reading the newspaper.

8. Leaping out of the plane, my parents watched the sky divers.

9. Scientists are working hard to develop new plants that are resistant to pests.

10. Heidi found the word's meaning looking in my dictionary.

Part 8   Each of the following sentences contains an error in usage. On the line provided, rewrite the sentence correctly. [2 points each]

1. Your absolutely correct.

_____

2. Please bring this book to the librarian.

_____

3. Your tape is somewheres in the hall.

_____

4. We were already to go when you called.

_____

5. Toby looks sort of tired today.

_____

6. We hadn't scarcely any gas in the mower.

_____

7. We have six dollars between the four of us.

_____

8. Mr. Cotton excepted the offer.

_____

9. The napkin is inside of the drawer.

_____

10. I know we should of called first.

_____

Assessment: Mastery Tests

Usage Mastery Test (Form B)

Part 1   In some of the following sentences, the verbs do not agree with the subjects. Draw a line through each incorrect verb. Then, on the line provided, write the correct form of the verb. Write **C** if the sentence is correct. [1 point each]

_____ 1. Twenty dollars aren't a lot of money for boots like these.

_____ 2. Here is the notes for the history test.

_____ 3. Chim and Adam wants to see the other film.

_____ 4. Neither of my parents are home right now.

_____ 5. One of the experiments are hard.

_____ 6. Don't anyone know what time it is?

_____ 7. *Radigan Cares* is a book about politics.

_____ 8. Nobody in my class know the answers.

_____ 9. Civics are not offered until high school.

_____ 10. All of the porch is covered with snow.

_____ 11. Mike and Domingo keep score.

_____ 12. Goldfish or a snake need little daily attention.

_____ 13. The yard full of ostriches were a surprise.

_____ 14. A secretary or a receptionist answer the telephone.

_____ 15. Here is some interesting topics for your report.

_____ 16. Fog and darkness have made traveling dangerous.

_____ 17. The girls on the track team is leaving in an hour.

_____ 18. Three months seem too short for summer vacation.

_____ 19. The burned toast don't taste very good.

_____ 20. Several was absent from the first class.

Part 2   Each of the following sentences is missing a pronoun. On the line provided, write a pronoun that will complete the sentence correctly. [2 points each]

1. Anyone who has completed _____ assignment may leave.

2. Many of our teachers have _____ meetings today.

3. Luke or Cornelius will give _____ speech today.

4. The elephant performed _____ trick.

5. Several of the passengers asked for _____ snacks.

Assessment: Mastery Tests

Usage Mastery Test (Form B)

Part 3 Each of the following sentences is missing a verb. Decide what form of the verb in parentheses will make the sentence clear and correct. Then, on the line provided, write the correct verb form. [1 point each]

1. (know) I should have _____ every answer on that test!

2. (eat) Who has _____ all the raisins?

3. (rise) A cheer _____ from the fans.

4. (work) The carpenters must have _____ overtime to finish.

5. (ring) The bell _____ before I finished my question.

6. (sit) After I _____ down, I felt better.

7. (bring) Julian had _____ some sandwiches with him.

8. (break) The water pipes _____ during the January cold spell.

9. (lie) Your clothes _____ on the floor all last week.

10. (hurt) That remark really _____ my feelings.

11. (swim) She could have _____ for another hour.

12. (go) Everyone _____ to the early show instead.

13. (speak) Had that bird ever _____ before yesterday?

14. (sell) Sorry, but we _____ that bike yesterday.

15. (write) I have _____ in my journal every day this week.

Part 4 Many of the following sentences contain pronoun errors. Draw a line through each incorrect pronoun. Then, in the space provided, write the correct pronoun. Write **C** if the sentence is correct. [1 point each]

_____ 1. Coach Wilson put Francisca and I into the game.

_____ 2. The announcement was a disappointment to we and our friends.

_____ 3. The creaking of the door terrified us.

_____ 4. The writer of the secret message must have been her.

_____ 5. They are always telling we students to study hard.

_____ 6. They and us were scheduled to paint scenery today.

_____ 7. Alameda can ride in the car with Wendy and she.

_____ 8. The first candidate talked about hisself the whole time.

_____ 9. You and him look like brothers.

_____10. Who wants the last piece of fruit?

Usage Mastery Test (Form B)

_____ 11. The runners asked him and I for the time.

_____ 12. Nina and them missed the last bus home.

_____ 13. Who did you ask to the dance?

_____ 14. The only soprano in the room was me.

_____ 15. Between you and me, I think Leo will win.

Part 5   The following sentences contain misplaced or incorrect modifiers. On the line provided, rewrite each sentence to make it clear and logical. [2 points each]

1. Leana is thoughtfuller than her sister.

_____

2. If that infection gets any more bad, you should see a doctor.

_____

3. The dog scared most people barking in the yard.

_____

4. Although Chen did good, he didn't win.

_____

5. Beeping loudly, Julian heard the smoke detector.

_____

6. Of all the news programs, this one is better.

_____

7. Covered with rust, Nina scrubbed the hinges.

_____

8. The room looked well after we painted it.

_____

9. The back row couldn't hardly hear the music.

_____

10. Perched on the side of a tree, I saw a woodpecker.

_____

Assessment: Mastery Tests

Usage Mastery Test (Form B)

Part 6   Read each sentence and decide which answer in parentheses is correct. Underline that answer. [1 point each]

1. The kitten is (real, very) cute.

2. LaVerne is (already, all ready) for the trip.

3. Will you (take, bring) me my gloves?

4. We have a long (way, ways) to go.

5. Jake (taught, learned) me how to cook.

6. They had only (themselves, theirselfs) to blame.

7. Esperanza (use, used) to practice every day.

8. I have (less, fewer) marbles than you have.

9. It looks (as if, like) it will rain.

10. (Whose, Who's) calling, please?

11. Please (accept, except) my apology.

12. You play tennis (good, well).

13. We (can, can't) hardly see in this fog.

14. Your sunglasses (broke, busted).

15. (Its, It's) time to go.

16. Do you feel (alright, all right)?

17. (You're, Your) an honest person.

18. He cannot go (unless, without) he finishes his chores.

19. (Sit, Set) the chair at this end of the table.

20. (Who's, Whose) book is this?

Assessment Tests

Usage Mastery Test (Form A)

Part 1 [1 point each, 15 points total]

1. have disappeared
2. doesn't think
3. C
4. Are
5. arrives
6. were
7. was
8. is
9. doesn't ring
10. has
11. speaks
12. was
13. C
14. were written
15. C

Part 2 [2 points each, 10 points total]

1. their
2. his
3. it
4. her
5. his

Part 3 [1 point each, 15 points total]

1. laid
2. lain
3. given
4. eaten
5. broke
6. fall
7. gone
8. knew
9. rose
10. swam
11. chosen
12. risen
13. burst
14. froze
15. led

Part 4 [1 point each, 10 points total]

1. I
2. She
3. themselves
4. me
5. We
6. me
7. us
8. us
9. he
10. them

Part 5 [2 points each, 10 points total]

1. One of the worst experiences I had was in fifth grade.
2. The first game was our easiest win of the season.
3. Of the two shirts, this one is less expensive.
4. C
5. He didn't have any money left for popcorn. *or* He had no money left for popcorn.

Part 6 [1 point each, 10 points total]

1. feverish
2. vigorously
3. well
4. slowly
5. surely
6. beautiful
7. carefully
8. bigger
9. quickly
10. easily

Assessment Tests

Part 7 [1 point each, 10 points total]

1. The castanets belong to my sister that I lent you.
2. Juggling oranges, we were impressed by the performer
3. Reba lent the magazine to her sister that she had bought.
4. Hearne noticed his broken shoelace climbing onto the bus.
5. C
6. Wood ducks live in trees with their mates.
7. Mr. Eng noticed the advertisement reading the newspaper.
8. Leaping out of the plane, my parents watched the sky divers.
9. C
10. Heidi found the word's meaning looking in my dictionary.

Part 8 [2 points each, 20 points total]

1. You're absolutely correct.
2. Please take this book to the librarian.
3. Your tape is somewhere in the hall.
4. We were all ready to go when you called.
5. Toby looks rather tired today.
6. We had scarcely any gas in the mower.
7. We have six dollars among the four of us.
8. Mr. Cotton accepted the offer.
9. The napkin is inside the drawer.
10 I know we should have called first.

Usage Mastery Test (Form B)

Part 1 [1 point each, 20 points total]

1. aren't isn't
2. is are
3. ants want
4. are is
5. are is
6. Don't Doesn't
7. C
8. know knows
9. are is
10. C
11. C
12. need needs
13. were was
14. answer answers
15. is are
16. C
17. is are
18. seem seems
19. don't doesn't
10. was were

Part 2 [2 points each, 10 points total]

1. his or her
2. their
3. his
4. its
5. their

Part 3 [1 point each, 15 points total]

1. known
2. eaten
3. rose
4. worked
5. rang
6. sat
7. brought
8. broke
9. lay
10. hurt
11. swum
12. went
13. spoken
14. sold
15. written

Assessment Tests

Part 4 [1 point each, 15 points total]

1. ~~I~~ me
2. ~~we~~ us
3. C
4. ~~her~~ she
5. ~~we~~ us
6. ~~us~~ we
7. ~~she~~ her
8. ~~hisself~~ himself
9. ~~him~~ he
10. C
11. ~~I~~ me
12. ~~them~~ they
13. ~~Who~~ Whom
14. ~~me~~ I
15. C

Part 5 [2 points each, 20 points total]

1. Leana is more thoughtful than her sister.
2. If that infection gets any worse, you should see a doctor.
3. The dog barking in the yard scared most people.
4. Although Chen did well, he didn't win.
5. Julian heard the smoke detector beeping loudly.
6. Of all the news programs, this one is the best.
7. Nina scrubbed the hinges covered with rust.
8. The room looked good after we painted it.
9. The back row could hardly hear the music.
10. I saw a woodpecker perched on the side of a tree.

Part 6 [1 point each, 20 points total]

1. very
2. all ready
3. bring
4. way
5. taught
6. themselves
7. used
8. fewer
9. as if
10. Who's
11. accept
12. well
13. can
14. broke
15. It's
16. all right
17. You're
18. unless
19. Set
20 Whose

Mechanics Pretests (Form A)

Pretest A   The following sentences contain errors in the use of capitalization. Cross out each incorrect letter form, and write the correct form above it. [20 points each]

1. My mother works for the Red cross.

2. Last fall, doug took chemistry, english, and social studies.

3. The Blanchard Memorial library is closed on Memorial day.

4. Many Muslims celebrate ashura, held to honor the grandson of muhammad.

5. In south Dakota, we visited a sioux village.

Pretest B   Each of the following sentences is missing at least one punctuation mark. Add the punctuation marks and circle them. [20 points each]

1. Has anyone seen Dr Newell or her son

2. Yes we have visited Fort Smith Arkansas.

3. We lived on Apple St for nine years

4. On March 9 1862 two ships met off Hampton Roads Virginia.

5. What a lovely sweater that is

Pretest C   Following are ten pairs of sentences. Of each pair, one sentence is correctly punctuated. On the line provided, write the letter of the correct sentence. [10 points each]

_____ 1. (a) The local train makes these stops, West Orange, Rahway and Newark.

(b) The local train makes these stops: West Orange, Rahway, and Newark.

_____ 2. (a) I voted for Dolores, Jack, and Lotte; my friend voted for Tom, Rosa, and Pete.

(b) I voted for Dolores, Jack, and Lotte, my friend voted for Tom, Rosa, and Pete.

_____ 3. (a) At 330 we ate, at 500 we slept, at 700 we ate again.

(b) At 3:30 we ate; at 5:00 we slept; at 7:00 we ate again.

_____ 4. (a) The main film feature was terrible: the second feature was even worse.

(b) The main film feature was terrible; the second feature was even worse.

Mechanics Pretests (Form A)

_____ 5. (a) Peas are legumes; carrots, on the other hand, are root vegetables.

(b) Peas are legumes; carrots on the other hand are root vegetables.

_____ 6. (a) A Night to Remember tells about the sinking of the Titanic.

(b) *A Night to Remember* tells us about the sinking of the *Titanic*.

_____ 7. (a) When you're finished, please put your pencils on the desks.

(b) When your finished, please put you're pencils on the desks.

_____ 8. (a) The students, at least the ones I met, made a total of twenty six posters.

(b) The students—at least the ones I met—made a total of twenty-six posters.

_____ 9. (a) I memorized the short poem "Andre, "which was written by Gwendolyn Brooks.

(b) I memorized the short poem *Andre,* which was written by Gwendolyn Brooks.

_____10. (a) Inside the museum everyones eyes were busy.

(b) Inside the museum, everyone's eyes were busy.

Pretest D   In the following passage, there are errors in punctuation and paragraphing. In the spaces provided, write the missing punctuation. Write ¶ to show that a new paragraph should begin. [10 points each]

> **Example:** The captain told the squad, _<u>"</u>__ Girls, this is a game
> we can win."
> <u>¶ "</u> You should score three points the first half,"
> Coach Gómez broke in.

"How(1) _____ asked a right half.

"That's simple. Get three quick goals (2) _____ Coach Gómez said.

(Is there ever a coach who does not say, "I want three goals(3) _____) If

we pass properly," said the captain(4) _____ we can score before they

get the ball (5) _____ Coach Gómez then added, "I also want you to

show good sportsmanship."

"Should we try to steal the ball(6) _____ asked a substitute player.

"Why not(7) _____ asked the captain.

"Lastly," said Coach Gómez(8) _____ I want you to remember these

three things(9) _____ Score first, keep them on the defensive, and never

let up on them (10)_____ With this the team members ran outside, certain

they would win.

Mechanics Pretests (Form A)

Pretest E   Following are five sentences with apostrophe, parentheses, or hyphen errors. Underline the parts of each sentence that are incorrect. On the line provided, write those parts correctly. [20 points each]

> **Example:**   One speaker on womens rights, Sojourner Truth
> (originally Isabella Van Wagener renamed herself.
> women's   Wagener)

1. Were going to try it again, but we'll add three quarters cup of milk. _____

2. Whos the person who painted all the 5s red? _____

3. Many entertainers, including Anna May Wong (born Lu Tsong Wong and

   Rip Torn born Elmore Torn), change their names. _____

4. Even though hed hoped for As, Kurt was happy with his grades. _____

5. Everyone worked hard on this play, so lets help guarantee it's success. _____

Pretest F   One word in each of the following groups of words is incorrectly spelled. Underline the incorrect word. Then, on the line provided, write the correct spelling of the word. [5 points each]

_____ 1. height, weight, cheif

_____ 2. succeed, supercede, proceed

_____ 3. unecessary, unavailable, unusual

_____ 4. happily, finelly, truly

_____ 5. said, paid, keyd

_____ 6. cried, tapping, driped

_____ 7. taxes, buzzes, foxs

_____ 8. switches, mixs, pays

_____ 9. knifes, tomatoes, solos

_____10. mothers-in-law, father-in-laws, drive-ins

_____11. ache, coler, friend

_____12. cannot, though, tonigt

_____13. aquire, argument, always

_____14. won't, trys, guess

_____15. womans, boys, puppets

_____16. built, erly, easy

_____17. half, cough, insted

Mechanics Pretests

_____ 18. heating, hiting, trying

_____ 19. changable, moveable, smiling

_____ 20. misspell, minite, mixing

Pretest G   Read each of the following sentences. In many of them, one word has been misused because it has been mistaken for another word much like it. Underline each incorrect word. Then, on the line provided, write the word that should have been used. Write **C** if there is no error. [10 points each]

1. An editor altared this manuscript. _____

2. We had fruit and sherbet for desert. _____

3. I thanked Mr. Chu for the compliment. _____

4. While you are hear, use this towel. _____

5. Soon, winter past and spring arrived. _____

6. Marla received a box of stationery for her birthday. _____

7. The blue chair is softer then the green one. _____

8. The whether report comes on right after the news. _____

9. Who's the man speaking to Officer Grant? _____

10. The town voted to except the gift of a new library wing. _____

Assessment: Pretests

Mechanics Pretests (Form B)

Pretest A   In the following paragraph, circle all letters that should be capitalized.
[2 points each]

for someone who lives on vine street near the mississippi river, i certainly have traveled a lot. my father and mother took me to europe, asia, the caribbean, and all over the united states while they were buying furniture for their antique store. my teachers at lakeland junior high school always said that it was all right for me to miss school because i would learn so much geography. i didn't have to wait for easter vacation or christmas; i could just go. sometimes my mother would come home on a friday, and off we would go on saturday morning. the grand canyon national park was one of my favorite places to be because i think that you can see to california. we took photographs there, but the pictures that are on my walls are from *national geographic*. this june we plan to travel with some english friends, who now live in west virginia, to tokyo, japan, where my aunt who is a cherokee lives. then we will visit washington, d.c., where i will see the white house and the smithsonian for the first time.

Pretest B   The following sentences are missing periods and other end marks. In the blanks provided, write each word that should be followed by a period or any other end mark, and include the correct punctuation. [10 points each]

Example: _Red River?_ Did you take these pictures of the Red River

_____ 1. Marty's mom always has great ideas

_____ 2. Do you like the music of Scott Joplin

_____ 3. Ms Singer wondered if you would volunteer

_____ 4. Watch out for that live wire

_____ 5. The bus just left

_____ 6. Must you play the radio so loudly

_____ 7. The museum is located on Dr Martin Luther King, Jr, Blvd

_____ 8 I am going to visit Mr Vidal today

_____ 9. Thank you for such a thoughtful gift

_____10. Wasn't Carl at the game last night

Mechanics Pretests (Form B)

Pretest C The following sentences are missing commas and semicolons. In the blanks provided, write each word that should be followed by a comma or semicolon, and include the correct punctuation. [5 points each]

Example: <u>Apples, raisins,</u> Apples raisins and grapes make a good salad.

_____ 1. My brother went shopping cooked dinner and washed the dishes.

_____ 2. Over the lake hung a huge hazy moon to light our way.

_____ 3. Mr. Echohawk a good friend of my mother's helps me with math.

_____ 4. Caroline pardon me have your test results arrived?

_____ 5. Yes Mario they came just last week.

_____ 6. The first time we tried, we did well but I wasn't surprised.

_____ 7. Our new address is 72 Maple Street Rochester New York 14612.

_____ 8. Inger designs the clothes her mother sews them.

_____ 9. No Antoan couldn't be responsible for that.

_____ 10. We followed the trail we went past the garage.

_____ 11. The world record in this event was held by Jesse Owens for several years however the record is now held by another outstanding athlete.

_____ 12. On June 15 1983 my father opened his first florist shop.

_____ 13. This revised updated plan of yours is brilliant!

_____ 14. Your use of materials for example is very artistic.

_____ 15. Yes I am going to try out for the dancing team.

_____ 16. Jaime the captain says that I have a good chance.

_____ 17. Did you hear the list of prizes ladies and gentlemen?

_____ 18. I carry the groceries into the house my sister puts them away.

_____ 19. Did you attend the International Folk Fair in St. Petersburg Florida?

_____ 20. She has assignments in geography Spanish and shop.

Pretest D The following passage is not written correctly. Changes in speaker are not always indicated by proper paragraphing, and some of the quotation marks and capital letters are missing. In the blanks provided, write correctly the words that require punctuation and capitalization. Use ¶ to show that a new paragraph should begin. [10 points each]

Examples: "Have you ever entered a contest? ___contest?"___ she asked. ___¶ "No,"___ "no," I said to myself.

The disc jockey continued explaining the rules of the contest. _____ the

1

Mechanics Pretests (Form B)

first person to name the magic number will win one thousand dollars!"

While she was talking, I lay in my bed, thinking of only one number. I said to my sister, "I think that I ought to call them." _____ sure, why not?" she
₂
mumbled. "But be quiet; I'm trying to sleep."

Well, I didn't call; I just lay there thinking about the number 12357.

A few minutes later the disc jockey said, _____ we have a winner!
₃
Mrs. H. B. Whitcomb has named our magic number, 12357!" _____ oh, no!"
₄
I yelled. "That could have been me!"

As you might imagine, my sister was quite awake by now, and she asked,

_____ why didn't you call?"_____ What could I say but "I don't
₅   ₆
know"?

She answered, _____ well, you certainly missed your chance."
₇

"I guess that I did _____ I replied, _____ but next time, I'll call.
₈   ₉
I may not win, but one thing is certain. If I don't try, I won't even have a chance to

win. _____
₁₀

Pretest E   The following sentences are missing colons, apostrophes, and hyphens. In the blanks provided, write each word that requires one of these marks of punctuation, and include the correct punctuation. [10 points each]

Example: <u>Thirty-three</u> <u>won't</u> Thirty three drums wont fit in the bus.

_____ 1. The tests questions include the following marks
hyphens, apostrophes, and colons.

_____ 2. Its easy to see that you like to use &s instead of writing out the
word *and*.

_____ 3. Eighty ninth Street is my dads new address.

_____ 4. My brothers car is sporty, but my sisters is a station wagon.

_____ 5. Isnt this play considered Lorraine Hansberrys best work?

_____ 6. Whats the function of its lowest common denominator?

_____ 7. Will Liangs friends be arriving before class starts at 230?

_____ 8. Its a drawing of one of Augusta Savages sculptures.

_____ 9. My baby brothers a real sleeper; he should have a mobile made
of Zs instead of airplanes over his crib.

_____10. Whos going to help repaint the clubs float for the parade?

Assessment: Pretests

Mechanics Pretests (Form B)

Pretest F In each of the following numbered items, there are three words. Two words are correctly spelled; one is incorrectly spelled. Find the incorrect word and spell it correctly in the blank provided. [5 points each]

_____ 1. fierce, apinion, medicine

_____ 2. particuliarly, vicinity, tongue

_____ 3. treasury, completly, performance

_____ 4. finaly, committee, bureau

_____ 5. acceptance, privilege, briliant

_____ 6. nervous, canidate, seize

_____ 7. posess, correspondence, guarantee

_____ 8. business, strength, picnik

_____ 9. criticize, mischif, heir

_____10. permanant, divine, muscle

_____11. college, benefit, unnecesary

_____12. temparary, theory, intelligence

_____13. recomend, satisfy, description

_____14. courteous, attacked, magizine

_____15. aisles, favorite, aparent

_____16. tragedy, sense, bicicle

_____17. scene, rythm, vacuum

_____18. foliage, mariage, mathematics

_____19. tries, villain, absense

_____20. studing, opportunity, advertisement

Assessment Tests

Mechanics Pretests

Pretest A [20 points each]

1. My mother works for the Red $\overset{C}{\text{cross}}$.
2. Last fall, $\overset{D}{\text{doug}}$ took chemistry, $\overset{E}{\text{english}}$, and social studies.
3. The Blanchard Memorial $\overset{L}{\text{library}}$ is closed on Memorial $\overset{D}{\text{day}}$.
4. Many Muslims celebrate $\overset{A}{\text{ashura}}$, held to honor the grandson of $\overset{M}{\text{muhammad}}$.
5. In $\overset{S}{\text{south}}$ Dakota, we visited a $\overset{S}{\text{sioux}}$ village.

Pretest B [20 points each]

1. Dr⊙... son⊙
2. Yes⊙... Fort Smith⊙
3. St⊙... years⊙
4. March 9⊙1862⊙... Hampton Roads⊙
5. is⊙

Pretest C [10 points each]

1. b
2. a
3. b
4. b
5. a
6. b
7. a
8. b
9. a
10. b

Pretest D [10 points each]

1. ?"
2. ,"
3. "? ¶"
4. ,"
5. ." ¶
6. ?"
7. ?"
8. ,"
9. :
10. ." ¶

Pretest E [20 points each]

1. We're ...three-quarters
2. Who's ...5's
3. Lu Tsong Wong)... (born Elmore
4. he'd... A's
5. let's... its

Pretest F [5 points each]

1. cheif — chief
2. supercede — supersede
3. unecessary — unnecessary
4. finelly — finally
5. keyd — keyed
6. driped — dripped
7. foxs — foxes
8. mixs — mixes
9. knifes — knives
10. father-in-laws — fathers-in-law
11. coler — color
12. tonigt — tonight
13. aquire — acquire
14. trys — tries
15. womans — women
16. erly — early
17. insted — instead
18. hiting — hitting
19. changable — changeable
20. minite — minute

Pretest G [10 points each]

1. altared — altered
2. desert — dessert
3. C
4. hear — here
5. past — passed
6. C
7. then — than
8. whether — weather
9. C
10. except — accept

Assessment Tests

Mechanics Pretests (Form B)

Pretest A [2 points each]

Ⓕ or someone who lives on Ⓥ ine Ⓢ treet near the Ⓜ ississippi Ⓡ iver, Ⓘ certainly have traveled a lot. Ⓜ y father and mother took me to Ⓔ urope, Ⓐ sia, the Ⓒ aribbean, and all over the Ⓤ nited Ⓢ tates while they were buying furniture for their antique store. Ⓜ y teachers at Ⓛ akeland Ⓙ unior Ⓗ igh Ⓢ chool always said that was all right for me to miss school because Ⓘ would learn so much geography. Ⓘ didn't have to wait for Ⓔ aster vacation or Ⓒ hristmas; Ⓘ could just go. Ⓢ ometimes my mother would come home on a Ⓕ riday, and off we would go on Ⓢ aturday morning. Ⓣ he Ⓖ rand Ⓒ anyon Ⓝ ational Ⓟ ark was one of my favorite places to be because Ⓘ think that you can see to Ⓒ alifornia. Ⓦ e took photographs there, but the pictures that are on my walls are from Ⓝ *ational* Ⓖ *eographic.* Ⓣ his Ⓙ une we plan to travel with some Ⓔ nglish friends, who now live in Ⓦ est Ⓥ irginia, to Ⓣ okyo, Ⓙ apan, where my aunt who is a Ⓒ herokee lives. Ⓣ hen we will visit Ⓦ ashington, Ⓓ . Ⓒ ., where I will see the Ⓦ hite Ⓗ ouse and the Ⓢ mithsonian for the first time.

Pretest B [10 points each]

1. ideas
2. Joplin?
3. Ms. volunteer.
4. wire!
5. left.
6. loudly?
7. Dr. Jr. Blvd.
8. Mr. today.
9. gift.
10. night?

Pretest C [5 points each]

1. shopping, dinner,
2. huge,
3. Mr. Echohawk, mother's,
4. Caroline, me,
5. Yes, Mario,
6. well,
7. Street, Rochester,
8. clothes;
9. No,
10. trail;
11. years; however,
12. 15, 1983,
13. revised,
14. materials, example,
15. Yes,
16. Jaime, captain,
17. prizes,
18. house;
19. St. Petersburg,
20. geography, Spanish,

Assessment Tests

Pretest D [10 points each]

1. "The
2. ¶ "Sure
3. "We
4. ¶ "Oh
5. "Why
6. ¶
7. "Well
8. did,"
9. "but
10. win."

Pretest E [10 points each]

1. test's marks:
2. It's &'s
3. Eighty-ninth dad's
4. brother's sister's
5. Isn't Hansberry's
6. What's
7. Liang's 2:30
8. It's Savage's
9. brother's Z's
10. Who's club's

Pretest F [5 points each]

1. opinion
2. particulary
3. completely
4. finally
5. brilliant
6. candidate
7. possess
8. picnic
9. mischief
10. permanent
11. unnecessary
12. temporary
13. recommend
14. magazine
15. apparent
16. bicycle
17. rhythm
18. marriage
19. absence
20. studying

Chapter 25: Capital Letters

Using Capital Letters A

The first word of a sentence always begins with a **capital letter.** The pronoun *I* is always capitalized, too.

The picture that **I** am painting is almost finished.

The first word of a direct quotation should be capitalized, whether or not the quotation starts the sentence.

Patrice said, "**P**lease help me plan the costumes for the school play."

A **proper noun** names a particular person, place, thing, or idea and always begins with a capital letter. A **common noun** names a kind or type of person, place, thing, or idea and does not begin with a capital letter unless it begins a sentence or is part of a title. Words such as *north* and *south,* are not capitalized when the words merely indicate direction. The word *earth* is not capitalized unless it is used along with the names of other heavenly bodies.

> **Proper nouns:** Denzel Washington, New Mexico, Ohio River, Christianity, the West
>
> **Common nouns:** actor, state, river, religion, north

Many proper nouns consist of more than one word. In these names, prepositions of fewer than five letters (such as *of, with, for*) and articles (*a, an, the*) are not capitalized.

the United States of America   Alexander the Great

Exercise A   Underline the letters that should be capitalized in the following sentences.

1. Last january, i moved away from arizona.

2. it takes several days to drive from utah to pennsylvania.

3. After dinner, my friend arlis and i swam in the gulf of mexico.

4. i took a picture of a statue of martin luther king, jr., in montgomery, alabama.

5. Pola said, "this is such a pretty city. let's stop for the night here."

Exercise B: Proofreading   The following paragraph contains six errors in capitalization, two spelling errors, and two errors in verb tenses. Can you find these errors? Proofread the paragraph to correct all the errors you can find.

On Wenesday, we drove to atlanta, Georgia, where we stoped for lunch. Then

we drive to Burlington, North carolina. My mother wanted to see the monument

to Charles drew, the famous doctor. We spend the night in a hotel on the

Roanoke river. Then, on thursday, we drove to Gettysburg, pennsylvania.

Using Capital Letters B

A **proper adjective** is formed from a proper noun. It is always capitalized.

Proper Nouns	Proper Adjectives
China	a Chinese scientist
William Shakespeare	a Shakespearean play
the Confederacy	a Confederate soldier
Venus	a Venusian leader

Do not capitalize the names of school subjects, except languages and course names followed by a number.

This morning my classes are art, French, and History II.

Exercise A   Underline the letters that should be capitalized in the following sentences.

1. My mother bought an african lamp made of teakwood for my aunt.

2. My japanese friend took latin american history 101 and enjoyed it.

3. Yesterday, a famous guest came to visit our music 102 class.

4. My British pen pal, Sarah, sent me an irish friendship ring.

5. I told my mother that the best way for me to practice speaking spanish is to talk

   on the phone to my peruvian friend every night.

Exercise B: Revising   On the lines provided, revise these sentences to correct all capitalization errors.

1. The spanish explorers sailed up the floridian coast. _____

   _____

2. According to the korean exchange student, Billy Joel is having an asian

   concert tour. _____

   _____

3. Isak Dinesen was a danish author who wrote a story about a european girl

   named Babette. _____

   _____

4. When I go to college, I plan to take Biology every semester and swimming

   I, II, and III. _____

   _____

5. Everyone who is in my english class is also in my Math class._____

   _____

Chapter 25: Capital Letters

Using Capital Letters C

Capitalize the important words in the titles of people, books, magazines, newspapers, short stories, poems, movies, plays, musical works, and television programs.

President Abraham Lincoln	*The Old Man and the Sea*
Aunt Flora	*"Ode to a Nightingale"*
Sports Illustrated	*"The Battle Hymn of the Republic"*
The New York Times	*Wheel of Fortune*

Do not capitalize a word showing a family relationship of it follows a possessive word.

My *uncle* Frank planned a birthday party for *Aunt* Flora.
Janine took her *grandmother* to Radio City Music Hall.

Exercise A   Underline the letters that should be capitalized in the following sentences.

1. At the party, uncle Derwood gave aunt Flora a subscription to *reader's digest*.

2. My grandpa gave her a tape of the musical play *cats*.

3. Before the game began, everyone stood and sang "the star-spangled banner."

4. In the *tampa tribune*, I read about a statement made by president Clinton.

5. My mother really liked Raul Julia in the movie *the addams family*.

Exercise B: Revising   On the lines provided, revise these sentences to correct all capitalization errors.

1. One of my favorite movies is *king kong*. _____

_____

2. The main characters sail to a remote Island to find kong, a giant ape-like creature. _____

_____

3. The adventurers steal away the creature from the island and return to new york. _____

_____

4. The creature manages to escape and takes fay wray, the star of the picture, to

   the top of the empire state building. _____

_____

5. Try to catch this old movie on that great television program *film classics*. _____

_____

Chapter 25: Capital Letters

Review (Form A)

Exercise A   Each sentence contains one error in capitalization. Circle the word that contains the error. Write it correctly on the line.

_____ 1. Last night i rented the movie *The Sound of Music*.

_____ 2. It is based on the life of Maria Von trapp.

_____ 3. The movie was filmed in the austrian city of Salzburg.

_____ 4. One movie critic said, "the scenery and music are stunning."

_____ 5. Julie Andrews plays the leading Role of Maria.

Exercise B   On the line provided before each sentence, write **CN** if the italicized word is a common noun. Write **PN** if it is a proper noun. Write **PA** if it is a proper adjective. Then circle any letters that should be capitalized.

_____ 1. The Marquis de Lafayette was a *french* soldier and diplomat.

_____ 2. He came to *america* in 1777 to join the staff of George Washington.

_____ 3. He helped the *american* colonists in their struggle for independence.

_____ 4. He persuaded *king louis XVI* to send soldiers and ships to help, too.

_____ 5. He fought in many *battles* of the American Revolution.

Exercise C   Rewrite each of these phrases, using capital letters as needed. If the phrase is capitalized correctly, write **C**.

1. the united states senate _____

2. a puerto rican catcher for the chicago white sox _____

3. 145 spring avenue, munster, indiana _____

4. tuesday, the fourteenth of november _____ _____

5. the book *gone with the wind* _____

6. a beautiful river in north dakota _____

7. a south american jungle _____

8. a pizza from the restaurant known as mama leone's _____

9. a summer trip to the beach _____

10. my uncle jolon _____

Chapter 25: Capital Letters

Review (Form A)

Exercise D   Circle each word that should begin with a capital letter.

1. Sophomores at lincoln high school take world history II.

2. Mount whitney is one of the highest mountains in north america.

3. The author of the book *A tale of Two cities* is charles dickens.

4. I saw an exhibit of paintings by the mexican artist josé orozco.

5. Then aunt clara began to sing the song "silver threads among the gold."

Exercise E   In each sentence, circle the word or words that contain errors in capitalization. Write the word or words correctly on the line.

_____ 1. The Cinemax Theater is two blocks North of our high school.

_____ 2. My Grandmother lives on the banks of The Ohio river.

_____ 3. There will be a full Moon on my birthday, september 14.

_____ 4. Harrison Ford stars in the Movie *Raiders Of The Lost Ark.*

_____ 5. Your aunt modene will take you to your appointment with dr. Block.

Exercise F   On the lines provided, rewrite these sentences, correcting all errors in capitalization.

1. Babe ruth was a great Baseball Player for the new york yankees. _____

_____

2. Native americans joined the Pilgrims at the first thanksgiving feast. _____

_____

3. The Planet Pluto is farthest from the Sun. _____

_____

4. The british composer Andrew lloyd webber wrote *Phantom Of The Opera.* _____

_____

5. Did you read Ellen Goodman's column in the sunday Issue of the *boston globe?* _____

_____

6. The butler insurance company has its Headquarters in akron, ohio. _____

_____

Chapter 25: Capital Letters

Review (Form B)

Exercise A   Each sentence contains one error in capitalization. Circle the word that contains the error. Write it correctly on the line.

_____ 1. My cousin Sheila asked, "what time does the play begin?"

_____ 2. She and i were planning to go to the Lillian Beaumont Theater.

_____ 3. I had seen the play *King Lear* there last november.

_____ 4. This time, Sheila had Tickets to see *Evita*.

_____ 5. It's the story of Eva Peron, a legendary figure in the history of argentina.

Exercise B   On the line provided before each sentence, write **CN** if the underlined word is a common noun. Write **PN** if it is a proper noun. Write **PA** if it is a proper adjective. Then circle any letters that should be capitalized.

_____ 1. Wolfgang Amadeus Mozart was born in Salzburg, austria.

_____ 2. By the age of four, Mozart had already shown great musical genius.

_____ 3. He toured the european courts, performing on the violin and organ.

_____ 4. This austrian became one of the world's greatest composers.

_____ 5. His operas include *the marriage of Figaro* and *The Magic Flute*.

Exercise C   Rewrite each of these phrases, using capital letters as needed. If the phrase is capitalized correctly, write **C**.

1. fresh water from the Salton sea _____

2. general ulysses s. grant _____

3. a hispanic baseball star, juan bonilla _____

4. a quarterback for the chicago bears football team _____

5. 897 cricket avenue, fort worth, texas _____

6. a picnic at the beach on long island _____

7. the book *the collected poems of william b. yeats* _____

8. a winter vacation in a warm climate _____

9. a legend about a monster in lake superior _____

10. my grandmother, minnie robinson _____

Chapter 25: Capital Letters

Review (Form B)

Exercise D Circle each word that should begin with a capital letter.

1. Many barges and ships pass through the panama canal.

2. Juniors at elkton high school must take world history II.

3. The larkspur hotel is just north of an exit on the pennsylvania turnpike.

4. The poet t. s. eliot wrote the poem "The love song of j. alfred prufrock."

5. The planets saturn and jupiter are much larger than earth.

Exercise E In each sentence, circle the word or words that contain errors in capitalization. Write the word or words correctly on the line.

_____ 1. My Uncle Patrick works as a dentist in Columbia, missouri.

_____ 2. On tuesday, brazilians will vote for a new president.

_____ 3. Drive west on Third avenue until you come to the Burger doodle.

_____ 4. We saw a partial eclipse of the Moon last Sunday Night.

_____ 5. Whitney Houston sang "the Star-spangled banner."

Exercise F On the lines provided, rewrite these sentences, correcting all errors in capitalization.

1. Robin williams played a modern peter pan in the movie *hook*. _____

_____

2. The birthday of queen elizabeth II is a Holiday in the united kingdom. _____

_____

3. The window of blum's bakery was full of italian bread and danish pastries. _____

_____

4. tennessee williams, a playwright from the south, wrote *The Night Of the Iguana*. _____

_____

5. In The *Philadelphia Inquirer*, I read about the gulf war. _____

_____

Answer Key

Practice and Reinforcement (1)
Using Capital Letters A

Exercise A

1. Last january, i moved away from arizona.
2. it takes several days to drive from utah to pennsylvania.
3. After dinner, my friend arlis and i swam in the gulf of mexico.
4. i took a picture of a statue of martin luther king, jr., in montgomery, alabama.
5. Pola said, "this is such a pretty city. let's stop for the night here."

Exercise B: Proofreading

On Wednesday, we drove to atlanta, Georgia, where we stopped for lunch. Then we drive to Burlington, North carolina. My mother wanted to see the monument to Charles drew, the famous doctor. We spend the night in a hotel on the Roanoke river. Then, on thursday, we drove to Gettysburg, pennsylvania.

Practice and Reinforcement (2)
Using Capital Letters B

Exercise A

1. My mother bought an african lamp made of teakwood for my aunt.
2. My japanese friend too latin american history 101 and enjoyed it.
3. Yesterday, a famous guest came to visit our music 102 class.
4. My british pen pal, Sarah, sent me an irish friendship ring.
5. I told my mother that the best way for me to practice speaking spanish is to talk on the phone to my peruvian friend every night.

Exercise B: Revising

1. The Spanish explorers sailed up the Floridian coast.
2. According to the Korean exchange student, Billy Joel is having an Asian concert tour.
3. Isak Dinesen was a Danish author who wrote a story about a European girl named Babette.
4. When I go to college, I plan to take biology every semester and Swimming I, II, and III.
5. Everyone who is in my English class is also in my math class.

Practice and Reinforcement (3)
Using Capital Letters C

Exercise A

1. At the party, uncle Derwood gave aunt Flora a subscription to *reader's digest*.
2. My grandpa gave her a tape of the musical play *cats*.
3. Before the game began, everyone stood and sang "the star-spangled banner".
4. In the *tampa tribune*, I read about a statement made by president Clinton.
5. My mother really liked Raul Julia in the movie *the addams family*.

Exercise B: Revising

1. One of my favorite movies is *King Kong*.
2. The main characters sail to a remote island to find Kong, a giant ape-like creature.
3. The adventurers steal away the creature from the island and return to New York.
4. The creature manages to escape and takes Fay Wray, the star of the picture, to the top of the Empire State Building.
5. Try to catch this old movie on that great television program *Film Classics*.

Answer Key

Chapter Review
Form A

Exercise A

1. Last night ⓘrented the movie *The Sound of Music*. I

2. It is based on the life of Maria Von ⟨trapp.⟩ Trapp

3. The movie was filmed in the ⟨austrian⟩ city of Salzburg. Austrian

4. One movie critic said, "⟨the⟩scenery and music are stunning." The

5. Julie Andrews plays the leading ⟨Role⟩of Maria. role

Exercise B

1. PA—⟨French⟩
2. PN—⟨America⟩
3. PA—⟨American⟩
4. PN—⟨King Louis⟩
5. CN

Exercise C

1. the United States Senate
2. a Puerto Rican catcher for the Chicago White Sox
3. 145 Spring Avenue, Munster, Indiana
4. Tuesday, the fourteenth of November
5. the book *Gone with the Wind*
6. a beautiful river in North Dakota
7. a South American jungle
8. a pizza from the restaurant known as Mama Leone's
9. C
10. my uncle Jolon

Exercise D

1. Sophomores at ⟨lincoln⟩⟨high⟩⟨school⟩take ⟨world⟩⟨history⟩II.
2. Mount ⟨whitney⟩is one of the highest mountains in ⟨north⟩⟨america.⟩
3. The author of the book *A ⟨tale⟩ of Two ⟨cities⟩* is ⟨charles⟩⟨dickens.⟩
4. I saw an exhibit of paintings by the ⟨mexican⟩ artist ⟨josé⟩⟨orozco.⟩
5. Then ⟨aunt⟩⟨clara⟩began to sing the song "⟨silver⟩⟨threads⟩⟨among⟩the ⟨gold.⟩"

Exercise E

1. The Cinemax Theater is two blocks ⟨North⟩of our high school. north
2. My ⟨Grandmother⟩lives on the banks of ⟨The⟩ Ohio ⟨river.⟩ grandmother, the, River
3. There will be a full ⟨Moon⟩on my birthday, ⟨september⟩14. moon, September
4. Harrison Ford stars in the ⟨Movie⟩ *Raiders ⟨Of⟩ ⟨The⟩ Lost Ark*. movie, *of*, *the*
5. Your aunt ⟨modene⟩will take you to your appointment with ⟨dr.⟩ Block. Modene, Dr.

Exercise F

1. Babe Ruth was a great baseball player for the New York Yankees.
2. Native Americans joined the Pilgrims at the first Thanksgiving feast.
3. The planet Pluto is farthest from the sun.
4. The British composer Andrew Loyd Webber wrote *Phantom of the Opera*.
5. Did you read Ellen Goodman's column in the Sunday issue of the *Boston Globe*?
6. The Butler Insurance Company has its headquarters in Akron, Ohio.

Answer Key

Chapter Review
Form B

Exercise A

1. My cousin Sheila asked, "(what) time does the play begin?" What
2. She and (I) were planning to go to the Lillian Beaumont Theater. I
3. I had seen the play *King Lear* there last (november.) November
4. This time, Sheila had (Tickets) to see *Evita.* tickets
5. It's the story of Eva Peron, a legendary figure in the history of (argentina.) Argentina

Exercise B

1. PN—(A)ustria
2. CN
3. PA—(E)uropean
4. PN—(A)ustrian
5. PN—(T)he (M)arriage of Figaro

Exercise C

1. fresh water from the Salton Sea
2. General Ulysses S. Grant
3. a Hispanic baseball star, Juan Bonilla
4. a quarterback for the Chicago Bears football team
5. 897 Cricket Avenue, Fort Worth, Texas
6. a picnic at the beach on Long Island
7. the book *The Collected Poems of William B. Yeats*
8. C
9. a legend about a monster in Lake Superior
10. my grandmother, Minnie Robinson

Exercise D

1. Many barges and ships pass through the (panama) (canal.)
2. Juniors at (elkton) (high) (school) must take (world) (history) II.
3. The (larkspur) (hotel) is just north of an exit on the (pennsylvania) (turnpike.)
4. The poet (t.) (s.) (eliot) wrote the poem "The (love) (song) of (j.) (alfred) (prufrock)"
5. The planets (saturn) and (jupiter) are much larger than (earth.)

Exercise E

1. My (Uncle) Patrick works as a dentist in Columbia, (missouri) uncle, Missouri
2. On (tuesday) (brazilians) will vote for a new president. Tuesday, Brazilians
3. Drive west on Third (avenue) until you come to the Burger (doodle.) Avenue, Doodle
4. We saw a partial eclipse of the (Moon) last Sunday (Night.) moon, night
5. Whitney Houston sang "(the) Star (spangled) (banner)." The, Spangled, Banner

Exercise F

1. Robin Williams played a modern Peter Pan in the movie *Hook.*
2. The birthday of Queen Elizabeth II is a holiday in the United Kingdom.
3. The window of Blum's Bakery was full of Italian bread and Danish pastries.
4. Tennessee Williams, a playwright from the South, wrote *The Night of the Iguana.*
5. In the *Philadelphia Inquirer,* I read about the Gulf War.

Chapter 26: Punctuation (End Marks, Commas, Semicolons, Colons)

Using End Marks

An **end mark** is a mark of punctuation placed at the end of a sentence. The three kinds of end marks are the *period,* the *question mark,* and the *exclamation point.*

Use a period at the end of a statement.
    Charles Dickens is my favorite author.

Use a question mark at the end of a question.
    Who can ever forget Oliver Twist?

Use an exclamation point at the end of an exclamation.
    What a likable character he is!

Use either a period or an exclamation point at the end of a request or a command.
    Please return this book for me.   (request)
    Don't put it on the wet table!   (command)

Use a period after most abbreviations.
(Note: Periods are not used for abbreviations such as VHF.)
    Dr. Zhivago   Video Corp.   UN
    Mrs. Miniver   1 qt.   PTA
    10 Downing St.   5:00 P.M.

Exercise A   Write periods and other end marks where they belong in the following sentences.

1. The library opens at 10:00 A M tomorrow

2. Did Randall finish the Stephen King mystery

3. Many movies are based on King's books

4. What scary movies they are

5. I missed seeing the latest one when it came to St Louis

6. Mrs Wilson and Towanna saw it three times

7. How I wish I could have seen it

8. Have you read anything by Sara Paretsky

9. State St is the setting of one story

10. Can you carry five lbs of nails

Exercise B: Revising   Write periods and other end marks where they belong in the following paragraph.

　　What a crazy day The Cedar Ave bus left early Wasn't I lucky that Dr and

Mrs Moreno came by and drove me We got to school by 8:00 A M , but it was

closed because of a heating problem Maybe the UNICEF program can be

presented tomorrow.

Chapter 26: Punctuation (End Marks, Commas, Semicolons, Colons)

Commas with Items in a Series

A **comma** separates words or groups of words so that the meaning of a sentence is clear.

Use commas to separate items in a series. A series is three or more items written one after another. The items in a series may be words, phrases, or clauses.

Words in a series:	Dad's garden produced *carrots*, *beans*, and *cucumbers*.
Phrases in a series:	I packed *a sleeping bag*, *a canteen*, and *dried food* for the camping trip.
Clauses in a series:	The mechanic *tuned the car's engine*, *checked the brake fluid*, and *changed the fuel filter*.

Use a comma to separate two or more adjectives that come before a noun.
Ten *hungry*, *chirping* birds landed near our blanket.

Exercise A   Insert commas where they belong in the following sentences.

1. The zoo director had to feed the animals guide visitors and keep the grounds safe and clean.

2. Mrs. Ortega won more votes than Mr. Harris Miss Steinberg or Dr. Gladstone.

3. Scallops oysters herring and shrimp are displayed in the fish market window.

4. One tall weary man dropped a gold coin into the kettle.

5. The chairperson's job was calling the meeting to order asking for the minutes and announcing new officers.

6. Todd's uncle sold an oak chest two tables a china lamp and four paintings.

7. Autos trucks and buses were stranded by the storm.

8. A sleek powerful submarine slipped into the sea.

9. Many white purple and yellow crocuses grew on the hill.

10. Howin's dogs are friendly obedient and loyal to him and his family.

Exercise B: Proofreading   The following paragraph contains six errors in comma usage, two spelling errors, and two errors in capitalization. Can you find the errors? Proofread the paragraph to correct the errors.

Have you heard abowt the new shopping Mall? It is a busy exciting place!

men wemen and children can find almost anything they need. It has all kinds of

specialty shops, such as those that sell only music boxes comic books health food

or baseball caps.

Commas with Compound Sentences

A **compound sentence** is made up of two independent clauses joined by a conjunction.

Use a comma before *and, but, for, or, nor, so,* or *yet* when it joins independent clauses.
   Joshua's uncle drove us to the skating rink, and he decided to skate.

When independent clauses are very short, the comma before *and, but,* or *or* may be left out.
   Mrs. Lu could have waited but she left.

Exercise A   Add a comma to each compound sentence that follows. Underline the conjunction in each sentence.

1. Our family planned a driving trip so we needed maps.

2. Mom looked carefully but she couldn't find Elgin.

3. She put on glasses for the print was tiny.

4. The scenery was great yet my sister was restless.

5. Is that normal or is something wrong with her?

6. Yoko is not a good traveler nor am I.

7. My cousin Cary writes music and he plays in a band.

8. He invited us to listen but we had no time.

9. Who woke us up and why must we leave early?

10. I'm too sleepy to answer so I won't even try.

Exercise B: Sentence Combining   Combine two sentences to make a compound sentence. Use *and, or, but, so,* or *yet*. Include commas as needed. Write on the lines provided.

1. I brought a new camera. It broke. _____

_____

2. It rained on Sunday. We were disappointed. _____

_____

3. The mountains were snowy. It didn't feel very cold. _____

_____

4. I can borrow skis. Maybe I can rent some. _____

_____

5. Floyd spotted a tower. Dad saw a deer. _____

_____

Commas with Interrupters

Use commas to set off an expression that interrupts a sentence. Use two commas if the expression is in the middle of a sentence. Use one comma if the expression comes first or last.

> The best player, *in my opinion,* is Roberto.
> *In my opinion,* the best player is Roberto.

Nonessential phrases and clauses add information that isn't needed to understand the meaning of the sentence.

Use commas to set off nonessential participial phrases or nonessential subordinate clauses.

> The picnic, *planned for months,* is on Thursday. (nonessential phrase)
> My aunt, *who is a former teacher,* will drive the bus. (nonessential clause)

Essential phrases and clauses cannot be left out of a sentence without changing the main idea. Essential phrases and clauses tell *which one(s).*

Do not use commas to set off essential phrases or clauses.

> The park *with the pool* is the one we chose. (essential phrase)
> Only students *who have paid their fees* can attend. (essential clause)

Use commas to set off an appositive or an appositive phrase that is nonessential.

> Dad's boss, *Mr. Tarkov,* will be an umpire.

Use commas to set off words used in direct address.

> *Marina,* may I borrow a pencil?   Yes, *Tina,* I have extras.

Exercise A   The five sentences that follow all have interrupters. Add commas where needed.

1. The Johnston City pool built ten years ago is where I swim.

2. Yes Tom people living in the city can use the pool free.

3. Of course people from the suburbs pay two dollars.

4. Did you see my neighbor Sheri Cato do a triple flip?

5. Mr. Epstein who is a retired firefighter teaches the beginners.

Exercise B   In the following sentences, decide whether the italicized words are essential or nonessential. Underline essential phrases and clauses. Add commas to the nonessential ones.

> **Examples:**   Parents *who know how to swim* can join the group.
>
>   Lana, *the one who's pouting,* wants her mother to swim with her.

1. A child *who is frightened* can usually be calmed.

2. Should we ask Mrs. Sims *who comes every day* to join us?

3. The lifeguard *wearing blue shorts* is the strictest one.

4. He once *in a fit of anger* ordered two children to leave the pool.

5. How would you *an experienced instructor* have disciplined them?

Chapter 26: Punctuation (End Marks, Commas, Semicolons, Colons)

Commas with Introductory Elements

Commas are punctuation marks that tell us to pause.

Use a comma after certain introductory elements.

Use a comma after *yes, no,* or any mild exclamation such as *well* or *why* at the beginning of a sentence.

> *Yes,* I'm the one who called.
> *Why,* I see you cut your hair!

Use a comma after an introductory participial phrase.

> *Coming from you,* that's a compliment.

Use a comma after two or more introductory prepositional phrases.

> *In the backyard by the alley,* I found this old horseshoe.

Use a comma after an introductory adverb clause.

> *After Tyrone stopped looking for his contact lense,* he accidentally stepped on it.

Exercise A   Insert commas where they belong in the following sentences.

1. Hiding behind the bush he scared me.

2. Under the picnic table beside the tent Frisky slept peacefully.

3. Well look who's here!

4. Beyond that mountain with a snowy peak there's a small cabin.

5. No it burned down last summer.

6. Although the air was muggy we turned off the air conditioner.

7. Oh look at all those birds.

8. Since their leaves stay green all year those trees are called "evergreens."

9. After we ate we explored the woods surrounding the campground.

10. Why I wish all views were as beautiful as this!

Exercise B: Proofreading   The following paragraph contains ten errors in comma usage. Insert commas where they are needed.

> Smiling from ear to ear Stephanie had wonderful news. Yes the Chicago
> Bears won their fifth game! In the second half of the game they were awesome.
> When she told us we yelled jumped for joy and hugged each other. I pasted team
> pictures in my bedroom inside my locker on the refrigerator and on my
> notebook cover. Well don't you want to see one?

Chapter 26: Punctuation (End Marks, Commas, Semicolons, Colons)

Other Uses of Commas

Did you know that commas are used more than any other punctuation marks? You have probably used commas in the following situations.

Use commas to separate items in dates and addresses.
> My grandfather was born on May 4, 1920.
> His first apartment was at 32 Walton Street, Dayton, Ohio.

Use a comma after the salutation of a friendly letter and after the closing of any letter.
> Dear Grandma,
> Sincerely yours,

Exercise: Revising   Read the following letter to find ten comma errors, five capitalization errors, and five misspelled words. Write the letter correctly on the lines provided.

december 31 1998

Dear Margo

I'm caching up on my letters. No I didn't forget your camp form. Their office

mooved from 1234 Howard St. Springfield Missouri. Now they're at 16 rogers

Road Deerfield Missouri. margo it wasn't a bother. my ant drove me. Camp starts

on june 15 1999. Good newz—they need counselors! I hop we both get jobs.

Your pal

Nichola

_____

_____

_____

_____

_____

_____

_____

_____

_____

_____

_____

_____

Chapter 26: Punctuation (End Marks, Commas, Semicolons, Colons)

Using Semicolons

A semicolon also helps you join thoughts. Use a semicolon between independent clauses if they are not joined by *and, but, or, not, for, so,* or *yet.*

Anna Mary Robertson Moses had a goal; she wanted to be an artist.
Some people encouraged her; others were critical.

Use a semicolon, rather than a comma, before a coordinating conjunction to join independent clauses that contain commas.

I called Chung Sook, Van, and Ray; and Sam called Marva.

Exercise A   Add a semicolon to each sentence that follows.

1. His mother is a painter his father is a sculptor.

2. Anna Mary Robertson Moses began painting in the 1930's she was in her late seventies.

3. You won't see her full name on her paintings instead, you'll see the name

    Grandma Moses.

4. Some people like folk art others like abstract art.

5. Simone, Rita, and Hector use charcoal Anita uses paints.

Exercise B   Some of the following sentences need semicolons. On the lines provided, write the semicolon and the words before and after it. If a sentence has correct punctuation, write C.

Examples: Jeremy and Thad returned early, LaVerne was late.   <u>early; LaVerne</u>
You help Dad, and I'll help Uncle Seymour.   <u>C</u>

1. First I practiced soccer, then I delivered papers.   _____

2. Dan, I know you're tired, but the laundry is waiting.   _____

3. Phillip, Homer, and Carla wrote poetry, Luis wrote a play.   _____

4. The long, steady rain continued, yet nobody cared.   _____

5. Helen, please sing soprano Jean will sing alto.   _____

6. Some of us marched others, like John, rode on a float. _____

7. Ethel saw the danger she shouted a loud, clear warning. _____

8. I like checkers, charades, and dominoes and he likes chess.   _____

9. Nicknames are fun some, however, can embarrass you.   _____

10. Lila forgot her umbrella Jewel, of course, had hers.   _____

Chapter 26: Punctuation (End Marks, Commas, Semicolons, Colons)

Using Colons

Use a colon before a list of items, especially after expressions such as *the following* or *as follows*.

> The things to buy for the picnic are as follows: fruit, drinks, cheese, and crackers.

Use a colon between the hour and the minute.

> 8:00 P.M.   2:15 A.M.

Use a colon after the salutation of a business letter.

> Dear Mrs. Cramer: To Whom it May Concern:

Use a colon between chapter and verse in Biblical references and between all titles and subtitles.

> Matthew 3:1–4

Exercise A   Write the missing colons in the following items.

1. The languages the exchange student speaks are as follows English, German, French, and Spanish.

2. Our bus leaves at 623 A.M.

3. Dear Mayor Winston

4. Please read Luke 3 7–8.

5. At 704 P.M. the spacecraft was launched.

6. Uncle Jerry likes the following authors Alex Haley, Mark Twain, and Willa Cather.

7. Our reading assignment is the following a short story by O. Henry, pages 4–18 in our text, and two newspaper editorials.

8. These students won awards Tasha Zimmer, Blake Sanders, and Sam Reyes.

9. Dear Sir or Madam

10. Remember these tips when you drive courtesy, caution, and judgment.

Exercise B: Proofreading   Find eleven errors in the business memo. Add four colons and three commas. Correct the spelling of one word and capitalize three letters. Write the memo correctly on the lines provided.

To All Employees

You are invited to a luncheon at 130 P.M. on friday. The speakers are as

follows dr. Perez Mr. Feldman and Mrs. Puccini. bring these supplies your

computer guide, a notebook and two sharp pencels.

_____

_____

_____

Chapter 26: Punctuation (End Marks, Commas, Semicolons, Colons)

Review (Form A)

Exercise A   Add periods, other end marks, and commas where needed in the following sentences.

1. Do you enjoy looking at the stars

2. What a wonderful sight to behold

3. Kurt maybe you have seen the Big Dipper

4. The Big Dipper a group of seven stars is in Great Bear.

5. That's a constellation isn't it

6. Were you able to see Halley's comet

7. It was named for Edmund Halley

8. Does *Halley* rhyme with *daily valley* or *crawly*

9. We heard Dr Seton tell about planets

10. How interesting he was

Exercise B   In the following sentences, twenty punctuation marks are missing. They are end marks, commas, and semicolons. On the lines provided, write each punctuation mark and the word that comes before it.

1. This museum now known as the Chamber of Horrors

   dates back to 1835.   _____

2. What a weird wonderful place   _____

3. Napoleon Mozart Washington, and Lincoln are in   _____

   the Great Hall.   _____

4. You can take a picture Ari but don't touch the models.   _____

5. Can I ask that tall uniformed guard a question   _____

6. Yes Jamie even the guards are made of wax   _____

7. Some of us know that's true others can hardly believe it. _____

8. A queen donated a gown a king gave his cape   _____

9. Fiberglass real hair and acrylic are important materials. _____

10. One guard whom I've seen before lives and breathes!   _____

Chapter 26: Punctuation (End Marks, Commas, Semicolons, Colons)

Review (Form A)

Exercise C: Proofreading   Read the following invitation to find fifteen punctuation errors. Add periods, commas, semicolons, and colons as needed.

You're invited to a Splash Party on Thursday May 26 1997.

Come to my house at 200 P M call if you need a ride.

I live at 224 Pine St Apartment 215.

Bring the following bathing suit clogs towel soap and pool pass.

If possible bring some tapes then we can dance.

Chapter 26: Punctuation (End Marks, Commas, Semicolons, Colons)

Review (Form B)

Exercise A Add a period, a question mark, or an exclamation point to each sentence.

1. Are you familiar with Gary Larson's work

2. What a talented cartoonist he is

3. Have you seen *The Far Side*

4. The characters are animals who act like people

5. Where did he get his ideas

6. When he was a child, Larson was afraid of the dark

7. He thought about things scary monsters might say

8. How original that is

9. Be sure to read his cartoon collections

10. You'll like the dogs who wear glasses

Exercise B Ten commas are missing from the following sentences. Write the necessary commas and the words that come before and after each one. Use the lines provided.

1. Megan what makes a sneaker comfortable?

_____

2. I think support comfort and cushioning are three important things.

_____

3. You also need to like the style the material the color and the price.

_____

4. Our team buys only one brand but it's not easy to get all sizes.

_____

5. In the summer of course it's easier to find bright pretty colors.

_____

Chapter 26: Punctuation (End Marks, Commas, Semicolons, Colons)

Review (Form B)

Exercise C: Proofreading   Read the following letter to find fifteen punctuation errors. Add periods, commas, semicolons, and colons as needed.

December 1, 1998

Dear Aunt Belle and Uncle Tyler

Have you heard the good news? I'm going to Finland on Feb 15 1999. My best friend whom you met last summer may join me. How thrilled I am!

I need to buy the following a knapsack some pillows and boots. Because the trip will be expensive I'm trying to get a job. Uncle Tyler do you think that I can work in your store? Maybe Mr Hoffman can help me get in shape for farming activities. I'm going to be working on a farm in Finland. Aunt Belle I need your advice I need lots of it.

Your nephew

Damont

Answer Key

Practice and Reinforcement (1)
Using End Marks

Exercise A

1. The library opens at 10:00 A.M. tomorrow.
2. Did Randall finish the Stephen King mystery?
3. Many movies are based on King's books.
4. What scary movies they are!
5. I missed seeing the latest one when it came to St. Louis.
6. Mrs. Wilson and Towanna saw it three times.
7. How I wish I could have seen it!
8. Have you read anything by Sara Paretsky?
9. State St. is the setting of one story.
10. Can you carry five lbs. of nails?

Exercise B: Revising (End marks may vary.)

What a crazy day! The Cedar Ave. bus left early. Wasn't I lucky that Dr. and Mrs. Moreno came by and drove me? We got to school by 8:00 A.M., but it was closed because of a heating problem. Maybe the UNICEF program can be presented tomorrow.

Practice and Reinforcement (2)
Commas with Items in a Series

Exercise A

1. The zoo director had to feed the animals, guide visitors, and keep the grounds clean.
2. Mrs. Ortega won more votes than Mr. Harris, Miss Steinberg, or Dr. Gladstone.
3. Scallops, oysters, herring, and shrimp are displayed in the fish market window.
4. One tall, weary man dropped a gold coin into the kettle.
5. The chairperson's job was calling the meeting to order, asking for the minutes, and announcing new officers.
6. Todd's uncle sold an oak chest, two tables, a china lamp, and four paintings.
7. Autos, trucks, and buses were stranded by the storm.
8. A sleek, powerful submarine slipped into the sea.

9. Many white, purple, and yellow crocuses grew on the hill.
10. Howin's dogs are friendly, obedient, and loyal to him and his family.

Exercise B: Proofreading

Have you heard about the new shopping Mall? It is a busy, exciting place! men women, and children can find almost anything they need. It has all kinds of specialty shops, such as those that sell only music boxes, comic books, health food, or baseball caps.

Practice and Reinforcement (3)
Commas with Compound Sentences

Exercise A

1. Our family planned a driving trip, so we needed maps.
2. Mom looked carefully, but she couldn't find Elgin.
3. She put on glasses, for the print was tiny.
4. The scenery was great, yet my sister was restless.
5. Is that normal, or is something wrong with her?
6. Yoko is not a good traveler, nor am I.
7. My cousin Cary writes music, and he plays in a band.
8. He invited us to listen, but we had no time.
9. Who woke us up, and why must we leave early?
10. I'm too sleepy to answer, so I won't even try.

Exercise B: Sentence Combining

(Sentences may vary. Short sentences may or may not have commas.)

1. I brought a new camera, but it broke.
2. It rained on Sunday, so we were disappointed.
3. The mountains were snowy, yet it didn't feel very cold.
4. I can borrow skis, or maybe I can rent some.
5. Floyd spotted a tower, and Dad saw a deer.

Answer Key

Practice and Reinforcement (4)
Commas with Interrupters

Exercise A

1. The Johnston City pool, built ten years ago, is where I swim.

2. Yes, Tom, people living in the city can use the pool free.

3. Of course, people from the suburbs pay two dollars.

4. Did you see my neighbor, Sheri Cato, do a triple flip?

5. Mr. Epstein, who is a retired firefighter, teaches the beginners.

Exercise B

1. A child *who is frightened* can usually be calmed.

2. Should we ask Mrs. Sims, *who comes every day*, to join us?

3. The lifeguard *wearing blue shorts* is the strictest one.

4. He once, *in a fit of anger*, ordered two children to leave the pool.

5. How would you, *an experienced instructor*, have disciplined them?

Practice and Reinforcement (5)
Commas with Introductory Elements

Exercise A

1. Hiding behind the bush, he scared me.

2. Under the picnic table beside the tent, Frisky slept peacefully.

3. Well, look who's here!

4. Beyond that mountain with a snowy peak, there's a small cabin.

5. No, it burned down last summer.

6. Although the air was muggy, we turned off the air conditioner.

7. Oh, look at all those birds.

8. Since their leaves stay green all year, those trees are called "evergreens."

9. After we ate, we explored the woods surrounding the campground.

10. Why, I wish all views were as beautiful as this!

Exercise B: Proofreading

Smiling from ear to ear,Stephanie had wonderful news. Yes,the Chicago Bears won their fifth game! In the second half of the game,they were awesome. When she told us,we yelled, jumped for joy,and hugged each other. I pasted team pictures in my bedroom,inside my locker,on the refrigerator and on my notebook cover. Well, don't you want to see one?

Practice and Reinforcement (6)
Other Uses of Commas

Exercise: Revising

December 31, 1998

Dear Margo,

I'm catching up on my letters. No, I didn't forget your camp form. Their office moved from 1234 Howard St., Springfield, Missouri. Now they're at 16 Rogers Road, Deerfield, Missouri. Margo, it wasn't a bother. My aunt drove me. Camp starts on June 15, 1999. Good news—they need counselors! I hope we both get jobs.

Your pal,

Nichola

Practice and Reinforcement (7)
Using Semicolons

Exercise A

1. His mother is a painter; his father is a sculptor.

2. Anna Mary Robertson Moses began painting in the 1930's; she was in her late seventies.

3. You won't see her full name on her paintings; instead, you'll see the name *Grandma Moses.*

4. Some people like folk art; others like abstract art.

5. Simone, Rita, and Hector use charcoal; Anita uses paints.

Answer Key

Exercise B

1. soccer; then
2. C
3. poetry; Luis
4. C
5. soprano; Jean
6. marched; others
7. danger; she
8. dominoes; and
9. fun; some
10. umbrella; Jewel

Practice and Reinforcement (8)
Using Colons

Exercise A

1. The languages the exchange student speaks are as follows: English, German, French, and Spanish.
2. Our bus leaves at 6:23 A.M.
3. Dear Mayor Winston:
4. Please read Luke 3:7–8.
5. At 7:04 P.M., the spacecraft was launched.
6. Uncle Jerry likes the following authors: Alex Haley, Mark Twain, and Willa Cather.
7. Our reading assignment is the following: a short story by O. Henry, pages 4–18 in our text, and two newspaper editorials.
8. These students won awards: Tasha Zimmer, Blake Sanders, and Sam Reyes.
9. Dear Sir or Madam:
10. Remember these tips when you drive: courtesy, caution, and judgment.

Exercise B: Proofreading

To All Employees:

You are invited to a luncheon at 1:30 P.M. on Friday. The speakers are as follows: Dr. Perez, Mr. Feldman, and Mrs. Puccini. Bring these supplies: your computer guide, a notebook, and two sharp pencils.

Chapter Review
Form A

Exercise A

1. Do you enjoy looking at the stars?
2. What a wonderful sight to behold!
3. Kurt, maybe you have seen the Big Dipper.
4. The Big Dipper, a group of seven stars, is in Great Bear.
5. That's a constellation, isn't it?
6. Were you able to see Halley's comet?
7. It was named for Edmund Halley.
8. Does *Halley* rhyme with *daily, valley,* or *crawly*?
9. We heard Dr. Seton tell about planets.
10. How interesting he was!

Exercise B

1. museum,   Horrors,
2. weird,   place!
3. Napoleon,   Mozart,
4. picture,   Ari,
5. tall,   question?
6. Yes, Jamie,   wax.
7. true;
8. gown;   cape.
9. Fiberglass,   hair,
10. guard,   before,

Exercise C: Proofreading

You're invited to a Splash Party on Thursday, May 26, 1997.

Come to my house at 2:00 P.M.; call if you need a ride.

I live at 224 Pine St., Apartment 215.

Bring the following: bathing suit, clogs, towel, soap, and pool pass.

If possible, bring some tapes; then we can dance.

Answer Key

Chapter Review
Form B

Exercise A

1. Are you familiar with Gary Larson's work?

2. What a talented cartoonist he is!

3. Have you seen *The Far Side*?

4. The characters are animals who act like people.

5. Where did he get his ideas?

6. When he was a child, Larson was afraid of the dark.

7. He thought about things scary monsters might say.

8. How original that is!

9. Be sure to read his cartoon collections.

10. You'll like the dogs who wear glasses.

Exercise B

1. Megan, what

2. support, comfort, and

3. style, the material, the color, and

4. brand, but

5. summer, of course, bright, pretty

Exercise C: Proofreading

December 1, 1998

Dear Aunt Belle and Uncle Tyler,

Have you heard the good news? I'm going to Finland on Feb. 15, 1999. My best friend, whom you met last summer, may join me. How thrilled I am!

I need to buy the following: a knapsack some pillows, and boots. Because the trip will be expensive, I'm trying to get a job. Uncle Tyler do you think that I can work in your store? Maybe Mr. Hoffman can help me get in shape for farming activities. I'm going to be working on a farm in Finland. Aunt Belle, I need your advice. I need lots of it.

Your nephew

Damont

Chapter 27: Punctuation (Other Types of Punctuation)

Underlining and Italics

Use **underlining** (italics) for titles of books, plays, periodicals, films, television programs, works of art, long musical compositions, ships, aircraft, and spacecraft. In printed matter, those titles appear in italics. (*This is italic type.*)

Books and plays:	The Adventures of Tom Sawyer A Raisin in the Sun
Periodicals:	The New York Times National Geographic
Films:	Aladdin Little Women
Television Programs:	Frasier Nova
Works of Art:	Mona Lisa Venus de Milo
Long musical compositions:	Rhapsody in Blue Nutcracker Suite
Ships, aircraft, spacecraft:	Queen Elizabeth II Endeavour

Use underlining (italics) for words, letters, and figures referred to as such.

Did you know that <u>aloha</u> means both "hello" and "goodbye"?

Kareem often forgets to cross his <u>t</u>'s and dot his <u>i</u>'s.

Exercise A   Underline the words and phrases that need underlining in the following sentences.

1. Mom buys the Wall Street Journal every morning.

2. Norman Rockwell created covers for the Saturday Evening Post.

3. Does your library rent Raiders of the Lost Ark?

4. Ranger Rick is my cousin's favorite magazine.

5. One of Verdi's operas is Madama Butterfly.

6. Time magazine had a article about Verdi last week.

7. Shalom can mean "welcome" as well as "farewell."

8. Have you seen photographs of Sputnik 1?

9. My little sister cannot pronounce l's.

10. Rodin's famous statue is called The Thinker.

Exercise B   Add underlining as needed in the following conversation.

"Are you going to watch reruns of The Simpsons? The Miami Herald wrote about them."

"So did Newsweek. But I have to finish my book report on To Kill a Mockingbird.

"That was a movie, too. We saw it after The Black Stallion."

Chapter 27: Punctuation (Other Types of Punctuation)

Direct and Split Quotations

Quotation marks are marks of punctuation that set off, or separate, words clearly.

Use quotation marks to enclose a **direct quotation**—a person's exact words. When you want to tell exactly what somebody said, you enclose those words with quotation marks.
  "The *Titanic* will never sink," said Mr. Colby.

Do not use quotation marks for an **indirect quotation**—a rewording of a direct quotation.
  Mr. Colby said that the *Titanic* will never sink.

A direct quotation begins with a capital letter.
  Mrs. Colby said, "This certainly is a fabulous ship."

When the expression identifying the speaker interrupts a quoted sentence, the second part of the quotation begins with a small letter.
  "Let's go," suggested his wife, "and join the others for dinner."

Exercise A   Decide if each sentence has a direct quotation or an indirect quotation. On the line provided, write **D** for direct or **I** for indirect. Then insert quotation marks as needed.

_____ 1. The captain announced that dancing begins at midnight.

_____ 2. How can we dance if the sea gets rough? Mrs. Colby asked.

_____ 3. My dear, her husband replied, we'll just rock with the waves.

_____ 4. What's that out there? Clive shouted.

_____ 5. A steward said that it looks like an iceberg.

Exercise B: Revising   Read the following news report to find where quotation marks and commas are missing. Also find two capitalization errors, two misspelled words, and one missing underline. Rewrite the report correctly on the lines provided.
              Example: The captain asked what's all the commotion about?
                          The captain asked, "What's all the commotion about?"

  Erly reports from england say that a ship is sinking. A telegraph operator

said I heard a distress signal. He was asked where it came from. I'm trying to

figure that out he answered but I'm not sure.

  It might be comming from the titanic another operator said.

_____

_____

_____

_____

_____

Chapter 27: Punctuation (Other Types of Punctuation)

Punctuating Quotations

A **direct quotation** is the exact words that somebody has said.

A direct quotation is set off from the rest of the sentence by a comma, a question mark, or an exclamation point, but not by a period.
  "Which cheese is your favorite**?**" Kara asked.
  Stanislav replied**,** "I'll take Swiss anytime!"

A period or a comma following a direct quotation should be placed inside the closing quotation marks.
  "Then maybe you know**,**" Kara said, "why Swiss has holes**.**"

A question mark or an exclamation point is placed inside the closing quotation marks when the quotation itself is a question or an exclamation. Otherwise, it should be placed outside.
  "As a matter of fact," answered Stanislav, "I do**!**" (The quotation is an exclamation.)
  Who said, "Cheese is nature's greatest product"**?** (The sentence, not the quotation, is a question.)

Exercise A   Insert the necessary quotation marks in the following sentences.

1. Did you hear a noise? asked Whitney.

2. No, I didn't hear a thing, Ramona answered.

3. Eli whispered, I'm worried.

4. Maybe someone is out there! exclaimed Whitney.

5. Let me go and check the back door, said Eli.

6. I'll go with you, volunteered Whitney.

7. By the way, asked Ramona, who said they were worried?

8. Eli teased, Are you afraid to stay by yourself?

9. No, silly! she answered.

10. Which person said, I'm worried?

Exercise B: Proofreading   Find ten errors of punctuation in the following conversation. Six quotation marks, two commas, and two end marks are missing. Can you find the errors? Insert punctuation marks where they are needed.

  "I know what causes holes in Swiss cheese said Stanislav. It's the gas!"

  Mrs. Kaplan wondered who said, It's the gas

  "I did" Stanislav remarked. "When bacteria is added for flavor, bubbles of

  gas are formed. He continued, When the cheese gets hard, the bubbles remain—

  as holes"

Other Uses of Quotation Marks

Dialogue is conversation. When you are writing dialogue, begin a new paragraph every time the speaker changes.

>"I wish I could attend the ball," said Cinderella.
>
>"Sorry, my dear. You must stay home and finish your chores," replied her stepmother.
>
>"It seems like I'm the only one working around here," Cinderella complained.

When a quotation consists of several sentences, put quotation marks only at the beginning and the end of the whole quotation.

>"Everybody knows this is totally unfair! But if I finish quickly, maybe I'll have a chance to go. Who knows? I might even dance with a prince."

Use single quotation marks to enclose a quotation within a quotation.

>"Did she say 'dance with a prince'?" one of the sisters asked.

Use quotation marks to enclose the titles of short works such as articles, short stories, poems, songs, episodes of television programs, and chapters and other parts of books.

>"How to Improve Your Bowling"   "The Gift of the Magi"
>"I've Been Working on the Railroad"   "Using End Marks"

Exercise A   Add quotation marks where they are needed in the following sentences.

1. The band plays Hail to the Chief for the president.

2. Jack London's To Build a Fire is the first story in this book.

3. Man on the Moon is *Nova*'s program tonight.

4. What's New in Videos is a daily column.

5. If you like videos, said Van, you should read this column.

Exercise B: Revising   Rewrite the following dialogue, breaking it into paragraphs and adding quotation marks as necessary.

I think your family doesn't like me, said Roman. "You might be right, Elinor

agreed, but it would help if you got a job. "Did you say got a job' or 'go to jog?

asked Roman. You know what I said, said Elinor, so stop pretending that you

don't understand!

_____

_____

_____

_____

_____

Chapter 27: Punctuation (Other Types of Punctuation)

Apostrophes to Show Possession

The **possessive case** of a noun or pronoun shows ownership or relationship.
   Paula's guitar   **our** skit

Singular nouns: To form the possessive case of a singular noun, add an apostrophe and an *s*.
   sun's rays   Father's scooter

Plural nouns: To form the possessive case of a plural noun that does not end in *s*, add an apostrophe and an *s*.
   people's votes   men's shirts

To form the possessive case of a plural noun ending in *s*, add only the apostrophe.
   the classes' election   the Petersons' snowmobile

Personal pronouns: Do not use an apostrophe with possessive personal pronouns.
   The red car is **theirs.**

Indefinite pronouns: To form the possessive case of some indefinite pronouns, add an apostrophe and an *s*.
   somebody's notes   everyone's idea

Exercise A   For each phrase that follows, change the italicized noun or pronoun to the correct possessive form. Use the lines provided.

              Example: four *weeks* supply   <u>four weeks' supply</u>

   1. three *doctors* opinions   _____

   2. *nobodys* business   _____

   3. *Chris* bicycle   _____

   4. the *mices* tricks   _____

   5. two *months* wait   _____

Exercise B: Proofreading   Find five errors in apostrophe usage, two capitalization errors, and four misspelled words in the following sentences. Correct the errors in punctuation and capitalization. Write the misspelled words correctly on the lines provided.

   1. The Mt. vernon girl's chorus sang tweny songs.

   2. One students' brother had an acsident.

   3. He triped over Mrs. johnsons' briefcase.

   4. The banjo is her's.

   5. Everyones' voice was horse.

1. _____   3. _____

2. _____   4. _____

Chapter 27: Punctuation (Other Types of Punctuation)

Apostrophes in Contractions

A **contraction** is a shortened form of a word, a number, or a group of words. The apostrophe in a contraction shows where letters or numerals have been left out.

I am — I'm	of the clock — o'clock
we have — we've	1998 — '98
they are — they're	I have — I've
where is — where's	let us — let's

When the word *not* is added to a verb, it is shortened to *n't*.

do not — don't	should not — shouldn't
are not — aren't	will not — won't

Exercise A   Write the contraction for each set of words. Use the lines provided.

1. where is _____

2. we are _____

3. they will _____

4. has not _____

5. she is _____

6. could not _____

7. you will _____

8. does not _____

9. might have _____

10. they are _____

Exercise B: Revising   The following sentences have errors in the use of apostrophes in contractions. An apostrophe may be missing or in the wrong place. Three words are misspelled. Can you find ten errors? Rewrite the sentences correctly on the lines provided.

1. Theres a hobby you may be interested in. _____

_____

2. Its' called in–line skateing, or "blading." _____

_____

3. Why have'nt I heard about it? _____

_____

4. Heres' a magazine article from October, 95'. _____

_____

5. Youll have to finish reading it by two 'oclock. _____

_____

Chapter 27: Punctuation (Other Types of Punctuation)

Contractions and Possessive Pronouns

Do not confuse contractions with possessive pronouns. Contractions have an apostrophe. Possessive pronouns do not.

> **Contraction:** *Who's* the lifeguard on duty?   (who is)
> **Contraction:** *Who's* been providing towels?   (who has)
> **Possessive Pronoun:** *Whose* clogs are these?   (Who owns the clogs?)

Contractions	Possessive Pronouns
it's (it is *or* it has)	its
they're (they are)	their
who's (who is *or* who has)	whose
you're (you are)	your

Exercise A   Identify the italicized words in the following sentences. On the lines provided, write **CON** for contraction or **PP** for possessive pronoun. Add apostrophes where missing.

> **Example:** <u>PP</u>   How do hurricanes get *their* names?

_____ 1. *They're* chosen by scientists from all over the world.

_____ 2. One person *doesnt* choose.

_____ 3. *Whose* idea was that?

_____ 4. Probably *its* the idea of an international group.

_____ 5. *There's* a list of names for each coast.

_____ 6. *Ive* heard about that.

_____ 7. My friend Hugo thinks *hes* famous now.

_____ 8. *Your* friend is right.

_____ 9. But they *wont* use that name again.

_____10. *Its* devastation will be remembered for a long time.

Exercise B   The following sentences have empty spaces. In each space, write a contraction or a possessive pronoun that makes sense. Choose from these five words:

> their   whose   couldn't   weren't   haven't

1. _____ you read about the hardships of the Nez Perce?

2. They lost some of _____ land to settlers.

3. _____ land is it now?

4. Many people _____ understand the problems.

5. They _____ sure if a treaty would help.

Chapter 27: Punctuation (Other Types of Punctuation)

Apostrophes in Plurals

Use an apostrophe and an *s* to form the plurals of letters, numerals, and symbols, and of words referred to as words.

Paula forgot to dot the *i*'s and cross the *t*'s.
Mr. Johanson writes *1*'s that look like *7*'s.
Use fewer *so*'s in your writing.

Exercise A For each sentence that follows, change the italicized items to their plural form. Use the lines provided.

Examples: __*A's*__ Did you get any *A* on your progress report?
__*2's*__ Begin counting by *2*.

_____ 1. Count the *yes* and the *no*.

_____ 2. How many *l* are in the word?

_____ 3. My telephone number has four *2*.

_____ 4. Sakura's *4* look like *9*.

_____ 5. There are too many *and* in that sentence.

_____ 6. Be sure to put loops in your *m* and *n*.

_____ 7. How many *5* are in 100?

_____ 8. Don't forget to write both *r* in the word.

_____ 9. All the *5* and *6* are blurred.

_____ 10. The *why* and *wherefore* will be covered later.

Exercise B: Proofreading Find five missing apostrophes in the following letter. Also find three misspelled words and two capitalization errors. Make the ten corrections.

dear Yoshi,

Im writting to tell you why *7s* are lucky! Theres a contest to guess how many

beans are in a jar. Youll never beleive that I won! my winning guess was 777.

Whats the prize? I won seven movie tickets. Let me know if you can use one.

Yur pal,

Emily

Name _____ Date _____ Class _____

Using Hyphens

A **hyphen** is used between syllables and with compound numbers.

Use a hyphen to divide a word at the end of a line. Follow these rules:

    (1) Divide a word only between syllables.
            Sometimes our family takes a sum-
            mer vacation.
    (2) Do not divide a one-syllable word.
            Unacceptable: They are bringing salad, ham, and rye bre–
            ad.
    (3) Do not divide a word so that one letter stands alone. If you are writing a word
    like *busy*, don't divide it like this: *bus-y*. Instead, carry the whole word to the
    next line.
            Before we left, we were
            busy at the farm.

Use a hyphen with compound numbers from twenty-one to ninety-nine and with
fractions used as modifiers.

    twenty-seven votes   two-thirds majority

Exercise A   Show how you would divide each of the following words at the end of a
line of writing. If it cannot be divided, write the entire word on the second line.

                  Examples: luggage   lug–_____   tiny   _____

                                     gage_____   tiny_____

1. rocky   _____   4. station   _____

             _____   _____

2. railroad   _____   5. through   _____

             _____   _____

3. track   _____

             _____

Exercise B   Rewrite the items in the following list using hyphens. Rewrite the
numbers as words. Rewrite the words, breaking them into syllables.

                  Examples: 25   twenty–five   foundation   foun–da–tion

1. backpack   _____   6. organic   _____

2. 85   _____   7. passenger   _____

3. Friday   _____   8. 33   _____

4. 1/2   _____   9. campfire   _____

5. 47   _____   10. 61   _____

Chapter 27: Punctuation (Other Types of Punctuation)

Using Parentheses

Parentheses are used to separate words from other words in a sentence.

Use parentheses to enclose material that is added to a sentence but is not considered of major importance.

Pablo Casals (1876–1973) played the cello and composed music.

Material enclosed in parentheses can be a single word or a short sentence.

Shoshanna (Shanna) and I turned in our reports together.

Two thirds of our class (most are athletes) voted for afternoon games.

Exercise A   Add parentheses where they are needed in the following sentences.

1. Our school's engineer he's Anne's uncle won an award for bravery.

2. He saved a boy from a family of ten from drowning.

3. We were paddling a canoe like this one the day of our school picnic.

4. Nigel fell overboard everyone was scared and shouted for help.

5. Of all the people children and adults at the picnic, only our school's engineer

   knew what to do.

Exercise B: Revising   Quotation marks, apostrophes, parentheses, and hyphens are missing from the following paragraph. Rewrite the paragraph, using correct punctuation. Remember to begin a new paragraph whenever the speaker changes.

Are you ready for your report? asked Chen. Yes, answered Latitia, Im going

to tell about an article three pages long I read. It's about a twelve year old boy

who climbed Mt. McKinley." Chen exclaimed, Isnt that the highest mountain in

North America? Latitia nodded, "Thats right; its over 20,000 feet high!

_____

_____

_____

_____

_____

_____

_____

_____

_____

_____

Chapter 27: Punctuation (Other Types of Punctuation)

Using Dashes

You already know how commas and parentheses are used to set apart thoughts in a sentence. Those words or phrases set apart from the main thought are *parenthetical expressions*.

Usually, commas and parentheses are fine for parenthetical expressions. But when stronger emphasis is needed, use dashes. A **dash** looks like a hyphen but is about twice the size. Use a dash to indicate an abrupt break in thought or speech.

It's your turn—even though it *is* your birthday—to do the dishes.
My favorite outing—if I can afford it—is a day at the amusement park.

Exercise A   Rewrite the following sentences, inserting dashes where they are needed. Use the lines provided.

1. The best gift you can give Mother will love it is a day free from of chores. _____

_____

2. I can't believe even though you said it that you'll agree to work. _____

_____

3. Aren't you surprised I know you think I'm lazy that I thought of it first? _____

_____

4. Let's not tell Dad he won't believe it anyway until she opens the card. _____

_____

5. Can you keep a secret it's hard to do, I know until next Monday? _____

_____

Exercise B   Insert one of the word groups, including dashes, in each sentence that follows. Write in the space provided. Be sure your sentences make sense.

—I know it's heavy—   —believe it or not—
—it was so dusty—   —I hope so—
—that is, if you agree—

1. I helped Grandpa change the filter _____ on the furnace.

2. Can we afford the fare _____ to go downtown?

3. Help me move this table _____ so we can exercise.

4. Addie Sue wants to join us _____ at camp this summer.

5. I have always dreamed of owning _____ a motorbike.

Chapter 27: Punctuation (Other Types of Punctuation)

Review (Form A)

Exercise A   Add underlining and quotation marks as needed in the following sentences.

1. Many Walt Disney films, such as Bambi and Jungle Book, are back again.

2. Sometimes I listen to Ravel's famous Bolero when I study.

3. Aunt Fran sent our family a subscription to Consumers Digest.

4. Dad suggested, Read the article called Best Buys in Bicycle Helmets.

5. Byron's long poem entitled Don Juan fills an entire book!

6. Here's my copy of Anne of Green Gables, said Mother.

7. USA Today covers the news of all fifty states.

8. Did Columbus sail on the Santa Maria or on another ship? asked Larry.

9. All in the Family is Uncle Emil's favorite television series.

10. Kelly exclaimed, Look whose picture is in Sports Illustrated!

Exercise B   Rewrite these expressions in the possessive case, inserting apostrophes as needed. Use the lines provided.

1. the strategy of the opponent   _____

2. the fears of the men   _____

3. the tracks of the deer   _____

4. the trips of the family   _____

5. the victories of the candidates   _____

Exercise C   Show how to divide each of the following words at the end of a line of writing. If the word cannot be divided, write all of the word on the second line.

1. pencil   _____

_____

2. notebook   _____

_____

3. shiny   _____

_____

4. principal   _____

_____

5. marks   _____

_____

Chapter 27: Punctuation (Other Types of Punctuation)

Review (Form A)

Exercise D: Proofreading   The following paragraph contains several errors. Apostrophes, parentheses, and dashes are missing or misplaced. Rewrite the paragraph correctly on the lines provided.

Our entire family likes to watch who does'nt? the Olympics. Even our pets a brown dog and a gray kitten seem to like the competition. Do you think they understand Im not sure if I always do whats going on? Most of the time we simply watch. My dads favorite event and mine, too is speed skating. Mom like's to watch alpine skiing (shes a great skier.

_____

_____

_____

_____

_____

_____

_____

_____

_____

_____

_____

_____

_____

_____

Chapter 27: Punctuation (Other Types of Punctuation)

Review (Form B)

Exercise A   Add underlining, quotation marks, and hyphens as needed in the following sentences.

1. Listen to this recording of The Rite of Spring.

2. When I was a child, said Aunt Minnie, the U.S. flag had forty eight stars.

3. The episode showing tonight is Crisis in Central City.

4. His article, How to Excel in Soccer, will be published soon.

5. Who said, It's one thing to build castles in the air; it's another thing to live in them?

6. One third of my cousin's shelf is filled with Seventeen magazines.

7. I need two more weeks, she said, to finish them all.

8. Poems like Edward Lear's The Owl and the Pussycat are nonsense poems.

9. When I return The Yearling, I'll owe about twenty five cents.

10. Did you finish reading it? Mrs. Casper asked.

Exercise B   Rewrite these expressions in the possessive case, inserting apostrophes as needed. Use the lines provided.

1. the giggles of the children _____

2. the lines of the poem _____

3. the shouts of the girls _____

4. the worries of the parents _____

5. the population of Alaska _____

Exercise C   Show how to divide each of the following words at the end of a line of writing. If the word cannot be divided, write all of the word on the second line.

1. things   _____

            _____

2. flagpole   _____

            _____

3. weary   _____

            _____

4. conduct   _____

            _____

5. enough   _____

            _____

Chapter 27: Punctuation (Other Types of Punctuation)

Review (Form B)

Exercise D: Proofreading   Twenty-one marks of punctuation have been left out of the following conversation. Add quotation marks, apostrophes, and underlining where needed. Rewrite the conversation correctly on the lines provided.

Dad, Grandma, and I were talking about cartoons. "Guess whos celebrating his sixtieth birthday—Goofy! said Dad. He went on to say, I read that in The New York Times.

"Isnt he pals with that popular mouse Mickey? asked Grandma.

Sure, I answered. Dad, Grandpa said that Goofy first appeared in a movie called Mickey's Revue. He was known as Dippy Dawg in those days.

Grandma nodded and said, That was in 1932."

"I remember him in the 1950s, said Dad. "He was in films that taught safety.

"Lets watch his daily TV show, I said. Its called Goof Troop."

_____

_____

_____

_____

_____

_____

_____

_____

_____

_____

_____

_____

_____

_____

_____

_____

_____

_____

_____

_____

_____

Answer Key

Practice and Reinforcement (1)
Underlining and Italics

Exercise A

1. Mom buys the <u>Wall Street Journal</u> every morning.
2. Norman Rockwell created covers for the <u>Saturday Evening Post</u>.
3. Does your library rent <u>Raiders of the Lost Ark?</u>
4. <u>Ranger Rick</u> is my cousin's favorite magazine.
5. One of Verdi's operas is <u>Madama Butterfly</u>.
6. <u>Time</u> magazine had an article about Verdi last week.
7. <u>Shalom</u> can mean "welcome" as well as "farewell."
8. Have you seen photographs of <u>Sputnik 1</u>?
9. My little sister cannot pronounce <u>l</u>'s.
10. Rodin's famous statue is called <u>The Thinker</u>.

Exercise B

<u>The Simpsons</u>, <u>Miami Herald</u>

<u>Newsweek</u>, <u>To Kill a Mockingbird</u>

<u>The Black Stallion</u>

Practice and Reinforcement (2)
Direct and Split Quotations

Exercise A

1. I
2. D—"How can we dance if the sea gets rough?" Mrs. Colby asked.
3. D—"My dear," her husband replied, "we'll just rock with the waves."
4. D—"What's that out there?" Clive shouted.
5. I

Exercise B: Revising

Early reports from England say that a ship is sinking. A telegraph operator said, "I heard a distress signal." He was asked where it came from. "I'm trying to figure that out," he answered, "but I'm not sure."

"It might be coming from the <u>Titanic</u>," another operator said.

Practice and Reinforcement (3)
Punctuating Quotations

Exercise A

1. "Did you hear a noise?" asked Whitney.
2. "No, I didn't hear a thing," Ramona answered.
3. Eli whispered, "I'm worried."
4. "Maybe someone is out there!" exclaimed Whitney.
5. "Let me go and check the back door," said Eli.
6. "I'll go with you," volunteered Whitney.
7. "By the way," asked Ramona, "who said they were worried?"
8. Eli teased, "Are you afraid to stay by yourself?"
9. "No, silly!" she answered.
10. Which person said, "I'm worried"?

Exercise B: Proofreading

"I know what causes holes in Swiss cheese," said Stanislav. "It's the gas!"

Mrs. Kaplan wondered who said, "It's the gas?"

"I did," Stanislav remarked. "When bacteria is added for flavor, bubbles of gas are formed." He continued, "When the cheese gets hard, the bubbles remain—as holes."

Practice and Reinforcement (4)
Other Uses of Quotation Marks

Exercise A

1. The band plays "Hail to the Chief" for the president.
2. Jack London's "To Build a Fire" is the first story in this book.
3. "Man on the Moon" is *Nova*'s program tonight.
4. "What's New in Videos" is a daily column.
5. "If you like videos," said Van, "you should read this column."

Answer Key

Exercise B: Revising

"I think your family doesn't like me," said Roman.

"You might be right," Elinor agreed, "but it would help if you got a job."

"Did you say 'get a job' or 'go to jog'?" asked Roman.

"You know what I said," said Elinor, "so stop pretending that you don't understand!"

Practice and Reinforcement (5)
Apostrophes to Show Possession

Exercise A

1. three doctors' opinions
2. nobody's business
3. Chris's bicycle
4. the mice's tricks
5. two months' wait

Exercise B: Proofreading

1. The Mt. Vernon girls' chorus sang twenty songs.
2. One student's brother had an accident.
3. He tripped over Mrs. Johnson's briefcase.
4. The banjo is hers.
5. Everyone's voice was hoarse.

twenty   accident   tripped   hoarse

Practice and Reinforcement (6)
Apostrophes in Contractions

Exercise A

1. where's
2. we're
3. they'll
4. hasn't
5. she's
6. couldn't
7. you'll
8. doesn't
9. might've
10. they're

Exercise B: Revising

1. There's a hobby you may be interested in.
2. It's called in-line skating, or "blading."
3. Why haven't I heard about it?
4. Here's a magazine article from October, '92.
5. You'll have to finish reading it by two o'clock.

Practice and Reinforcement (7)
Contractions and Possessive Pronouns

Exercise A

1. CON
2. CON—doesn't
3. PP
4. CON—it's
5. CON
6. CON—I've
7. CON—he's
8. PP
9. CON—won't
10. PP

Exercise B

1. Haven't
2. their
3. Whose
4. couldn't
5. weren't

Practice and Reinforcement (8)
Apostrophes in Plurals

Exercise A

1. *yes's, no's*
2. *1's*
3. *2's*
4. *4's, 9's*
5. *and's*
6. *m's, n's*
7. *5's*
8. *r's*
9. *5's, 6's*
10. *why's, wherefore's*

Answer Key

Exercise B: Proofreading

dear Yoshi,

I'm writing to tell you why 7's are lucky! There's a contest to guess how many beans are in a jar. You'll never believe that I won! my winning guess was 777. What's the prize? I won seven movie tickets. Let me know if you can use one.

Yur pal,

Emily

Practice and Reinforcement (9)
Using Hyphens

Exercise A

1. rocky
2. rail–
   road
3. track
4. sta–
   tion
5. through

Exercise B

1. back–pack
2. eighty–five
3. Fri–day
4. one–half
5. forty–seven
6. or–gan–ic
7. pas–sen–ger
8. thirty–three
9. camp–fire
10. sixty–one

Practice and Reinforcement (10)
Using Parentheses

Exercise A

1. Our school's engineer (he's Anne's uncle) won an award for bravery.
2. He saved a boy (from a family of ten) from drowning.
3. We were paddling a canoe (like this one) the day of our school picnic.
4. Nigel fell overboard (everyone was scared) and shouted for help.
5. Of all the people (children and adults) at the picnic, only our school's engineer knew what to do.

Exercise B: Revising

"Are you ready for your report?" asked Chen.

"Yes," answered Latitia, "I'm going to tell about an article (three pages long) I read. It's about a twelve–year–old boy who climbed Mt. McKinley."

Chen exclaimed, "Isn't that the highest mountain in North America?"

Latitia nodded, "That's right; it's over 20,000 feet high!"

Practice and Reinforcement (11)
Using Dashes

Exercise A

1. The best gift you can give—Mother will love it—is a day free from chores.
2. I can't believe—even though you said it—that you'll agree to work.
3. Aren't you surprised—I know you think I'm lazy—that I thought of it first?
4. Let's not tell Dad—he won't believe it anyway—until she opens the card.
5. Can you keep a secret—it's hard to do, I know—until next Monday?

Exercise B

(Answers may vary. Sample responses are given.)

1. I helped Grandpa change the filter—it was so dusty—on the furnace.
2. Can we afford the fare—I hope so—to go downtown?
3. Help me move this table—I know it's heavy—so we can exercise.
4. Addie Sue wants to join us—that is, if you agree—at camp this summer.
5. I have always dreamed of owning—believe it or not—a motorbike.

Chapter Review
Form A

Exercise A

1. Many Walt Disney films, such as Bambi and Jungle Book, are back again.
2. Sometimes I listen to Ravel's famous Bolero when I study.

Answer Key

3. Aunt Fran sent our family a subscription to <u>Consumers Digest</u>.

4. Dad suggested, "Read the article called 'Best Buys in Bicycle Helmets.'"

5. Byron's long poem entitled <u>Don Juan</u> fills an entire book!

6. "Here's my copy of <u>Anne of Green Gables</u>," said Mother.

7. <u>USA Today</u> covers the news of all fifty states.

8. "Did Columbus sail on the <u>Santa Maria</u> or on another ship?" asked Larry.

9. <u>All in the Family</u> is Uncle Emil's favorite television series.

10. Kelly exclaimed, "Look whose picture is in <u>Sports Illustrated</u>!"

Exercise B

1. the opponent's strategy
2. the men's fears
3. the deer's tracks
4. the family's trips
5. the candidates' victories

Exercise C

1. pen–
cil
2. note–
book
3. shiny
4. prin–   *or*   princi–
cipal   pal
5. marks

Exercise D: Proofreading

Our entire family likes to watch—who doesn't?—the Olympics. Even our pets (a brown dog and a gray kitten) seem to like the competition. Do you think they understand—I'm not sure if I always do—what's going on? Most of the time we simply watch. My dad's favorite event (and mine, too) is speed skating. Mom likes to watch alpine skiing (she's a great skier).

Chapter Review
Form B

Exercise A

1. Listen to this recording of <u>The Rite of Spring</u>.

2. "When I was a child," said Aunt Minnie, "the U.S. flag had forty-eight stars."

3. The episode showing tonight is "Crisis in Central City."

4. His article, "How to Excel in Soccer," will be published soon.

5. Who said, "It's one thing to build castles in the air; it's another thing to live in them?"

6. One third of my cousin's shelf is filled with <u>Seventeen</u> magazines.

7. "I need two more weeks," she said, "to finish them all."

8. Poems like Edward Lear's "The Owl and the Pussycat" are nonsense poems.

9. When I return <u>The Yearling</u>, I'll owe about twenty–five cents.

10. "Did you finish reading it?" Mrs. Casper asked.

Exercise B

1. the children's giggles
2. the poem's lines
3. the girls' shouts
4. the parents' worries
5. Alaska's population

Exercise C

1. things
2. flag–
pole
3. weary
4. con–
duct
5. enough

Answer Key

Exercise D: Proofreading

Dad, Grandma, and I were talking about cartoons. "Guess who's celebrating his sixtieth birthday—Goofy!" said Dad. He went on to say, "I read that in <u>The New York Times</u>."

"Isn't he pals with that popular mouse Mickey?" asked Grandma.

"Sure," I answered. "Dad, Grandpa said that Goofy first appeared in a movie called <u>Mickey's Revue.</u> He was known as Dippy Dawg in those days."

Grandma nodded and said, "That was in 1932."

"I remember him in the 1950's," said Dad. "He was in the films that taught safety."

"Let's watch his daily TV show," I said. "It's called <u>Goof Troop.</u>"

Using a Dictionary to Check Spellings

You use words every day—in reading, writing, and speaking. It's important to understand what you read. It's also important for others to understand your writing. A dictionary is a valuable aid for checking your spelling.

Maybe you're thinking, "How do I look up a word if I don't know how to spell it in the first place?" Try the following steps.

(1) Suppose you want to check the spelling of *articulate*. First, say the word slowly, pronouncing each syllable: *ar · tic · u · late*.

(2) Ask yourself: "Do I already know some words that begin with the sound *ar?*" You probably know *are* and *art*.

(3) In a dictionary, find the pages that contain words beginning with the letter *a*. Skim until you find those that begin with *ar*.

(4) Think about the next syllable: *tic*. Doesn't it sound like *tic* and *tick*, words you may know? Continue to skim until you find words that begin with *artic*.

(5) Now add *u*, and finally, *late*—a word you already know how to spell.

Exercise A   Read the following sentences to find spelling errors. Write each misspelled word correctly on the line provided. Use a dictionary if you need it.

_____ 1. Did you watch the documentry about bats?

_____ 2. There are many difrent kinds of bats.

_____ 3. One egspert said that photos make bats look vicious.

_____ 4. If the bat was caged, it probly was scared.

_____ 5. A scientist's labotory isn't a bat's favorite roosting place!

Exercise B   Look up the following words in a dictionary. Rewrite each word, dividing it into syllables. Use the lines provided.

1. atrocious _____

2. frightened _____

3. habitat _____

4. research _____

5. scientist _____

Chapter 28: Spelling

Using Spelling Rules A

Some words confuse even the best spellers. Many people stop and ask themselves questions like these:"Is *weird* spelled with *ei* or *ie* ?" "Does *succeed* end in *ceed, cede,* or *sede?*" Spelling rules can sometimes help you answer such questions.

(1) When spelling words with a long *e* sound, write *ie.*

> be**lie**ve, y**ie**ld, ch**ie**f, p**ie**rce

> Exception: When the long *e* sound comes after *c,* write *ei.*

> re**cei**ve, de**cei**ve, **cei**ling

(2) Write *ei* when the sound is not long *e,* especially when the sound is long *a.*

> **ei**ght, sl**ei**gh, w**ei**gh

(3) Most words that end with the "seed" sound are spelled with a *-cede* ending.

> pre**cede**, con**cede**

> Exceptions: The only word ending in *-sede* is *supersede.*
> The only words ending in *-ceed* are *exceed, proceed,* and *succeed.*

Exercise A   In each sentence that follows, a word is italicized. If the word is spelled correctly, write **C.** If the word is misspelled, rewrite it correctly. Use the lines provided.

_____ 1. Jason's *chief* interest is magic tricks.

_____ 2. It all began when he *recieved* a book for his birthday.

_____ 3. Would you *beleive* that it was about famous magicians?

_____ 4. There's a *breif* story about Harry Blackstone, Jr.

_____ 5. In one *weird* trick, he turned his wife into a tiger!

_____ 6. The audience was *releived* when she came out for a bow.

_____ 7. Some tricks are called "*slieght* of hand."

_____ 8. Jason tried to hide *eight* scarves in his sleeve.

_____ 9. He *iether* lost one or miscounted.

_____10. I guess he didn't *succede* with that trick!

Exercise B   Notice five incomplete words in the following paragraph. Fill in the missing letters so that each word is spelled correctly.

> Here's something to do in your l ____ sure time. Maybe you and a fr ____ nd

> can start a service. Offer to take an elderly n ____ ghbor shopping. After you load

> the shopping cart, proc ____ to the checkout line. Let's hope this idea will

> y ____ ld success!

Using Spelling Rules B

A **prefix** is a letter or group of letters added to the beginning of a word to change its meaning. A **suffix** is a letter or group of letters added to the end of a word to change its meaning.

When adding a prefix to a word, do not change the spelling of the word itself. Some commonly used prefixes are *dis–, il–, im–, in–, mis–, over–, re–, un–.*

Here are some words with prefixes.

      discount (dis + count)   retake (re + take)
      input (in + put)   unsure (un + sure)

When a suffix is added to a word, the spelling of the word itself may or may not change. When adding the suffix *–ness* or *–ly* to a word, do not change the spelling of the word itself.

      kindness (kind + ness)   total (total + ly)

Exceptions: For most words that end in *y,* change the *y* to *i* before *–ly* or *–ness.*
      daily (day + ly)   loneliness (lonely + ness)

Exercise A   For each item below, add the prefix or suffix given to form a new word Use the lines provided.

1. in + direct = _____

2. dis + locate = _____

3. re + open = _____

4. il + legal = _____

5. un + safe = _____

6. over + take = _____

7. main + ly = _____

8. mis + print = _____

9. im + possible = _____

10. busy + ness = _____

Exercise B   Each sentence that follows has a blank where a word is needed. Fill in the missing word, after you read the directions in parentheses.

          Example: Behruz had to _____ his suitcase. (un + pack)
          Behruz had to ___unpack___ his suitcase.

1. Please _____ the clock. (re + wind)

2. Aunt Manuela was upset about _____ the stew. (over + cooking)

3. _____ is one habit I must work on. (Neat + ness)

4. Did I _____ your name on the invitation? (mis + spell)

5. Helga and her sister _____ opened their gifts. (happy + ly)

Chapter 28: Spelling

Using Spelling Rules C

A **suffix** is a letter or group of letters added to the end of a word to change its meaning. Some common suffixes are *–ing*, *–ed*, *–er*, *–able*, *–ful*, *–hood*, *–ment*, *–ly*, *–less*, *–ness*.

When adding a suffix to a word, you may need to change the spelling of the word itself. The following rules will help you remember those spelling changes.

Words ending in e

(1) Drop the final silent *e* before a suffix beginning with a vowel.

        like + able = likable   skate + ing = skating

(2) Keep the final *e* before a suffix beginning with a consonant.

        care + ful = careful   state + ly = stately

Exceptions: argue + ment = argument   true + ly = truly

Words ending in y

(3) For words ending in *y* preceded by a consonant, change the *y* to *i* before any suffix that does not begin with *i*.

        happy + ness = happiness   carry + er = carrier

(4) Words ending in *y* preceded by a vowel do not change their spelling before a suffix.

        play + ed = played

Exceptions: lay + ed = laid   pay + ed = paid

Words ending in a consonant

(5) Double the final consonant before adding *–ing*, *–ed*, or *–er* to a one-syllable word that ends in a single consonant preceded by a single vowel.

        swim + ing = swimming   chop + ed = chopped

(6) With a one syllable word ending in a single consonant that is not preceded by a single vowel, do not double the consonant before adding *–ing*, *–ed*, or *–er*.

        roam + ing = roaming   peel + er = peeler

Exercise A   For each word that follows, write the correct spelling, adding the suffix given.

1. merry + ment = _____   4. argue + ing = _____

2. trap + ed = _____   5. crazy + er = _____

3. love + able = _____   6. help + ful = _____

Exercise B: Proofreading   Find four misspelled words in the following paragraph. Rewrite them correctly on the lines.

     Have you ever payed for a haircut you hated? Did you think about cuting it

yourself? Try this: Find a magazine picture of a style you like. Bring it to your

styleist so he or she can copy it. Maybe you'll end up lookking like a star!

1. _____   3. _____

2. _____   4. _____

Chapter 28: Spelling

Forming the Plurals of Nouns

The **singular** form of a word stands for one of something. The **plural** form stands for more than one.

house—*houses,* dish—*dishes,* child—*children.*

Observe the following rules for spelling the plural of nouns.

(1) To form the plural of most nouns, add –*s*.
> tree—trees   nest—nests

(2) Form the plural of nouns ending in *s, x, z, ch,* or *sh* by adding –*es*:
> tax—tax**es**   wish—wish**es**   boss—boss**es**

(3) Form the plural of nouns ending in *y* preceded by a consonant by changing the *y* to *i* and adding -*es*:
> baby—bab**ies**

(4) Form the plural of nouns ending in *y* preceded by a vowel by adding –*s*.
> tray—trays   monkey—monkey**s**

(5) Form the plural of most nouns ending in *f* by adding –*s*. The plural of some nouns ending in *f* or *fe* is formed by changing the *f* to *v* and adding –*s* or –*es*.
> belief—beliefs   wolf—wol**ves**

(6) Form plurals of nouns ending in *o* preceded by a vowel by adding –*s*. The plural of many nouns ending in *o* preceded by a consonant is formed by adding –*es*.
> banjo—banjos   hero—hero**es**

(7) The plural of a few nouns is formed in irregular ways.
> mouse—m**ice**   foot—f**eet**

(8) Form the plural of compound nouns consisting of a noun plus a modifier by making the modified noun plural.
> brother-in-law—brother**s**-in-law

(9) The plural of a few compound nouns is formed in irregular ways.
> tie-up—tie-up**s**   drive-in—drive-in**s**

(10) Some nouns are the same in the singular and the plural.
> deer—deer

(11) Form the plural of numerals, letters, signs, and words referred to as words by adding an apostrophe and –*s*.
> 1900—1900**'s**   A—A**'s.**

Exercise   Write the plurals of the following items. Use the lines provided.

1. branch   _____

2. elf   _____

3. rodeo   _____

4. mix   _____

5. country _____

6. mother-in-law _____

7. man   _____

8. drive-in   _____

9. turkey   _____

10. 1800   _____

Chapter 28: Spelling

Words Often Confused A

Some words are easily confused because they sound alike. However, these words have different meanings and spellings. Study these commonly confused words.

advice, advise   *Advice* means "a recommendation for action" (noun). *Advise* means "to recommend a course of action" (verb).

affect, effect   *Affect* means "to act upon" or "to change" (verb). *Effect* means "result" or "consequence" (noun).

already, all ready   *Already* means "previously." *All ready* means "all prepared" or "in readiness."

altogether, all together   *Altogether* means "entirely." *All together* means "everyone in the same place."

Exercise   Read each sentence and decide which word or phrase in parentheses is correct. Underline the correct word or words.

> **Examples:** Would you (advice, <u>advise</u>) me to buy this jacket?
>
> Yes, take my (<u>advice</u>, advise) and buy it.

1. How did your test score (affect, effect) your final grade?

2. I (already, all ready) got an A for the semester!

3. Will you follow Dwayne's (advice, advise) and buy the jacket?

4. I was (already, all ready) to buy it, but then I saw another one.

5. My mood (affects, effects) what I buy.

6. Did Miss Rubio (advice, advise) you to take cheerleading?

7. She needs us (altogether, all together) for daily practice.

8. What were the (affects, effects) of the war with Iraq?

9. It's (altogether, all together) too silly for me!

10. Do you need more time, or are you (already, all ready)?

Chapter 28: Spelling

Words Often Confused B

Homonyms are words that are pronounced the same, but their meanings and spellings are different. Study the following homonyms.

capital, capitol   *Capital* is "a city" or "the location of a government." *Capitol* refers to a building or statehouse.

coarse, course   *Coarse* means "rough, crude, not fine" (adjective). *Course* means "path of action, series of studies" (noun). It's also used in the expression "of course."

hear, here   *Hear* means "to receive sounds through the ears" (verb). *Here* means "in this place" (adverb).

peace, piece   *Peace* refers to quiet order and security. *Piece* means "a part of something."

plain, plane   *Plain* is "simple; unadorned" (adjective); or "a flat area of land" (noun). *Plane* is "a flat surface; a tool; an airplane" (noun).

Exercise A   For each sentence below, underline the correct word in parentheses.

1. Our computer (coarse, course) sometimes baffles me.

2. Miranda, did you (hear, here) about the test?

3. I'm writing about Washington, the (capital, capitol) of the United States.

4. You know what a spreadsheet is, of (coarse, course).

5. Grandma says, "It's as (plain, plane) as the nose on your face!"

6. She thinks this fabric is too (coarse, course) for curtains.

7. Look at that (peace, piece) of material on the shelf.

8. Uncle Henry uses a hammer and a (plain, plane).

9. The (capital, capitol) has a gold dome.

10. Ruben saw it from the window of the (plain, plane).

Exercise B   Fill in the each space with a word that makes sense. Choose words from the list at the top of the page.

1. Is Montgomery the _____ of Alabama?

2. Of _____ , many people remember the bus boycott.

3. Did you _____ about Rosa Parks?

4. She was arrested for disturbing the _____ .

5. We took a _____ called "Human Rights."

Words Often Confused C

Study the following word pairs that are often confused.

quiet, quite   *Quiet* means "still and peaceful; without noise" (adjective).
Quite means "wholly or entirely; to a great extent" (adverb).

shone, shown   *Shone* means "gleamed; glowed" (verb, past tense of *shine*).
Shown means "revealed" (verb, past participle of *show*).

threw, through   *Threw* means "tossed; cast" (verb, past tense of *throw*).
Through means "by way of; as a result of" (preposition).

weak, week   *Weak* means "feeble; not strong" (adjective).
Week refers to "seven days" (noun).

Exercise A   In each sentence below underline the correct word in parentheses.

1. My walkie-talkie is too (weak, week) to pick up voices.

2. Try to be as (quiet, quite) as a mouse.

3. The criminal (threw, through) away the evidence.

4. It will take a (weak, week) to get my watch repaired.

5. I was able to reach him (threw, through) a friend.

6. Your statement is not (quiet, quite) true.

7. You've already (shone, shown) me how to work the math problem.

8. I think the batteries in my radio are (weak, week).

9. The lights in the harbor (shone, shown) brightly.

10. Our teacher asked us to be (quiet, quite).

Exercise B   For each sentence below, underline the correct word in parentheses.
Then, write a new sentence using the other word correctly.

1. Will the recycling drive last all (weak, week)? _____

_____

2. We were (shone, shown) how to sort the glass. _____

_____

3. Loretta (threw, through) some glass in the wrong bin! _____

_____

4. I'm too (weak, week) to lift that bundle of papers. _____

_____

5. I agree that it's (quiet, quite) heavy. _____

_____

Chapter 28: Spelling

Commonly Misspelled Words

Sometimes we misspell words because they look different from what we expect. Many words have silent letters. Some may sound like other words, but they are spelled differently. The following words are commonly misspelled.

again	cough	minute	tonight
answer	doctor	often	trouble
built	friend	paid	using
color	instead	special	wear

Exercise A   Each sentence that follows has a misspelled word. Write the word correctly on the line provided.

_____ 1. How offen do you visit your grandparents?

_____ 2. They usually come to see us insted.

_____ 3. Mom and Dad bilt a guest room.

_____ 4. He put in speshal things for people in wheelchairs.

_____ 5. They'll have no trouble useing the sink.

_____ 6. Grandpa's docter gave Dad medicine.

_____ 7. The medicine is for Grandpa's coff.

_____ 8. Tonite Mom and Dad are cooking for ten of us.

_____ 9. They won't have a minite to spare!

_____ 10. Can Regina anser all the phone calls?

Exercise B: Proofreading   There are ten spelling errors in the following paragraph. Circle the misspelled words. Then write them correctly on the lines provided.

The time has come agin for our class picnic. We're useing the same park as last year. There should be fun every minut. Can you make name tags of two colers insted of one? Then we'll know who payed their fees. Tell your frends to ware hiking shoes so they won't have trubbel walking. Ansur by May 15!

1. _____	6. _____
2. _____	7. _____
3. _____	8. _____
4. _____	9. _____
5. _____	10. _____

Chapter 28: Spelling

Review (Form A)

Exercise A   For each item that follows, add the prefix or write the plural form of the word. Use the lines provided.

1. re + write =   _____

2. un + healthy =   _____

3. box   _____

4. im + mature =   _____

5. mis + inform =   _____

6. in + complete =   _____

7. wolf   _____

8. over + turn =   _____

9. 10   _____

10. man   _____

Exercise B   Add a suffix to each italicized word in the following sentences. Choose from these suffixes: *–able, –less, –ness, –ment, –ly*. Write the complete word on the line provided. Remember that the spelling of the original word may change.

Example: <u>hopeless</u>   It was *hope* for Marta to win, since she didn't practice.

_____ 1. In all *fair*, the judge will hear the case.

_____ 2. Much to our *astonish*, Manfred won a trophy!

_____ 3. *Final*, the team has a chance for first place.

_____ 4. A sudden storm caused a *postpone* of the picnic.

_____ 5. Who owns that *adore* little kitten?

_____ 6. My cousin's directions were *worth*, so we got lost.

_____ 7. The clock in the hall chimes *hour*.

_____ 8. What *busy* do you have at the bank?

_____ 9. Ana was *care* to lose your umbrella.

_____10. Aunt Thelma won the *achieve* award.

Chapter 28: Spelling

Review (Form A)

Exercise C   Two words or phrases appear in parentheses in each of the following sentences. Underline the correct word or words.

1. The legislature meets on the second floor of the (capital, capitol).

2. Willard took his sister's (advice, advise) and went to the party.

3. The coach said we're not (quiet, quite) ready to compete.

4. Are you (already, all ready) for your trip?

5. I hope you counted every (peace, piece) of luggage.

6. When I had the flu, I felt very (weak, week).

7. The small (plane, plain) flew over the Grand Canyon.

8. Can you (hear, here) me?

9. I hope to take a cooking (coarse, course) this summer.

10. That might (affect, effect) your job.

Exercise D: Proofreading   There are five spelling errors in the following paragraph. Circle the misspelled words. Then write them correctly on the lines provided.

      Koala bears are getting speshul attention. I gess people are payed by zoos to bring them in. Now the police are takeing the koalas' fingerprints. Even tho their palms have no prints, the tips of their fingers show a pattern.

1. _____

2. _____

3. _____

4. _____

5. _____

Chapter 28: Spelling

Review (Form B)

Exercise A   For each item that follows, add the prefix or write the plural form of the word. Use the lines provided.

1. un + real = _____

2. deer _____

3. C _____

4. mis + spell = _____

5. over + worked = _____

6. hoof _____

7. re + tell = _____

8. woman _____

9. fox _____

10. in + secure = _____

Exercise B   Add the suffixes *–ness, –hood, –ment, –ful, –ly* to the list of words below to form new words that correctly complete each sentence.

happy

joy

child

engage

formal

1. My older sister Holly has known her boyfriend since _____ .

2. Holly and Dirk talked about their _____ last night.

3. They'll announce it _____ in the newspaper.

4. We hope the wedding turns out to be a _____ event.

5. The whole family is sharing their _____ .

Chapter 28: Spelling

Review (Form B)

Exercise C   Read the following paragraphs. Underline the correct word from each pair in parentheses.

Have you heard of the play *Macbeth,* by William Shakespeare? The (principal, principle) character, Macbeth, is (altogether, all together) too ambitious for his own good. When he hears a prediction that he will be the new king, he (accepts, excepts) it as the truth. His wife, Lady Macbeth, greatly (affects, effects) Macbeth's (coarse, course) of action.

When the king visits Macbeth's castle, Macbeth and his wife are ready to (procede, proceed) with their plan. While the king sleeps, Macbeth slips (past, passed) the guards and does a (terrible, terible) deed.

Macbeth thinks that nothing now can (altar, alter) his plan to be king. He gains the throne but loses his (peace, piece) of mind. Lady Macbeth loses her sanity.

Answer Key

Practice and Reinforcement (1)
Using a Dictionary to Check Spellings

Exercise A

1. documentary
2. different
3. expert
4. probably
5. laboratory

Exercise B

1. a · tro · cious
2. fright · ened
3. hab · i · tat
4. re · search
5. sci · en · tist

Practice and Reinforcement (2)
Using Spelling Rules A

Exercise A

1. C
2. received
3. believe
4. brief
5. C
6. relieved
7. sleight
8. C
9. either
10. succeed

Exercise B

leisure
friend
neighbor
proceed
yield

Practice and Reinforcement (3)
Using Spelling Rules B

Exercise A

1. indirect
2. dislocate
3. reopen
4. illegal
5. unsafe
6. overtake
7. mainly
8. misprint
9. impossible
10. business

Exercise B

1. rewind
2. overcooking
3. Neatness
4. misspell
5. happily

Practice and Reinforcement (4)
Using Spelling Rules C

Exercise A

1. merriment
2. trapped
3. lovable *or* loveable
4. arguing
5. crazier
6. helpful

Exercise B: Proofreading

1. paid
2. cutting
3. stylist
4. looking

Answer Key

Practice and Reinforcement (5)
Forming the Plurals of Nouns

Exercise

1. branches
2. elves
3. rodeos
4. mixes
5. countries
6. mothers-in-law
7. men
8. drive-ins
9. turkeys
10. 1800's *or* 1800s

Practice and Reinforcement (6)
Words Often Confused A

Exercise

1. affect
2. already
3. advice
4. all ready
5. affects
6. advise
7. all together
8. effects
9. altogether
10. all ready

Practice and Reinforcement (7)
Words Often Confused B

Exercise A

1. course
2. hear
3. capital
4. course
5. plain
6. coarse
7. piece
8. plane
9. capitol
10. plane

Exercise B

1. capital
2. course
3. hear
4. peace
5. course

Practice and Reinforcement (8)
Words Often Confused C

Exercise A

1. weak
2. quiet
3. threw
4. week
5. through
6. quite
7. shown
8. weak
9. shone
10. quiet

Answer Key

Exercise B

(Answers will vary for the second part of the exercise. Sample responses are given.)

1. <u>week</u> That shelf looks too weak to hold those jars.
2. <u>shown</u> Chris polished the tray until it shone.
3. <u>threw</u> Stop the cars before they come through the gate.
4. <u>weak</u> We'll be on duty the whole week!
5. <u>quite</u> It's so quiet today!

Practice and Reinforcement (9)
Commonly Misspelled Words

Exercise A

1. often
2. instead
3. built
4. special
5. using
6. doctor
7. cough
8. Tonight
9. minute
10. answer

Exercise B: Proofreading

(Incorrect words in paragraph should be circled.)

1. again
2. using
3. minute
4. colors
5. instead
6. paid
7. friends
8. wear
9. trouble
10. answer

Chapter Review
Form A

Exercise A

1. rewrite
2. unhealthy
3. boxes
4. immature
5. misinform
6. incomplete
7. wolves
8. overturn
9. 10's
10. men

Exercise B

1. fairness
2. astonishment
3. Finally
4. postponement
5. adorable
6. worthless
7. hourly
8. business
9. careless
10. achievement

Exercise C

1. capitol
2. advice
3. quite
4. all ready
5. piece
6. weak
7. plane
8. hear
9. course
10. affect

Answer Key

Exercise D: Proofreading

(Incorrect words in paragraph should be circled.)

1. special
2. guess
3. paid
4. taking
5. though

Chapter Review
Form B

Exercise A

1. unreal
2. deer
3. C's
4. misspell
5. overworked
6. hooves
7. retell
8. women
9. foxes
10. insecure

Exercise B

1. childhood
2. engagement
3. formally
4. joyful
5. happiness

Exercise C

1. principal
2. altogether
3. accepts
4. affects
5. course
6. proceed
7. past
8. terrible
9. alter
10. peace

Mechanics Mastery Test (Form A)

Part 1   Read each phrase and imagine it is to be used within a sentence. Decide which phrase is correctly capitalized. On the line provided, write its letter, **A** or **B**. [1 point each]

	A	B
_____ 1.	the Big Ten Conference	the Big ten Conference
_____ 2.	at ten O'clock	at ten o'clock
_____ 3.	one Spring in the Rocky Mountains	one spring in the Rocky Mountains
_____ 4.	foreign car convertible	Foreign car convertible
_____ 5.	Prime Minister Margaret Thatcher	prime minister Margaret Thatcher
_____ 6.	my Algebra I and Science classes	my Algebra I and science classes
_____ 7.	Harvard University	Harvard university
_____ 8.	Death Valley national monument	Death Valley National Monument
_____ 9.	driving west to California	driving West to California
_____10.	reads Greek and Latin	reads Greek and latin
_____11.	in October, yom kippur	in October, Yom Kippur
_____12.	the Secretary of Defense	the Secretary Of Defense
_____13.	read *The New York times*	read *The New York Times*
_____14.	invited Barb's Mother	invited Barb's mother
_____15.	my high school	my High School
_____16.	a French Poodle	a French poodle
_____17.	along lake Michigan	along Lake Michigan
_____18.	at Twenty-Third Street	at Twenty-third Street
_____19.	natives of the Southwest	natives of the southwest
_____20.	the book *A Dream Of Africa*	the book *A Dream of Africa*

Part 2   The following letter is missing end punctuation, commas, colons, parentheses, and semicolons. Add the missing punctuation. Then, underline the word or figure immediately before the punctuation you added. [1 point for each mark]

Example: Dear Mrs. Kostas   Dear Mrs. <u>Kostas</u>:

1. No we haven't a cottage available in July our peak month

2. however, in August we could give you a two-room cabin

3. It's on the lake Please let us know at once if this would be

Mechanics Mastery Test (Form A)

4. suitable. You may rent it for one to five weeks, through August

5. August 3–31 and September You asked about five points the cottages the

6. mosquitoes, the weather, the crowds at Leech Lake and a

7. guarantee of good fishing every day We can guarantee only the

8. Minnesota mosquitoes Leech Lake is normally peaceful and uncrowded

9. Our local guides can usually find good fishing they can't manage the

10. weather

11. If you make reservations, plan to arrive after 2 00 in the afternoon At that

12. time the cabins will be ready. Will we see you then I hope so

Sincerely,

Lum Twilliger

Part 3　In many of the following sentences, there are errors in the use of quotation marks. In the spaces provided, write any corrections. If the sentence is correct, write **C**. 1 point each]

Example:　Have you read the chapter The Battle of Bull Run?
<u>"The Battle of Bull Run"?</u>

1. The pilot said, "Our flight has been grounded because of fog. _____

2. Juanita named her poem "One Last Victory." _____

3. Mother called, Come now; we must be going." _____

4. "The paper carrier has come to collect payment, I told them. _____

5. He replied, "I was singing my favorite song, 'Home on the Range. _____

6. The driver asked, "How far to the nearest motel"? _____

7. We must read the chapter entitled Australia for geography class. _____

8. The captain shouted, "What a spectacular catch you made! _____

9. The dentist asked me to open my mouth a little wider. _____

10. Who said "Give me liberty or give me death? _____

Part 4　Each group of expressions contains one expression that has an apostrophe error. Underline the expression that has the error. [1 point each]

Example: (a) Joan's house　(b) <u>is it her's</u>　(c) the crew's victory

1. (a) isn't old enough　(b) it's theirs　(c) a mans' coat

2. (a) thats all right　(b) his bicycle　(c) Frank's brother

3. (a) too many *and*'s　(b) weve rested　(c) I'm here

Mechanics Mastery Test (Form A)

4. (a) whose going?   (b) that dog's bark   (c) the child's toys

5. (a) a penny's worth   (b) two weeks' rest   (c) it's paw

6. (a) it's almost over   (b) where theres room   (c) the pencil's owner

7. (a) *i*'s look like *e*'s   (b) she's tired   (c) two dog's food

8. (a) everybody's cooperation   (b) some of your's   (c) the jury's verdict

9. (a) the water's edge   (b) it wouldnt help   (c) that's the answer

10. (a) babies' hats   (b) baby's hats   (c) so many hat's

Part 5   Read each of the following sentences. In most of them, a word has been misused because it has been mistaken for another word much like it. Underline each incorrect word. Then, on the line provided, write the word that should have been used. Write **C** if there is no error. [1 point each]

1. The book contained good advise for travelers. _____

2. I know the capitol of every state. _____

3. The house looked old and desserted. _____

4. My counselor at school gave me a placement test. _____

5. Of coarse you may ride with us! _____

6. Once the sun shown, we were warm enough. _____

7. Hans didn't swim to the raft because it was to far from shore. _____

8. Olga asked whether you're going to take the train. _____

9. The truck that past us was speeding! _____

10. Reba is lucky that all her cloths from last year still fit her. _____

Part 6   Each of the following groups of words contains one word that is misspelled. Underline that word. Then, write the correct spelling of the word on the line provided. [1 point each]

_____ 1. ache, absence, acceptence

_____ 2. again, accomodate, believe

_____ 3. docter, apparent, theory

_____ 4. genuine, luxery, color

_____ 5. instead, arguement, similar

_____ 6. experement, schedule, tries

_____ 7. anxiety, trouble, amoung

Mechanics Mastery Test (Form A)

_____ 8. dont, attacked, conscience

_____ 9. basis, suprize, seems

_____ 10. genius, definite, colledge

_____ 11. governer, necessary, depth

_____ 12. physical, intrest, bicycle

_____ 13. benifit, icicles, opinion

_____ 14. mischief, refferred, meant

_____ 15. divide, minute, desireable

_____ 16. often, attendence, once

_____ 17. seperate, success, violence

_____ 18. yield, familar, vacuum

_____ 19. intelligence, eighth, tradgedy

_____ 20. brief, equippment, similar

Part 7   On the line provided, write the plural of each word. [1 point each]

1. donkey   _____

2. tax   _____

3. wish   _____

4. country   _____

5. wolf   _____

6. hero   _____

7. trio   _____

8. foot   _____

9. mother-in-law   _____

10. 1900   _____

Assessment: Mastery Tests

Mechanics Mastery Test (Form B)

Part 1   Read each phrase and imagine it is to be used within a sentence. Decide which phrase is correctly capitalized. On the line provided, write its letter, **A** or **B**. In some cases, neither phrase is correctly capitalized. In each of these cases, write **N** in the space provided. [1 point each]

	A	**B**
_____ 1.	our Junior High school	our junior high school
_____ 2.	Jefferson City, Missouri	Jefferson city, Missouri
_____ 3.	along Lake Calhoun	along lake Calhoun
_____ 4.	on Fifty-eighth Street	on Fifty-Eighth Street
_____ 5.	go South on Main Street	go South on Main street
_____ 6.	member of the Dramatic club	member of the Dramatic Club
_____ 7.	a Memorial Day observance	a Memorial Day Observance
_____ 8.	in the fall of the Year	in the Fall of the year
_____ 9.	during World war I	during World War I
_____10.	spanish diplomats	Spanish Diplomats
_____11.	neither God nor Jehova	neither god nor Jehova
_____12.	in typing or Latin class	in Typing or Latin class
_____13.	beside judge Prasad	beside Judge Prasad
_____14.	Tuesday, the seventh of March	Tuesday, the Seventh of March
_____15.	president Wood of the United Fund	president Wood of The United Fund
_____16.	from my Grandmother	from my grandmother
_____17.	Crunchy Oaties cereal	crunchy oaties cereal
_____18.	the Edmonton hotel on Frank Avenue	The Edmonton Hotel on Frank avenue
_____19.	Mount Rushmore National Memorial	Mount Rushmore national Memorial
_____20.	member of the senate	member of the Senate

Part 2   Each of the following sentences is missing an end mark and at least one comma, semicolon, or colon. Add the missing punctuation to each sentence. Then underline the word that comes before the mark you added. [2 points each]

    Example: Well can we go   <u>Well</u>, can we <u>go</u>?

1. Because of the rain everyone ran back into the school

2. Our best players Trishia and Virgil won special awards

3. The signs were unnecessary though because of the noises smells and smoke

Assessment: Mastery Tests

Mechanics Mastery Test (Form B)

4. I voted for Tyler, Delores and Lotte my friend Babs voted for Tyler Lotte and me

5. Are you taking swimming lessons again Phil

6. No I most certainly will not

7. These items will go in my backpack a compass a candle dried fruit and matches

8. Some people left early some stayed until the very end

9. Is that train by the way the red one

10. Don't go yet the manager would like to speak with you

Part 3   The following sentences are missing either quotation marks or underlining (italics), or both. On the lines provided, rewrite each sentence correctly. [2 points each]

1. Willis asked, Did President Truman really say, If you can't stand the heat, get out

   of the kitchen? _____

   _____

2. Doyle's story The Adventure of the Crooked Man is in a book called The

   Memoirs of Sherlock Holmes. _____

   _____

3. Gail asked who had borrowed her copy of Junior Natural History magazine. _____

   _____

4. Mr. Andrews asked, Have you read Frost's poem Stopping by Woods on a

   Snowy Evening? _____

   _____

5. One chapter of Alice's Adventures in Wonderland, said Gil is called Pig and

   Pepper. _____

   _____

Part 4   On the line provided, write each word or group of words requiring an apostrophe or a hyphen, and insert the correct punctuation. [1 point each]

   Example: Normas birthday is twenty one days away.
                 Norma's, twenty-one

1. Im sure shes having a party, but whos invited? _____

2. Its supposed to be a secret, but her parents closest friends are taking her out to

   dinner. _____

3. Lets plan a party on a day thats not her birthday. _____

Assessment: Mastery Tests

Mechanics Mastery Test (Form B)

4. Youll help with the invitations, wont you? _____

5. Doesn't Norma spell her last name with two *c*s and two *r*s? _____

6. I'll make a list, but lets limit the number of guests to twenty five. _____

7. Isn't that the number of students in Ms. Johnstons class? _____

8. If everyones invited from class, we wont have room for other friends of hers. _____

9. Whos on the list now that its up to thirty five people? _____

10. We havent decided whose house we'll use for the party. _____

Part 5   Most of the following sentences have one word that is either misspelled or misused. Underline each incorrect word. Then, on the line provided, write the word correctly. If the sentence is correct, write **C**. [1 point each]

_____ 1. The family that formally lived here moved to Utah.

_____ 2. After the ride, Grant lead the horse back to the corral.

_____ 3. I know its late, but we want to finish tonight.

_____ 4. Leave the equipment in hear when you're done.

_____ 5. The university said that references were unecessary.

_____ 6. Around here the weather is very changeable.

_____ 7. The speaker began with a humerous statement about winning.

_____ 8. My scedule has already been typed.

_____ 9. The absense of legal counsel may be a problem.

_____ 10. The professor taught my English coarse last year.

_____ 11. I can almost guarantee you will like the taste of this desert.

_____ 12. Fortunatly, my principal is trained in first aid.

_____ 13. This Febuary was particularly cold and uncomfortable.

_____ 14. Rita through nineteen strikes in the first inning.

_____ 15. Please do not altar anything in the laboratory.

_____ 16. Saturday night's concert was briefer than the one in the afternoon.

_____ 17. We stood with the other foriegn visitors outside the capitol.

_____ 18. At camp, one of the councilors gave a talk on water safety.

_____ 19. The museum referred the professor to it's library.

_____ 20. The audience thought my speech was quite humorous.

Mechanics Mastery Test (Form B)

Part 6   On the line provided, write the plural of each word. [2 points each]

1. telephone   _____

2. Gómez   _____

3. shelf   _____

4. story   _____

5. studio   _____

6. lady-in-waiting _____

7. salmon   _____

8. pitch   _____

9. child   _____

10. tray   _____

Assessment Tests

Mechanics Mastery Test (Form A)

Part 1 [1 point each, 20 points total]

1. A	11. B
2. B	12. A
3. B	13. B
4. A	14. B
5. A	15. A
6. B	16. B
7. A	17. B
8. B	18. B
9. A	19. A
10. A	20. B

Part 2 [1 point for each punctuation mark, 20 points total]

1. <u>No</u>, we haven't a cottage available in <u>July</u>, our peak <u>month</u>;
2. however, in August we could give you a two-room <u>cabin</u>.
3. It's on the <u>lake</u>. Please let us know at once if this would be
4. suitable. You may rent it for one to five weeks, through <u>August</u>
5. (August 3-<u>31</u>) and <u>September</u>. You asked about five <u>points</u> : the <u>cottages</u>, the
6. mosquitoes, the weather, the crowds at Leech <u>Lake</u>, and a
7. guarantee of good fishing every <u>day</u>. We can guarantee only the
8. Minnesota <u>mosquitoes</u>. Leech Lake is normally peaceful and <u>uncrowded</u>.
9. Our local guides can usually find good <u>fishing</u>; they can<u>'</u>t manage the
10. <u>weather</u>.
11. If you make reservations, plan to arrive after <u>2:00</u> in the <u>afternoon</u>. At that
12. time the cabins will be ready. Will we see you <u>then</u>? I hope <u>so</u>.

Part 3 [1 point each line, 10 points total]

1. fog."
2. C
3. "Come
4. payment,"
5. Range.'"
6. motel?"
7. "Australia"
8. made!"
9. C
10. death"?

Part 4 [1 point each, 10 points total]

1. (c) <u>a mans' coat</u>
2. (a) <u>thats all right</u>
3. (b) <u>weve rested</u>
4. (a) <u>whose going?</u>
5. (c) <u>it's paw</u>
6. (b) <u>where theres room</u>
7. (c) <u>two dog's food</u>
8. (b) <u>some of your's</u>
9. (b) <u>it wouldnt help</u>
10. (c) <u>so many hat's</u>

Part 5 [1 point each, 10 points total]

1. <u>advise</u> — advice
2. <u>capitol</u> — capital
3. <u>desserted</u> — deserted
4. C
5. <u>coarse</u> — course
6. <u>shown</u> — shone
7. <u>to</u> (far) — too
8. C
9. <u>past</u> — passed
10. <u>cloths</u> — clothes

Assessment Tests

Part 6 [1 point each, 20 points total]

1. <u>acceptence</u>—acceptance
2. <u>accomodate</u>—accommodate
3. <u>docter</u>—doctor
4. <u>luxery</u>—luxury
5. <u>arguement</u>—argument
6. <u>experement</u>—experiment
7. <u>amoung</u>—among
8. <u>dont</u>—don't
9. <u>suprize</u>—surprise
10. <u>colledge</u>—college
11. <u>governer</u>—governor
12. <u>intrest</u>—interest
13. <u>benifit</u>—benefit
14. <u>refferred</u>—referred
15. <u>desireable</u>—desirable
16. <u>attendence</u>—attendance
17. <u>seperate</u>—separate
18. <u>familar</u>—familiar
19. <u>tradgegy</u>—tragedy
20. <u>equippment</u>—equipment

Part 7 [1 point each, 10 points total]

1. donkeys
2. taxes
3. wishes
4. countries
5. wolves
6. heroes
7. trios
8. feet
9. mothers-in-law
10. 1900's (*or* 1900s)

Mechanics Mastery Test (Form B)

Part 1 [1 point each, 20 points total]

1. B	11. A
2. A	12. A
3. A	13. B
4. A	14. A
5. N	15. N
6. B	16. B
7. A	17. A
8. N	18. N
9. B	19. A
10. N	20. B

Part 2 [2 points each, 20 points total]

1. <u>rain,</u> ...<u>school.</u>
2. <u>players,</u>... <u>Virgil,</u> ...<u>awards.</u>
3. <u>unnecessary, though,</u> ...<u>noises, smells,</u> ... <u>smoke.</u>
4. <u>Delores,</u> ...<u>Lotte;</u> ...<u>Tyler, Lotte,</u> ... <u>me.</u>
5. <u>again, Phil?</u>
6. <u>No,</u> ...<u>not!</u>
7. <u>backpack:</u> ...<u>compass,</u> ...<u>candle, dried fruit,</u>... <u>matches</u>
8. <u>early;</u> ...<u>end.</u>
9. <u>train,</u> ...<u>way,</u> ... <u>one?</u>
10. <u>yet;</u> ...<u>you.</u>

Part 3 [2 points each, 10 points total]

1. Willis asked, "Did President Truman really say, 'If you can't stand the heat, get out of the kitchen'?"
2. Doyle's story "The Adventure of the Crooked Man" is in a book called *The Memoirs of Sherlock Holmes.*
3. Gail asked who had borrowed her copy of *Junior Natural History* magazine.
4. Mr. Andrews asked, "Have you read Frost's poem 'Stopping by Woods on a Snowy Evening'?"
5. "One chapter of *Alice's Adventures in Wonderland*," said Gil, "is called 'Pig and Pepper.'"

Assessment Tests

Part 4 [1 point each, 10 points total]

1. I'm ...she's ...who's
2. It's ...parents'
3. Let's ...that's
4. You'll ...won't
5. *c*'s ... *r*'s?
6. let's ...twenty-five
7. Johnston's
8. everyone's ...won't
9. Who's ...it's ...thirty-five
10. haven' t

Part 5 [1 point each, 20 points total]

1. <u>formally</u> —formerly
2. <u>lead</u> —led
3. <u>its</u>—it's
4. <u>hear</u> —here
5. <u>unecessary</u>—unnecessary
6. Correct
7. <u>humerous</u> —humorous
8. <u>scedule</u>—schedule
9. <u>absense</u>—absence
10. <u>coarse</u> —course
11. <u>desert</u>—dessert
12. <u>Fortunatly</u> —Fortunately
13. <u>Febuary</u> —February
14. <u>through</u>—threw
15. <u>altar</u>—alter
16. Correct
17. <u>foriegn</u>—foreign
18. <u>councilors</u> —counselors
19. <u>it's</u> —its
20. Correct

Part 6 [2 points each, 20 points total]

1. telephones
2. Gómezes
3. shelves
4. stories
5. studios
6. ladies-in-waiting
7. salmon
8. pitches
9. children
10. trays

Most standardized tests require that you use a No. 2 pencil. Each mark should be dark and completely fill the intended oval. Be sure to completely erase any errors or stray marks. If you do not have a pencil, follow your teacher's instructions about how to mark your answers on this sheet.

1

Your Name: _____
(Print)   Last   First   M.I.

Signature: _____

Class: _____ Date: ____ / ____ / ____
(Print)   Month   Day   Year

2 Your Name

First 4 letters of Last Name				First Init.	Mid. Init.

(columns of ovals A through Z)

3 Date

Month		Day		Year	
Jan.					
Feb.					
Mar.	0	0	0	0
Apr.	1	1	1	1
May	2	2	2	2
June	3	3	3	3
July		4	4	4
Aug.		5	5	5
Sept.		6	6	6
Oct.		7	7	7
Nov.		8	8	8
Dec.		9	9	9

4 Grade

0 1 2 3 4 5 6 7 8 9

5 Age

0 1 2 3 4 5 6 7 8 9

For each new section, begin with number 1. If a section has more answer spaces than questions, leave the extra spaces blank.

Grammar and Usage Test

Section 1

1 A B C D E   6 A B C D E   11 A B C D E
2 A B C D E   7 A B C D E   12 A B C D E
3 A B C D E   8 A B C D E   13 A B C D E
4 A B C D E   9 A B C D E   14 A B C D E
5 A B C D E   10 A B C D E   15 A B C D E

Section 2

1 A B C D E   6 A B C D E   11 A B C D E
2 A B C D E   7 A B C D E   12 A B C D E
3 A B C D E   8 A B C D E   13 A B C D E
4 A B C D E   9 A B C D E   14 A B C D E
5 A B C D E   10 A B C D E   15 A B C D E

Mechanics Test

Section 1

1 A B C D E   6 A B C D E   11 A B C D E
2 A B C D E   7 A B C D E   12 A B C D E
3 A B C D E   8 A B C D E   13 A B C D E
4 A B C D E   9 A B C D E   14 A B C D E
5 A B C D E   10 A B C D E   15 A B C D E

Section 2

1 A B C D E   6 A B C D E   11 A B C D E
2 A B C D E   7 A B C D E   12 A B C D E
3 A B C D E   8 A B C D E   13 A B C D E
4 A B C D E   9 A B C D E   14 A B C D E
5 A B C D E   10 A B C D E   15 A B C D E